Praise for *Angling ___*

"After over sixty years in the sport Bob DeMott is to me the best trout fisherman I've ever met along with Tom McGuane. His expertise shows on every page of *Angling Days*. Any trout fisherman who can read will want to pick up a copy."

—Jim Harrison, author of *Dead Man's Float*

"This irresistibly readable book is presented as a compilation of entries to a fishing journal kept by Bob DeMott for over a quarter of a century. Those entries track a long, attention-paying self-education in the high art of trout fishing. . . . Along the way, DeMott entertains us with lively prose, deft cameos of guides and fishing pals, elegant depictions of riverscapes, and an erudition in angling literature as capacious yet unpretentious as a thirty-year-old fishing vest. *Angling Days: A Fly Fisher's Journals* belongs on the bookshelf of everyone who fishes for trout and values fine writing."

—Charles Gaines, author of *The Next Valley Over* and *Waters Far and Near*

"A rich book indeed, the work of a passionate and cultivated writer who can actually fish and sees the place of angling in a thoughtful life. DeMott has a lot to tell us about how the game is played, and what it means. A cultivated, unpretentious and useful contribution to our literature."

—Tom McGuane, author of *The Longest Silence*

"We get a wonderful tour of a thoughtful angling life in this book, a biogeography of DeMott's need to fish...to experience the present moment and to plumb the depths of important memories."

—Chris Camuto, *Gray's Sporting Journal*

"Fishing is Robert DeMott's chosen metaphor, but one gets the feeling that he could write with grace about any other contest between obligation and escape, and every other test that requires us to be more expansive in our thinking and imagination. We habitually reach for the familiar and the inventive, the useful and transcendent in fishing. In *Angling Days* DeMott has given us the whole possibles bag."

—Marshall Cutchin, publisher of *MidCurrent*

"Generous, erudite, and relentlessly readable, like sitting down with the author over burgers and beers to relive a fine shared day of obsessive fly fishing."

—James R. Babb, editor emeritus, *Gray's Sporting Journal*

"One of the best books ever written on fly fishing and all that this sublime sport evokes. Working against a changing backdrop of glorious scenery and varied action, DeMott weaves a reflective, self-deprecating, and vivid story of one man's fishing life that captures the moods and metaphysics of trout fishing as beautifully as any writer ever has. Compelling at every turn and sparklingly written throughout, this book is a must-have for any fly fisherman, one to be savored more than once."

—William Souder, author of *Under a Wild Sky: John James Audubon and the Making of The Birds of America*, and *On A Farther Shore: The Life and Legacy of Rachel Carson*

"Bob DeMott's *Angling Days* is a richly textured chronicle of the fly fisher's life at its most enterprising and provocative. We wait a long time between books that are this satisfying—and this much fun."

—Paul Schullery, author of *The Fishing Life* and member of the Fly Fishing Hall of Fame

Angling
Days

A Fly Fisher's Journals

ROBERT DeMOTT

Skyhorse Publishing

Skyhorse Publishing books may be purchased in bulk at special discounts for sales promotion, corporate gifts, fund-raising, or educational purposes. Special editions can also be created to specifications. For details, contact the Special Sales Department, Skyhorse Publishing, 307 West 36th Street, 11th Floor, New York, NY 10018 or info@skyhorsepublishing.com.

Skyhorse® and Skyhorse Publishing® are registered trademarks of Skyhorse Publishing, Inc.®, a Delaware corporation.

Visit our website at www.skyhorsepublishing.com.

10 9 8 7 6 5 4 3 2 1

Library of Congress Cataloging-in-Publication Data is available on file.

Cover design by Tom Lau
Cover water color credit: Mary Hendrix, based on a photograph by Paul Schullery.

Print ISBN: 978-1-5107-3225-4
Ebook ISBN: 978-1-63450-824-7

Printed in the United States of America

For

James R. DeMott (1917–2007) &
Nicholas Agustin Ramadan (2008–)

The pure serene of memory . . .
A ripple widening from a single stone
Winding around the waters of the world.

—Theodore Roethke, "The Far Field"

Also by Robert DeMott

Works
Steinbeck's Reading (1984; 2007)
News of Loss: Poems (1995)
Steinbeck's Typewriter: Essays on His Art (1996; 2012)
Dave Smith: A Literary Archive (2000)
The Weather in Athens: Poems (2001)
Brief and Glorious Transit: Prose Poems (2007)
Angling Days: A Flyfisher's Journals (2016)

Edited Anthologies
From Athens Out (1974) [with Carol Harter]
*Artful Thunder: Versions of the Romantic Tradition in
    American Literature* (1975) [with Sanford Marovitz]
After The Grapes of Wrath: *Essays on John Steinbeck* (1995)
    [with Donald Coers and Paul Ruffin]
Conversations with Jim Harrison (2002)
Afield: American Writers on Bird Dogs (2010) [with Dave Smith]
Astream: American Writers on Fly Fishing (2012)
Conversations with Jim Harrison: Revised and Updated (2019)

Editions of John Steinbeck's Writings
Working Days: The Journals of The Grapes of Wrath, *1938–1941* (1989)
The Grapes of Wrath (1992; 2006)
John Steinbeck: Novels and Stories, 1932–1937 (1994)
To a God Unknown (1994)
John Steinbeck: The Grapes of Wrath *and Other Writings, 1936–1941* (1996)
John Steinbeck: Novels, 1942–1952 (2001)
John Steinbeck: Travels with Charley *and Later Novels, 1947–1962* (2007)
    [with Brian Railsback]
Sweet Thursday (2008)

Table of Contents

Part II (2002–2015)   107

Part III (2016-2018)   193

Journal Notebooks, 1989-2015. Credit: Fred C. Tom

". . . meditation and water are wedded for ever."

—Herman Melville, *Moby-Dick* (1851)

"Perhaps, among my many ulterior motives, one is the discovery of language. Or has writing about fishing, which cannot occur without first fishing, become quite as important to me as the act itself? 'Wouldn't think of disassociating fishing from Art,' said the happy John Marin- 'one and the same thing with me.'"

—Nick Lyons, *Spring Creek* (1992)

Acknowledgments

Stay too long in your chamber and you acquire "rust," Thoreau claimed. In my case, to leaven fifty-plus years of regimented, lock-step college life—first as an undergraduate and graduate student, then as a public university teacher—I required a correspondingly steady but less predictable nonacademic and non-ivory tower diet of trout streams, duck marshes, and upland coverts to keep a sane perspective. Changeup is good. A parallel life is good. As John Graves says, "My focus, it seems, belonged elsewhere."

Some people come out of the closet, some people come out of the shadows, and some, like me, come out of the woods and water. Reach a certain age—in my case seventy-two—and it is natural to want to sum up and make a reckoning of accounts. In tracing the background of the sporting part of my life, I am mindful of Herman Melville's comment that "no man is his own sire," a truism that puts the lie to our current fascination with "selfies." There are always one or more kindly souls involved in the drama of our making.

I have been aided and abetted by so many people that as I enter more deeply the shadowy realm of geezerdom, the fact that the number of my reliable, in-any-weather outdoor partners has diminished drastically appears almost tragic. People with whom I hunted and/or fished on a regular basis for long periods of time have become infirm or died, while many others either left town, switched obsessions, or gave up fishing/hunting altogether. I try to make sense of these inevitabilities, but depending on the darkness of the day, don't manage to do so very successfully. Reach three score and ten and the view backward looks more appealing and certainly a good deal richer than the view forward, though of course one has to be ready for anything. It's the way of the world. The point is not nostalgia for its own indulgent sake, then, but an opportunity to sum up and pay respects and give thanks before who-knows-what will make that impossible.

During the past six decades, many people have been part of my outdoor life. Nothing new in that. I learned something from every one of them, especially from my uncle, Anthony Ventrella, my mother's older brother, who set the stage during my youth in New England. He and his brothers Pete and Bob, realists of the first order, gave me a practical, nuts-and-bolts education and an unwavering commonsense foundation about hunting and fishing that I've been building on ever since.

While Tony, Pete, and Bob are present in my sporting obsessions in physical ways, my father, Jim, that good, wise man, is present in a deep, soulful way. He was an inveterate gardener and avid sports fan, who, though he only dabbled in spin fishing for trout, knew full well why it was important to be outdoors on a more or less regular basis. I know, because I owe this same tendency in myself to my father as well as to my uncles. Perhaps it is genetic. But even if it is a matter of nurture, the effect has been the same.

And though my father bought me my first fishing rod, my first pair of hockey skates, and helped me purchase my first shotgun, he did not teach me to shoot accurately, cast a fly rod efficiently, or handle a hunting dog knowingly—all skills my uncles were better equipped at conveying. Rather, in creating the context in which those skills became not just possible but continuous and ongoing, my father granted me permission to keep doing what I loved, and that, to my mind, is the greatest present of all and the most difficult to repay, as well as the easiest to acknowledge.

I am also grateful for Jim Harrison's fellowship. Those days fishing Montana's Yellowstone and Big Hole Rivers have been tips of the iceberg, and his claim that we survive "only by seeking an opposite field" has been a personal touchstone of conduct. Ditto for Nick Lyons, godfather to all who read and write about outdoor sports, particularly fly fishing, who has been supportive and instructive beyond anything I could have imagined. Either man might have been the older brother I never otherwise had.

Gifted anglers Kent Clements, my cousin-in-law Earl DuBack, Bob Hendrix, Dennis Hess, Dan Lahren, Harold and Katie Perkins, and that stalwart Lars Lutton, with whom I go back decades, are in or behind this angling record in more ways than they will ever know. So are generous friends Walter Bennett, Guy de la Valdéne, Jerry Dennis, Chris Dombrowski, Ron Ellis, Bruce Guernsey, Ted Leeson, Tom McGuane, Craig Mathews, Craig Nova, Paul Schullery, and Dave Smith—all contributors to *Afield* and/or *Astream*, who have each proven that fishing/hunting and writing are not mutually exclusive activities, and in fact exist to enrich each other. Our conversation is as likely to be about literature and culture as it is about the sport *du jour*. That, I believe, is the way it should be.

Over the past sixty-plus years, these people brightened days on many waters: Greg Belcamino, Robert Bertholf, John Capowski, Tim Coffman, Dave Delisi, Dave Fulton, Tom Heyes, RJ Kerwood, Jeff Laszlo, John McKinney, Robert McWilliams, John Mitchell, Bob Mizono, Rodger Ornduff, Gregg Orr, Steve Potenberg, Rock Ringling, Mike Ryan, Dr. Erroll Singh, Philip Smith, cousin Phil Ventrella, Pat Washburn, Joe Webb, Jim and Julie Wellington, plus many fellow members of the Blennerhassett (WV) Chapter of Trout Unlimited. All furnished their part toward the whole, whether they knew it or not. So did Dave Breitmeier, Patrick Daigle, Bob Jacklin, John Juracek, George Kelly, John McDaniel, Leon Sagaloff, John Sampson, Mike Saputo, Tim Tollet, and Rick Wollum, all superb guides and the best angling pros the sport has to offer. I am grateful as well to Fred C. Tom at Lamborn's Studio in Athens, to Tony Lyons, Jay Cassell, and Veronica Alvarado at Skyhorse, and to Mary Hendrix for her artwork. To my mother, Colletta, in her hundredth year, continuing good cheer and love.

Patrick Skeen, manager of Daron and Lisa Dean's Elk Springs Resort in Monterville, West Virginia, and his staff always made me welcome, as has my angling partner Rodger Gaulding, master of the soft hackle swing, whose Rivers of the West cabins in Cameron, Montana, have been a convenient and comfortable (and connected) base for many consecutive summers. Gil and Mary Willis at Elk River Inn in Slatyfork, West Virginia, where even the most advanced smartphone cannot reach my hideout, have been helpful and accommodating, as have Roger and Mary Nelson at Nelson's Spring Creek Ranch in Livingston, Montana. Charlotte Fabrizio Meade, former owner of the Gateway Lodge Bed and Breakfast in Highmount, New York, deserves special thanks for her generosity. So does Joyce Bahle, who often let me roost at her family's charming cabin in Suttons Bay, Michigan. Many parts of this book were either ruminated on or written at those half dozen inviting places.

Earlier versions of some sections of this book appeared in *American Fly Fisher, Astream: American Writers on Fly Fishing, Bulletin of the Anglers' Club of New York, The Contemporary Sportsman, Fly Rod and Reel, Gray's Sporting Journal, Quarter After Eight, Southwestern American Literature, Trout,* and *Yale Anglers' Journal.* My gratitude to all who made recycling possible, with special thanks to Marshall Cutchin at *MidCurrent,* and Tracy McClain at *Sulphur,* who understand that catching isn't all there is to fishing.

F. Scott Fitzgerald said there are no second acts in American life, but I am happy to say that sometimes what goes around comes around. I am blessed to have rediscovered a life partner in Kate Fox (we caught and released each other more than thirty years ago). She understands this part of my existence and, as a poet, a quick study in fly fishing, a willing copilot in drift boat exploits, and an inveterate dog lover, shares it as well.

I hope this book of fishing and remembering, this collection of backcasts, will strike a chord years hence with my grandson Nico, to whom Walt Whitman's great poem, "Crossing Brooklyn Ferry," was surely intended: "And you that shall cross from shore to shore years hence are/more to me, and more in my meditations, than you/might suppose." What follows is a reckoning, a roll call of some aspects of my outdoorsy angling life, viewed from over my shoulder. I loved these experiences, these memories, these people, these places, these rivers, and hope he will too.

Robert DeMott
Athens, Ohio
February 2016

A Note to the 2019 Edition

I am deeply gratified by the popular and critical reception of *Angling Days* and am honored to see it appear in expanded paperback format, with Part III added. My thanks once again to Tony Lyons and Jay Cassell at Skyhorse Publishing for their stewardship. I regret that Jim Harrison (1937-2016), who figures prominently in and out of this book, did not live to see this edition. His life-long search for the genuine as an artist and angler, recorded in everything he wrote, continues to inspire.

RD
October 2018

Preface

When it comes to fishing, Athens, Ohio, in the rural southeastern quarter of the state, is plug, hardware, and live-bait country. Fly fishing is an afterthought at best. Nothing caused looks of amazement and now and then verbal exclamations more quickly than angling for rock bass on Federal Creek or the Hocking River, or pumpkinseed, redear and bluegill sunfish, or largemouth bass on Dow Lake or Lake Snowden using a fly rod. I know because I've done plenty of it. Trout Unlimited, the International Federation of Fly Fishers, Theodore Gordon Flyfishers, and other cold-water organizations have zero presence in this hinterland portion of the state (my TU chapter is in Parkersburg, West Virginia). The nearest major fly shops—one in Columbus, Ohio (Mad River Outfitters) and one in Parkersburg, West Virginia (Angler's Xstream)—are seventy-five and forty-five miles away, respectively.

Trouting opportunities here are so slim as to be almost nonexistent. Ohio's DNR dumps rainbows in some area lakes that are mostly harvested within days. Forty minutes away, there's Clear Creek, a small but very welcoming and pleasantly shaded cool-weather stream with long riffles and glides and a number of deep runs and pools, that winds through the piney, rhododendron-draped hills south of Lancaster. Clear Creek is stocked each autumn with small brown trout, some of which hold over from year to year but never seem to get very big. Still, it offers pleasing though limited sport in an intimate setting.

There's the Mad River near Dayton and the Clear Fork near Mansfield. Both are public fisheries with spotty reputations that are two- to three-plus hours away. There are also private clubs in Northwest Ohio that charge thousands for initiation and annual fees to access their groomed and stocked water. Except for enjoyable occasions when I've been a privileged guest at Briarwood Sporting Club in Bellefontaine or Rockwell Springs Trout Club in Castalia, these private outfits are financially beyond my means. I avoid Lake Erie's seasonal steelhead fisheries on Ohio's North Coast because I dislike urban combat fishing.

So when sanity, curiosity, and wanderlust dictate getting away, I hit the road out of Athens to other destinations for my trout fix. In my case that means making the 200-plus-mile drive to West Virginia's Elk River system nearly every other weekend in the spring, and beyond that to the trout streams of Maryland, Pennsylvania's Cumberland Valley (especially Falling Springs Branch Run), Connecticut, Michigan, and even farther afield to the Southwest and West, especially Montana. Besides angling for resident—and often wild—trout, it's the indefinable elements—spiritual renewal, increased well-being, fresh perceptions, new stories, restored energy—I bring back from away that keep me content in my troutless home domain.

Ohio University, where I taught for forty-four years, has kept me rooted in rural southern Ohio. The job was my first priority and all else followed in due course as time and inclination and proportion allowed. I came for the employment fresh out of graduate school and have stayed on years past my retirement for reasons of personal preference and situational compatibility.

So it's reassuring to know that the trouting experience is a movable feast that travels well. I suspect that for many of us with feet planted in both indoor and outdoor realms, life should not be a case of *either/or*, but *both/ and*. Both homebody reality and wild inheritance are necessary for balance. The longed-for goal is to inhabit the elusive arena where nature and culture, wildness and art, society and self intersect. It's the Holy Grail of quotidian life. The far field we journey toward is as much memory, language, and consciousness as any other manner of physical place or material result. In erranding into the wild, in lighting out for distant trout waters four hours away or four days away, I am always seeking my home, everywhere and at once, whether it is outside with a fly rod in hand or inside with a pen in hand. Sometimes I'm lucky enough to find it.

The Trouting Journals

"Memories are a major part of fishing."

—Ernest Schwiebert, *Remembrances of Rivers Past* (1972)

Since I retired from full-time teaching at Ohio University in 2007, fly fishing in its varied guises and dimensions has become increasingly a kind of habit of being, a personal identity marker, an alternate way of apprehending the world. In *Upland Stream: Notes on the Fishing Passion*, W. D. Wetherell lists thirteen reasons why human beings fish, all of them plausible and informative, but the fact is we probably do it for a hundred other different reasons, too, and my guess is that, among them, we love the intimate process of fishing, the simple rituals and preparations associated with the act, the tactileness and physicality of the equipment, the freedom and challenge of being on or near the water, the adrenaline rush and sense of well-being that comes from doing something for ourselves outside the ho-hum work-a-day routine. And last but not least there is the pleasure of recollecting that time on the water.

Among the unalloyed blessings of traveling in Fly-Fish Nation is that when I am not actually fishing forty to fifty days a year, I am equally happy to be reading about it or, if I really want to stretch myself, to be writing about it. Directly or indirectly, whether with rod or pen in hand, I find myself, especially as I pass into old age, spending an inordinate part of each day invested in fly fishing and its related forms of memory, thought, word, and deed. These conglomerate forms of fishing strike me as being of imagination all compact and create a particular angle on the green world.

I admit I can't pass by a river without wondering whether it is as healthy as it should be, whether it holds trout, whether its insect hatches are bountiful and easy or difficult to imitate, and whether I'd be happier living near it than somewhere else. Daydream stuff, fantasy stuff, but a tolerable momentary respite from (if not an actual rebuttal to) an increasingly politicized, dehumanized, technocratic world, which, now that I think of it, is probably the same "modern" world we've been living in and bemoaning for the past 200 years, but which recently appears somehow to have gotten more egregious, poisonous, and fractious. "We fly-fish in part," Chad Hanson says in *Trout Streams of the Heart,* "because we all harbor a sense of loss." In that case, we yearn for something better and different, something restorative. But like most other deep-seated cognitive patterns that veer toward passionate and even obsessive compass points, this angling stance is at best a paradoxical one, discovered as the fisher fishes.

For me, the appeal and power of a fly-fishing purview—if I can give a name to the thing that has colonized my imagination for more than five decades—comes from a lapidary space where cross currents mix and mingle in their at-onceness. Fly fishing can be at turns conservative and avant-garde, naïve and critical, active and reflective, practical and aesthetical, pedestrian and lyrical, pristine and invasive, artificial and natural, experiential and literary, commodified and romantic, brutish and spiritual, misguided and dead-on. Although binaries sometimes cancel each other out, living in these paradoxes strikes me as a thoroughly agreeable condition that keeps me on my toes. "Fish and find out," British philosopher A. A. Luce advised in *Fishing and Thinking.*

In other words, we pay our money and make our choices: we believe in catch and release, but every so often we like to eat what we catch. Sometimes John Keats's unheard melodies are sweetest, sometimes not. After all, best not to forget that, with so many fly-fishing apps downloadable to our smartphones and electronic devices, and with video logs, glossy photo mags, fly-fishing film tours, and angling blogs proliferating at an unheard-of clip, these probably *are* the good old days for many people.

But once an English prof, always an English prof. Whipping the water with a fly rod is one half of the fun. The other half is reading and writing about it. The latter impulses connect to a stained-glass window marking Izaak Walton's burial site in the Chapel of St. John the Evangelist (aka Prior Silkstead's Chapel) at England's Winchester Cathedral: the old master himself with a book in hand, lounging bankside among his fishing paraphernalia. "Study to be quiet," the window's legend reads. The words, from the First Epistle of St. Paul to the Thessalonians in the New Testament, are also the concluding words of Walton's *Compleat Angler.*

I realize that classicism can be a problematic stronghold, and I hope I am not being imperially nostalgic, pining for a way of life gone forever. But it strikes me that St. Paul's admonition is equally as memorable and valid and deserving for fishing writers or writing fishers as Lefty Kreh's "Never leave rising fish," Russell Chatham's "No one ever shot himself in the middle of an evening hatch," or Lee Wulff's "Game fish are too valuable to be caught only once." Then and now, language defines the essence of our sport as much as action. Even Nick Adams, amid an abundance of trout and solitude in Hemingway's "Big Two-Hearted River," "wished he had brought something to read."

For the past forty-five years I have been an inveterate jotter and life-writer of one form or another. I have kept *zibaldone*, mish-mash commonplace ledgers with the titles of and excerpts from books I've read; personal calendar-style diaries of day-to-day life; extended journals of foreign travels, road trips, museum visits, emotional ups and downs, affairs of the heart, psychological self-examination; field books with drawings and observations on nature; vest-pocket pads with shorthand notes and sketches; upland hunting diaries; notebooks with rough drafts of poems, lines, images, sentences, ideas for further development; and, to keep the ego in check, a log book in which I pasted all my rejection slips from editors. Some crazy-quilt notebooks contain all of these topics in one. At times I have scribbled in three or four different varying sized notebooks at once, eager—perhaps even desperate—to set down as much as I could of the inner and outer life of an otherwise ordinary person. But even a private vice like scribomania has a rationale: to find out where I am, I always felt I needed to know where I had been. Thus, a life project was born.

I came late to journaling, an impulse I owe to Henry David Thoreau and John Steinbeck, two of my literary heroes. In 1969 I wrote my PhD dissertation on Thoreau's major works, and I was as impressed as much as anything else in his canon by the extensive, detailed journal he maintained nearly daily from 1837 to his death in 1864 and which had the simplest of beginnings. Few of us can match Thoreau's record of sustained attentiveness and observation, few of us ever attain to his historical significance, but the idea of keeping watch on areas of interest in my life appealed to me greatly, not as a vainglorious exercise but as an incessant learning experience.

Fast-forward to the late 1980s: I was readying for Viking Press *Working Days*, the unpublished daily journal Steinbeck kept while composing his masterpiece, *The Grapes of Wrath*, which he launched in early February 1938, with a simple statement, "It seems necessary to write things down." In the world of social awareness and civic empowerment, fly fishing is not on a par with political activism, but self-recording angling experiences appealed to me anyway as a method of engagement. Since then, over the subsequent decades, all my short quick-view diaries and my long narrative journals—with cumulative entries totaling in the thousands—have become a memory bank, a savings account, a reservoir of experience, a ground of being, and now, in my seventh decade, a springboard toward recapturing aspects of the past before they recede entirely from view. The shorthand jottings and the long handwritten narrative entries are not there only as ends in themselves, but as enticements to flesh out those primary experiences in meaningful, personal ways.

Thus *angling days, writing nights:* what follows here is a reified selection of forty-plus episodes gleaned from thousands of pages and countless entries on fishing that date back decades and fill twenty-plus handwritten volumes chronicling not so much a life *in* fly fishing, as a life *with* fly fishing. There is no attempt to be exhaustive, no attempt to put down each and every timely entry in lock-step fashion. Instead these entries are the tips of the icebergs. For every sampled entry here, there are many more below the waterline. Even among these examples, however, a narrative of progress, a learning curve of angling education, however incomplete and tenuous, eventually arises out of the year-by-year welter. I mean incomplete as in adjunct, unfinished, rough-edged, amateurish, but also incomplete as in limited in range and narrow in skill sets, compared to those rare men and women who have mastered a whole portfolio of angling procedures in both fresh and salt water. Few of us, myself included, are in that category of heightened, all-around expertise, so I have to be content with my narrowband, trout-centric focus. It is what it is and I embrace it.

Although I have never caught a steelhead (winter or summer), a permit, or a musky on a fly, even an incomplete angler has qualities, fixities, and enthusiasms. Basic factual material—dates, times, places, names, actors in the day's events, size and number of fish encountered—are transcribed verbatim from the original journals, though as with all retrospective inscription, the shape of each entry is not always spontaneous, but is also a product of later rumination, reflection, deliberation, and attention, sometimes recollected in tranquility, and sometimes not. Sometimes the shape of the entry arrived as it is given, scribbled *en plein air* so to speak at some trout stream's edge; sometimes the shaping and smoothing of rough edges came later as the language itself torqued down, like a fly reel under an ever-increasing drag setting.

In many original entries, ellipses were deliberately added to signify areas meant to be filled in later, such as exact quotations from and references to books I'd been reading. Infelicities of spelling, grammar, and naming were regularized later as well. Titles that accompany dated entries were added later too. Memory and imagination flourished in the interstices. Fact versus fiction is always a slippery, contested ground the moment pen is set to paper and often language takes us in directions experience and memory (the latter is inherently flawed and partial) by themselves cannot, at which point the best one can do is hold on for the ride. There is "fishing truth" (what happens on stream) and there is "angling tale truth" (what happens at the writing desk). The former is necessary for intellectual accuracy; the latter is necessary for emotional feel. I don't mean to trivialize historical reality or to grant lying *carte blanche* (despite the popular notion that all fishermen are liars), but rather to suggest that facticity, because it sometimes occludes density and texture and nuance, is a starting point, not always an end result.

Walt Whitman called memories "silent backward tracings," which might help explain why some of the following entries have a way of breaking out of chronological bounds and looping behind, like a backcast, before continuing on in their present mode, for memory is fluid, not static, and is given to overrunning its banks. Cast a fly rod over a stream and before you know it, you are focused on the task at hand as well as myriad things that led up to that moment. Fishing Forty Rod Creek in Daniel, Wyoming, took me back to earlier days on Weatherby Brook in Danby Four Corners, Vermont. Shuttling between present and past gives new meaning to "double hauling."

Ultimately, it's possible to consider these entries as small interconnected autobiographical sketches or brief personal memoirs or little discursive essays or (to sound a contemporary note) serial blog pieces. But whatever name they go by, each one is a section of tippet tied with a blood knot on a lengthening leader, all of which comprise an angle, a line of approach, a window, a set of ruminations, on one average person's more or less obsessive amateur fly-fishing life. Each entry can stand on its own, but each also profits from commerce with all the others.

Although I have fished in various places here and occasionally abroad during my life, an inordinate number of entries that follow here occurred in Montana. Throughout the 1990s and beyond, when my professorial life—course preparation, student research direction, thesis and dissertation advising, committee meetings and organization, and my own research and publishing projects—demanded full-time attention, I found that a summer excursion to Montana was often the only extended fishing I'd have in any given year.

The geophysical area I've frequented year after year is a small dot on the enormous Greater Yellowstone Ecosystem map, but it has become the Valhalla in my otherwise limited fly-fishing world. One sliver of it, twenty or so miles of the Madison River below Quake Lake (between the Gravelly Range to the west and the Madison Range to the east), is my *ne plus ultra* angling location where summer after summer, by fishing and schooling my-self thirty days in a row, I learned more about angling for trout than in any other place. Long story short: Montana's trout captured my heart.

Call it the Thoreauvian model: travel deeply in one place or region rather than widely and see what results. Even so, such immersions are relative and fractional. I am still a tourist (though a regular one) and neither claim to be a Montana hand (you must live there year-round to be considered a proper Montanan), nor claim to glorify Montana itself as the "last best place" (it's an imperfect, contradictory, and broadly varied state like every other). But grant this: due to far-reaching fisheries management practices that date back to the early 1970s and resulted in a sustainable stream-bred trout popu-lation in the state's premier rivers, Montana's public fishing is in a category of its own. That and the appeal of the often stunning geographical settings of southwestern Montana are sufficient to draw me back repeatedly. My attach-ment to Montana never wanes. Part of my identity is centered there.

I have tried not to cherry-pick or emphasize glory moments at the ex-pense of unremarkable, mundane, and embarrassing ones, because all those moments—the good, the bad, and even the ugly—comprise the total fab-ric of my fishing life. To suggest otherwise would be a falsehood because everything impinges on everything else. The Izaak Walton–inspired pastoral fishing memoir, though still much beloved by me and many others for its pure escapism and somewhat innocent focus on the natural world, is going away, and in its place it is possible to see why a kind of creative hybrid genre, with its edgy tone and blend of autobiography, fictive techniques, and lyrical style, has evident appeal. Linking outdoor experiences with the inner emotional contexts surrounding and informing those sporting moments is the new wave. Context counts. The story behind the story, or adjacent to it anyway. These experiences aren't always separate in life; why should they be separate in books? "Merge the fisher and the writer, merge the river and the word," W. D. Wetherell wisely advises in *Vermont River.*

General consensus says it is improper to make a noun into a verb, though such usage is occurring more often now in some quarters. I like the present progressive, gerundal form of a noun, such as "journaling" or "trouting," because it gives a sense of movement, of being in motion, of traveling toward an end that can never be fully reached. In that sense, then, no matter their content, style, or temperament, journals (and the act of journaling, like the act of fishing itself), are all about process rather than product, a path toward the horizon rather than arrival at a destination. That *journals* shares a linguistic root element with *journeys* strikes me as more than just coincidence.

But more than that, I was pleased to discover recently that *trouting,* used as a verb, has precedence and history in English from William C. Stewart's "Trouting with the Fly" in *The Practical Angler* in 1857 to Ed Shenk's eminently readable *Fly Rod Trouting* in 1989. I stand on their shoulders with gratitude and not a twinge of guilt. But where the term *trouting* has been characteristically synonymous with a kind of genteel, leisurely pastoral outdoor pursuit enjoyed by leisurely, pastoral gentle folk, I use the term in a broader sense as a focal metaphor for the whole contextual surround and ongoing process of fly fishing for trout (and other game fish along the way), so that it is as much a mind-set, or subconscious orientation, as it is a physical activity. Getting in to the trouting zone is as much mental and interior as it is physical and exterior. "Fishing and philosophy, trout and truth" are linked together, Professor Luce quipped to his students at Trinity College, Dublin.

Although I had been fly fishing more or less frequently since the mid-1950s, my fly-fishing/trouting journal habit started as simply and casually as an afterthought on 12 June 1989, with a brief entry about catching trout on dry flies in the Norwalk River in Wilton, Connecticut, where I was visiting family. I folded the account into a larger diary I was keeping at the time, as much for the tranquility of the afternoon (a delicious interlude in an otherwise fractious emotional period) as for its quality of *déjà vu*.

I had been fishing the humble Norwalk (and its neighbor the Saugatuck) since I was a kid on a bicycle, and though I long ago had moved away from Connecticut, I always considered it my first "home" river. Even the occasional braying Metro North passenger train stopping a few yards away at the Cannondale Station on its shuttle between New York City and Danbury couldn't spoil the effect. "Peaceful, beautiful, enjoyable, lovely" was how I summed up the fishing, before jotting a wistful note to myself: "I want to live near a trout stream." From the very first, fishing was a respite and a therapy along with all of its other potentially redemptive qualities.

Norwalk River trout were all stockers, with an occasional holdover fish from the previous year, and to find a half-dozen pale-skinned browns rising to a Parachute Adams that day was extremely pleasurable and noteworthy. And though it has never come to pass that I've been able to reside permanently next to a trout stream, since 1989 I have made an annual summer pilgrimage to Western waters to live, even briefly, in their presence.

The following year, 1990, with extended entries and accompanying photographs about excellent fishing on Montana's Bighorn and Madison Rivers, my trout journaling habit took root. In 1994 I quit incorporating angling entries into my regular diaries and started keeping a separate fly-fishing journal, one per year, devoted entirely to angling. For a quarter of a century or more, each standard letter size (8.5" × 11") notebook (now and then a lined ledger, but most often blank artist's sketchbooks) has run between 100 and 150 pages and beyond.

I must have been absent in grammar school when penmanship and proper writing style were being taught because my handwriting, which is illegible at worst and poor at best, is a hybrid of cursive and printing styles too wayward and wandery to obey the confines of a lined ledger page. I understand the convenience a medium-sized lined book like Tully Stroud's *Trout Chaser's Journal: A Diary for Trout and Salmon Fishermen* holds for the casual angler, but for me, only the wide-open lineless, marginless spaces of a blank book will suffice. Plus there's enough space to draw maps and sketches, paste or tape in photographs, maps, printed documents, and excerpts from fishing books and magazines, and other flavorful odds and ends, like pressed flowers, bird feathers, and damaged flies.

From the start, because I prefer the immediacy and tactile intimacy of a pen, and the freedom of free-handing, my journals have always been written by hand rather than typed on a computer. Occasionally I scribbled streamside when the spirit moved me. Stop fishing, walk to the truck, get out the pen and sketchbook, and start writing, then go back to fishing. From that time forward I never went astream without having my journal nearby, or a small inexpensive vest-pocket notebook that could be later transcribed or transposed into the larger volume.

Most of the time, however, I wrote each day after fishing, oftentimes even if it meant staying up late to complete the writerly task. Once in a while, too tired to wield a pen, I deferred my entry to the next day, usually but not always first thing the following morning. The point was to write as soon after the fishing as possible, when some lingering sense of the visible moment was still fresh. Other anglers tied flies by the dozens, or took photographs by the dozens, or filled pads with drawings by the dozens; I wrote journal entries. I lack even a hint of sketching and painting ability, so I was destined never to be able to produce the kind of whimsical and brilliantly-illustrated diary that British angler Muriel Foster kept from 1913 to 1949. For me, rod and pen complete each other in a kind of call-and-response way. Both tools urge each other on and keep the circle unbroken.

From age four on in my southwestern corner of Connecticut I fished and fished and fished. New Canaan was a launch point. At the public Mill Pond Park near Route 123, in the company of my older cousin, Jack Lapolla, I caught my first fishes—brown bullhead (horned pout) and sunfish—on a cane pole three times as tall as I was, rigged with waxed twine and a snelled Eagle Claw hook baited with an earthworm. It would be many years before I learned that Thoreau had a similar experience a century earlier on the more famous Walden Pond, where he pulled a "horned pout squeaking and squirming to the upper air." Thoreau claimed, in a truly metaphysical gyration, that he "caught two fishes as it were with one hook," and I have come to believe that, as I am still actively fishing nearly seven decades later, those two fish caught me.

I fished in fresh and salt water with live bait (earthworms, night crawlers, sand worms, blood worms, small frogs, grasshoppers) and artificial lures

(C.P. Swing, Mepps, Jitterbug, Hula Popper, Flatfish, Dardevle, lead jigs, popping bugs) by every conceivable means—cane pole, spinning rod, ultra-light spinning rod, bait casting rod, fly rod, surf rod—for panfish, yellow perch, suckers, largemouth bass, smallmouth bass, pickerel, bullheads, mackerel, snapper blues, striped bass, weakfish, and flounder, but it was trout that led me on in ways I could not have imagined. Renowned naturalist John Burroughs said in his classic 1870 essay, "Speckled Trout," that he had "been a seeker of trout" from his boyhood, and a similar enthusiasm has been mine as well. Trout as a species and fly fishing for them became an aperture through which I viewed an intriguing and increasingly large area of my avocational life. Trout have remained my signature fish for reasons I don't always fully understand or even care to dissect too closely. A particular fish becomes our special fish or our favorite quarry for reasons that have nothing to do with reason. Romanticism, sentimentality, affect, nostalgia, yes, but not logic, Harold Blaisdell suggested in 1959 in *The Philosophical Fisherman.*

Perhaps it has something to do with size—because most trout are scaled in the right proportion to their habitat; perhaps it has something to do with beauty—because all trout are colored like resplendent hand-painted artifacts; perhaps it has something to do with geography—because trout tend to live in Earth's desirable places; perhaps it has something to do with environment—because trout are prime indicators of water's organic health, in which we all have a stake; perhaps it has something to do with books and paintings—because the extensive written and iconographic records on trout are among the absolute glories of sporting literature and art. And then perhaps it is as simple as saying that in their welcoming familiarity as a species, trout suit my sensibility, speak directly to my temperament. I understand other anglers' similar and sometimes exclusive fascination with tarpon, salmon, bonefish, or permit as exalted species that signify the meaning of what the fly-fishing pursuit and mania are all about, and I say more power to them—fish and men—but I am content and comfortable to keep my focus most of the time, anyway, riveted on trout. That's my story of monogamous attraction and I'm sticking to it.

To progress from wanting to catch just one trout, to wanting to cast only to the most difficult and challenging of them (my current state of play) is a typical angler's arc of evolution. It's the aqueous plot many of us follow through our angling days. But the deeper I went into fly fishing as a serious pursuit rather than an occasional or irregular pastime, the more I felt compelled to be correspondingly diligent about researching its texts and documents and recording my riverine experiences.

If trout lead us on, so does writing. Anglers are never content simply to say how many fish they fooled, but prefer to elaborate on the how and why of each watery seduction. Our need to regale is not simply a matter of being enamored of elemental facticity—numbers involving the measurement of weight, length, girth, and so on—but a matter of recreating an entire context, a whole history of each piscatorial event. There are times when the fish don't matter so much by themselves (after all, many of us end up releasing them alive anyway), but only as part of a larger history, an immersion in and involvement with a process in water and words that is somehow more extensive than the meager individual self.

Fishermen are notorious liars, or so the folk wisdom goes; but really we are all relentless elaborators, seeking explanations for why we fish and what we fish for. To put it another way, the river that "runs through it" might of course be the Big Blackfoot in northern Montana (or any home river you care to name), but it is also the river of narrative, the rush and tumble of language, the unimpeded flow of a contextual story that binds together experience, gives it emphasis and vitality, and creates a running thread of participatory, immersive knowledge. Fly fishing is tailor-made for our story-obsessed culture.

So, if the fishing wasn't always spectacular or off the charts or worth the effort, writing about it always was. More than that, there were days, I admit, when I could not say which mattered more—fooling a nice trout under difficult conditions or giving the moment its due in words. Both the fishing and the journaling kept me writing. They are both part and parcel of my personal fishing plot and I often cannot tell them apart; I often cannot say which catch is more satisfying or for that matter, which is more difficult. I discovered a life-defining project, and I became, in Melville's words, a "fast-fish" myself, hooked as I was by the twin acts of fishing and writing, both of which struck me as being open-ended, incomplete processes rather than final products. The journey never ends, which of course is part of its inherent appeal. The plot is always thickening: there's always another trout rising around the next bend, always another chance for angling success or failure.

A late relative of mine on my mother's side, an artist, children's book author/ illustrator, and Atlantic salmon angler named Albert Aquino, created a cover for the March 1963 issue of *Field & Stream*. His impressionistic scene foregrounded a very portly cartoon-like fish, its hugely disproportionate mouth wide open, about to strike an utterly realistic green and blue streamer fly called an "Aquino Special." In the background, standing waist deep in the rolling river, the fish's adversarial counterpart, a comic-strip fisherman smiling broadly, fly rod held conspicuously aloft, anticipates the strike. Humor aside, the point of the illustration is that we never know whether the fisherman gets what he thinks he wants, never know whether he catches the fish. Our angler (the fish, too) is forever in a state of anticipation, the uncertainty of the about-to-happen, so that the answer to the question the picture poses (will he hook up or won't he?) is always deferred and left open to the imagination of each viewer.

The cover brought a storm of protests from *Field & Stream*'s readers, who were apparently accustomed to more sharply executed mimetic images of the fishing moment, and who objected strenuously to what might now be considered an example of painterly *jouissance*, a blissful aesthetic indulgence. I was a sophomore in college when Al's cover came out. Encountering a real streamer fly in an imaginary river with imaginary fish (to paraphrase liberally Marianne Moore's famous Modernist poem, "Poetry") was more (or less) than subscribers in the early '60s expected regarding their beloved sport. But somehow that metaphoric quality struck me then as it still does now as perfectly fitting to underscore the essentially fabular and inconclusive nature of angling to which the journal genre as a by-product is perfectly fitted.

Of course I created a leviathan. Fishing and journal keeping went through the inevitable "process of evolution" from simple to complex that British radiologist J. C. Mottram predicted a century ago in his great (and overlooked) *Fly Fishing: Some New Arts and Mysteries*. In a chapter called "The Keeping of a Fishing Log," he claims there "is more in fishing than fish," and part of the "more" is keeping a record of close observations that enhances both the pleasurable and instructional aspects of angling. My entries gradually grew longer and more complex, required larger notebooks, and consumed more time, so that during the past several years my annual fishing journal has approached (and at times exceeded) 150 pages. Yet even while each personal journal has become fatter than the one before—became more prose narrative than unadorned log—I can't wean myself from the recording habit. It has become my vice, if not my curse. But not, I hope, in a bad way. My angling experiences don't seem real unless I make them into sentences, which is itself a twisted but obviously necessary kind of fascination. In this I am like all unreconstituted and unrepentant obsessives who are caught and not yet released, and I cannot imagine a life free from my pursuit or my pursuit apart from my life, for who can tell the fisher from the fishing, or the writer from the writing?

Part I (1989–2001)

"You are aware, in a horizonless and slightly mesmerized way, like listening to the double bass in orchestral music, of the fish below there in the dark. . . . And the whole purpose of this concentrated excitement, in this arena of apprehension and unforeseeable events, is to bring up some lovely solid thing like living metal from a world where nothing exists but those inevitable facts which raise life out of nothing and return it to nothing."

—Ted Hughes, *Poetry in the Making* (1967)

On Grayling Creek

26 July 1989

I'm in a small cabin at Parade Rest Ranch, on the banks of Grayling Creek just out of West Yellowstone, Montana. A comfy little spot off Highway 287, except that there was a 4.2 earthquake yesterday hereabouts, and oh yes, there is apparently a female grizzly that has taken up residence on the ridge behind the ranch to the north, and we've all been warned to keep a wary eye. That is not an encounter I care to have.

I've been looking over road and topo maps, reading fly-shop catalogs, trying to get a feel for the area, which is truly vast. West Yellowstone has the Big Four—Jacklin's, Bud Lilly's, Blue Ribbon Flies, and Madison River Outfitters. All are well stocked, friendly, and mostly, but not always, courteous to outsiders and amateurs like myself. Also International Fly Fisher's Federation is here, making West Yellowstone a center for trout fishing in the United States. You can't drive a mile in any direction without hitting trout water. West is still a rough-edged town, though it's grown since Dad and I came through here five years ago on the drive back from California. Some of the roads have been paved since then, though I'm not sure whether that's a good thing. Surely the world can do with less homogenization.

Stormy all day with spectacular lightning shows. It's breathtaking because I can see the weather fronts advancing from miles away. You think you're ready for what's coming, but you're not. *Bam!* Just like that, wind, rain, and hail are in your face. Wetness should keep fires from starting, unlike tinder-dry 1988 when Yellowstone National Park burned by the millions of acres. Already green swaths of new growth are springing up in the park, like a promise of redemption among these huge, eerie stands of blackened, skeletal, crazy-leaning timber. People are starting to understand the recuperative effects of fire, though I wonder how all that ash, silt, and exposed dirt will damage the park's streams once that junk gets in the water. I can't imagine tons of siltation will be good for the environment.

Cool night. I've got the wall heater on low but the windows open to catch a late-night breeze. Battery-powered radio tuned to the only channel I can get, KZBQ, a country station from Pocatello, Idaho. Some needs are being met: a welcoming letter from home waiting for me when I checked in; decent meals and all the iced tea and sandwiches I can carry out the door for lunch; rainbow trout rising to gayly bedecked Royal Trudes and Lime Humpys in Grayling's runs and riffles; and at night, perhaps best of all, the sound of its water to fall asleep by. Nothing more relaxing than the soothing gurgle of running water.

Pitch dark outside. No ubiquitous urban glow to distort the scene. Last evening, sat on the porch at dusk with my neighbors, Dick and Al, two over-the-top Californians who looked like Laurel and Hardy (one has been married four times, the other is an interior designer for Vegas casinos), and we smoked cigars and drank—me beer from a bottle, they whiskey from engraved silver cups, no less! They come out here for a catered week every year and seem to enjoy life to the fullest. Ah, the merry fast-lane life! No money worries or philosophical discontents with them, as far as I could tell. The porch is cheek by jowl with Grayling Creek. The day refused to give up its hold, and as the last light lingered, it draped from the porch eaves, until bats and nighthawks showed up and whirled us all into full darkness.

Woke this morning with a splitting headache and eye strain that thankfully lessened as the day progressed. I doubt it was the beer—I only had a couple last night. More likely it was from peering into river glare trying to follow my fly yesterday on the Madison, which I floated from West Fork to Palisades. At $165 the float trip was an indulgence and I am thinking that I can treat myself to two of them each summer without plunging into debt. The rest of the time I'll have to be on my own.

Anyway, the float turned out to be an intense, all-day experience: my first time ever on that storied river, and only the third float trip I've ever taken in my life—the first was beneath the brow of the Tetons on the drop-dead scenic Snake River in Wyoming five years ago with my father along, and the second just a few days ago on the upper Green River around Pinedale, Wyoming, with a young guide, Rich McCaskill, also out of Jack Dennis's stocked-to-the-rafters fly shop, a cathedral of sporting gear, in Jackson. Otherwise, the bulk of my fishing has been traditional—on foot from a stream bank, or now and then out of a canoe or small rowboat on a Connecticut or Vermont lake, or from Uncle Bob Ventrella's powerboat around the Norwalk islands in Long Island Sound. I've reached my financial limit, though. No more guided trips until next year.

In the bow of a drift boat there's so much that's new, so much yet to be absorbed. I felt like I was on a treadmill at high speed: reading water on the move, managing the drift of the fly, mending properly to defeat drag, detecting the take (hard on the eyes following an indicator or a bouncy dry fly in the glare), and trying not to appear an utter greenhorn in front of the guide. All anxiety producers for a newbie who never took an organized fly-casting or fishing lesson in his life. You don't want to concentrate so exclusively on the fishing that you miss the scenery, which exists on a scale incalculable and ever-wondrous to an Easterner, whether you've seen it before or not. Best to listen to the guide and follow instruction. Admonishments to myself: Don't be thin-skinned, don't take offense or umbrage if the guide offers correction. Act as though you've got everything to learn and nothing to lose. Be a good student of the game and when in doubt, make it up as you go.

I learned a boatload yesterday from my guide, Bob Adams, about nymphing, which I admit I had never done much of back east in my earlier angling life. But it seems to be a way to go out here: Prince Nymph, this year's hot fly (Adams carries a box full of them in various sizes), fastened below a neon-yellow indicator as the flag of earnest angling purposefulness. It is a rig especially designed to troll up bottom-hoovering native whitefish, of which there were at least ten (they reminded me of suckers we used to catch in the Norwalk River when I was a kid), and which for a neophyte put a bend in a fly rod that sends a quiver of excitement, momentarily anyway, straight to the heart.

But repetitious or not, following the bouncing indicator, I managed half-a-dozen goodly trout, the best being an 18-inch brown, one of the nicest I've ever gotten, with glorious buttery colored sides and dime-sized spots and a fight worthy of a middleweight contender. I'd almost forgotten a trout could be that beautiful. Adams, who's a teacher in California, appeared as pleased about that fish as I was and let out a hearty whoop when it was netted. I wonder if he knew his enthusiasm was infectious? I can't get over the fact that at one point in a shallow section of the Madison, he jumped out of the boat and walked behind it slowly working us downstream so I could cast unhurriedly to holding water on either side. Talk about personal service! I got tired and felt guilty just watching him ferry the boat.

Today I fished alone and hit the Madison hard around Slide Inn, which is becoming my favorite area. And did a stupid thing—in a rush to avoid being fried by lightning, I caught my Sage rod in the rear gate of my Blazer and broke it. Barreled into West Yellowstone and bought a 6-weight, 9-foot J. Kennedy Fisher for $210, a bargain price since most other high-end rods, like Winstons and Powells, are in the $300 range. Maybe someday. Right now this is all more money than I planned on spending, and now I'm hoping *Working Days* goes into paperback soon and I get some compensatory moola to stuff in the fishing wallet.

Hardy LRH Lightweight

28–29 July 1989

Taking stock, summing up: Left Athens 1,900 miles ago, give or take a few hundred miles. Truck loaded with camping gear and fishing equipment, plus maps, books, notebooks, binoculars, and a typewriter (which I have yet to use). My intention was to do some prep work for my fall-term classes, draft a couple of lectures I'm giving in California next month and the Soviet Union in October, and catch up on reading. Grandiose intellectual plans! Recent road travel and the allure of fishing have eclipsed my academic intentions and professional obligations, revealing (1) the true depths of my laziness, and (2) how easily I am seduced by activities that are way more fun. Except, I've made a slight dent in Kenneth Lynn's doorstop Hemingway biography to see what he says about Hemingway's "Big Two-Hearted River," always my litmus test to gauge whether a Hemingway authority knows what he or she is talking about. So far, so good.

Early on, Old Papa fished bait with a fly rod and still changed everything. I was ignorant of that thirty-five years ago. I thought I'd invented a new angling method when I caught chain pickerel at Hailey's Pond in Norwalk using my fly rod rigged with a live frog. Those greedy wolves hit the frogs like torpedoes and I can still see the explosion and the swirl. *Blam!* They put a bend and a throb in my old fiberglass rod and I had to hang on for dear life. Pickerel so voracious that minutes after being caught and released they would come cruising back through the lily pads for more frog. Always with a smile on their wolfish faces. They had a devilish, slinky way of moving in the water that made them look like they were levitating. I can't explain it exactly, but there was something haunting about their movements. I once caught the same toothy little bastard three times in a row. It might have been more often than that, too, but I ran out of bait. It couldn't have been more than a foot long, but it had aggression in spades. For a time pickerel were my favorite quarry, especially after I discovered a frog-colored Flatfish in a size light enough to fling with my fly rod.

Last week on the drive out here, I pulled off Route 80 at Rock Springs, Wyoming, and cruised around—it isn't so much a town or even a city as it is intimidating sprawl—an oil-and-gas mecca open to the widest of Western skies, the "heartless Wyoming sky," Richard Ford calls it in *Rock Springs*, his knockout story collection of a few years ago. A human being seems dwarfed, reduced to the tiniest fragment, another wind-blown speck of dust among a million others. Depending on one's mood, that can be good or bad.

Rumination on time's fleeting passage, as if there is anything new in that! *Tempus fugit* and all that. Ask not for whom the bell tolls, etc., etc. Truth is, to reenter a formerly visited scene, as I have done by driving out here from Ohio and passing through some territory I have visited briefly several times before, brings some inevitable and unavoidable connections. Twenty years ago this month I came west the first time—a post-PhD graduation present to myself. Bob Bertholf and me in a rented VW bus, on the road through Colorado, Wyoming, Montana, Idaho, Oregon, and Washington. Some days the High Plains wind blew so hard in our grille we couldn't get that sewing machine–engined car to go over forty miles an hour, and the distances from point A to B increased exponentially with every rotation of the wheels.

The long hours in that boxy car without radio or air-conditioning seemed dreamlike in their starkness. I often felt like I was floating through space, like one of those wind-hovering prairie falcons we saw. I remember my first western trout—an 11-inch cutthroat that inhaled a Muddler Minnow alongside a midstream boulder in the Wind River. Heavy current made the fish seem much larger than it was, though I can't say I was disappointed when it came to hand. Nothing spectacular, but the first one, no matter its size, is as good as it gets. Under its chin, the brilliant orange slash mark—like an incipient Nike swoosh—blazed in my mind for a long time.

There were several days of pleasant camping next to the Encampment River (the name alone enough to draw us there) in Wyoming's Medicine Bow Mountains. And a few firm-bodied trout caught for the purpose of serving as dinner, cooked on an open fire. Spectacularly delicious those wild cold-water Wyoming trout, seasoned only with salt and pepper, butter, and fresh lemon. Gourmet dining reduced to its simplest elements. Oh, and Saltines and Cheez-Its on the side, not exactly gourmet touches, but good enough in a pinch. And of course beer. I learned a great deal about wine from Bertholf, but I was always pleased to know he could down a beer with the rest of us *hoi poloi*. At night great horned owls *hoo-hooing* in the cathedral of firs and pines all around us: their deep nighttime vibrato serenaded us, as though we were honored guests in their house.

Fishing these last few days has been slow but not uneventful. Pleased with my new Fisher rod. Seems lighter in hand than my now-busted Sage, which I will send back for repair when I get home. I'm not a gear junkie, but thank God for fly rods and fly reels—what a melding of aesthetic form and pure function. Physical objects, sure, but metaphors for slow-handedness and intimate, scaled-down proportions. Retrograde items worked by hand, without frills, bells, whistles, doodads, mechanical or electric aid. The simplicity of this equipment is arresting and speaks to something deep in me, some little sequestered island of unadorned resoluteness that I never realized I had. Part of me is definitely a Luddite, the part that loves fly fishing.

I've been using my Wheatley fly box for thirty years, my single-action Hardy LRH reel for twenty. Simple as they are in design, each item is more than itself: each is a touchstone for a whole complex of personal memory and private history. Little talismans, I guess. The reel was a Christmas present from first wife Michele, who worked overtime, bless her heart, to earn the money to surprise me. One summer, at a time when we were simpatico and divorce was still in the future, we backpacked part of the Appalachian Trail together. Michele was not exactly an outdoor gal but she was a good sport with a great sense of humor, and in order for her to agree to a hike that lasted longer than a single day, it fell to me to carry the bulk of our camping gear, while to her fell the task of packing her makeup, some extra clothes, and the all-important candy bars ("to keep up our strength," she insisted).

I was a sucker for her beauty, her long legs and raven hair, and for her entreaties, all of which of course she knew and counted on, and so we went, thus burdened. I did not have a fly rod short enough for small stream work, so I rigged my LRH reel on a 2-piece, 5-foot fiberglass spinning rod and we caught perfectly formed and brilliantly colored native brook trout on bushy dry flies in the tight quarters of Vermont's pristine, brush-lined mountain streams. On topo maps those trickling streams were nothing but thin blue squiggly lines without names. There was something utterly delicious about disappearing that deep into the forest to do as we pleased. Even lovemaking was special, carried on as it was beyond the margins of the printed map.

So Wheatley and Hardy: like sex, no planned obsolescence there. Both still completely functional, delightfully tactile, resonant to the senses: the satisfying snap-click of the fly box lid; the one-of-a-kind ratchet sound of the reel. No Apple computer on Earth gives me the same rush.

Today I worked a meadow section of the Gallatin River next to Route 191 near Specimen Creek. In a book I've been reading, *Fishing Yellowstone Waters*, Charles Brooks calls the Gallatin a "friendly" stream and indeed it is a pleasure to fish. Then I came down to the Madison at the Slide Inn area. A few nicely colored rainbow trout on a low-drifting Prince. It's those two little white goose biots that give the fly its pop, I think. Early evening there were fish rising quite actively, some right at my feet. The "sudden silent trout are all lit up hanging, trembling.. . ." Virginia Woolf says in *To the Lighthouse*. She used to fish with her father and brother and wrote in an autobiographical sketch of her "passion for the thrill and the tug." Alas, no tug thrill for me tonight, which only makes me miss it more. I could not find the proper match and so faced refusal after refusal from those trembling fish whose silence spoke volumes. Frustrating! The experience drove home what an amateur I really am at this angling business even though I have been at it, off and on, for decades. You would think I would've learned more in all that time. The bottom line: enthusiasm and passion but not much skill to speak of. But then

I have fought the fraudulence, inadequacy, and pretense in me all my life. This trip, though, this trip seems to be a definite marker between my early angling life and a more committed one that's likely to follow, hoping never to cease, to paraphrase Walt Whitman. It's been like going back to school. It feels like these are the first days of a new life.

Fishing washes the slate clean, puts the other part of my life in perspective. Where do I draw the line, though, between vocation and avocation? Between the work-a-day existence that pays the bills and the sporting life that fills the heart and lifts the spirit? Starting for Ohio tomorrow with full awareness that I need much more time to get this Western fishing figured out, because right now, in the moment, it seems to be the most important thing imaginable. I no longer have to teach Ohio University's summer session to make ends meet, so the long-term goals, if I can arrange them, would be to spend a month out here each summer, then write about fishing. Every scrap of fishing would be research for the writing. I don't envision quitting my day job and going full bore into a fishing life of some sort, though I probably would if I had a day job I hated. But that isn't the case. Teaching is my A game; the outdoor stuff is C+ or maybe B− with plenty of room for improvement, the promise of which spurs me on. Teach nine months, take three months off in the summer, part of it out here, and recharge the professorial batteries. That would be sweet if it comes to pass.

Maybe starting this journal, such as it is, will be a step toward creating a future *Book of Fishing and Remembering*, subtitled *Ohio Prof's Secret Angling Life Revealed.* Or *Fishing Plots: Pages from a Fly Fisher's Days.* Right now, though, it's too soon to tell where this all leads, and the best I can do is to remain hopeful and keep plugging away when time and energy allow. To which I can only add, *We'll see. . . .*

Did the Hemingway thing and gave a small box of flies each to my neighbors Al and Dick. I don't think either of them ever read *The Sun Also Rises,* but one of my favorite passages occurs when the Englishman Wilson-Harris gives Jake Barnes and Bill Gorton a selection of hand-tied trout flies after they had fished together on the Irati River in Spain's Pyrenees: "'I only thought if you fished them some time it might remind you of what a good time we had.'" Amen!

A Rod, Not a Pole

6 October 1991

Whiling away a TWA flight from Denver to St. Louis where I connect to Columbus. Lots of time to scribble this recent stuff down and account for it, sketchy or not. Came out to Colorado a few days ago to Rocky Mountain National Park to present a talk at the annual Western American Literature Conference, my favorite professional gathering. I hobnobbed with some of my former graduate students, now happily launched on careers of their own, and had a good long chat with Louis Owens about writing and fishing, twin loves for both of us.

This is a conference where I find colleagues with more of a country than city bent. And a kind of infectious enthusiasm for their subject. Not too many academic confabs where I can discuss fly-fishing literature as though it mattered and is on equal footing with highbrow books and not a cast-off, low-rent mongrel. The talk among the cognescenti concerned Norman Maclean's 1976 novella, *A River Runs Through It*, and the buzz is that it is being made into a movie by Robert Redford, who was turned on to the book by Thomas McGuane. If that's true, it will have a distinguished lineage. Who better to kick-start the deal than McGuane, writer and angler *nonpareil*?

I was part of the WAL discussions the last few days, by dint of having taught *River* to a freshman class last year. One mild spring day I took the class outside and demonstrated fly casting on the lawn in front of the English Department, then had each one try it following Maclean's specific instructions.

I love that kind of hands-on approach to literary texts. Writing is a physical construct as well as a mental act. It takes art out of the ether and grounds it in the here-and-now where the ineluctable laws of physics and tailing loops operate.

Well, mostly anyway: Maclean doesn't acknowledge Montana's constant wind. You can't fish there a day without having to contend with a blow of some sort. Then there's the problem of character: who in their right mind would want to fish with that maniac Paul? And, oh yeah, that shadow casting mumbo jumbo is hard to swallow, though if I remember right, almost eighty years ago in *The Dry Fly and Fast Water*, George LaBranche claimed a hatch could be simulated. But I'm not buying it. I remain skeptical. I'm on the side of Harold Blaisdell in *The Philosophical Fisherman*. He called creating a hatch "bunk."

Otherwise, what's not to like about Maclean's book? I think the casting lessons, and a brief lecture and slide show on trout food and hatches made a difference in my students' level of understanding. I know they liked whipping the rod around. And no one, not even the urban kids from Cleveland and Cincinnati, used the word *pole* instead of *rod* in their writing assignments. A small triumph for fly-fishing English teachers everywhere.

Best of all, WAL holds its annual confabs in scenic places. There's nothing like going to a professional meeting with the sound of bugling elk coming through your window every morning. Many times, though I'm sure it isn't on purpose, WAL chooses meeting sites close to good trout fishing, so on those occasions I usually pack my fly rod and stay on an extra day at my own expense. If I am a designated presenter at the conference, Ohio University's research fund covers my official travel and conference room and board, but the extra stuff is on my dime and easy to arrange with some judicious planning, so that no one is cheated or swindled. It's my personal quirk. Why not take advantage of getting to distant waters?

And while arrangements and schedules and conference dates and venues don't always fall out in my favor, I've been piggybacking fishing and scholarly business off and on since a 1970 Steinbeck conference in Oregon. When I got off the plane in Corvallis, the person assigned to pick me up recognized me by the fly-rod case I was carrying. After the conference I fished some of the local mountain streams. Fishing was slow—the streams were all in April spate—but I saw a part of the vernal Northwest I might never have seen. (The place gave "green" a new meaning.) Fishing made the whole conference attendance rigmarole palatable and enjoyable. Soothed the fevered and overworked brain, taxed with too much literary theory and pedagogical discourse. Next year's WAL conference is in Reno, which means, with some nimble planning, I might be able to get a day on the East Fork of Walker River, which I have heard has fine fishing.

I shuttled down to Denver to a motel near Stapleton and fished yesterday with Rick Wollum, a guide out of The Flyfisher in Denver I met a few years ago. Rick picked me up at the motel at 8 a.m. and I didn't get back until 9 p.m. last night. Long day but worth every minute. Last time, in 1988, we fished a section of the South Platte River near Spinney Reservoir, and I had my first truly impressive Western fly-fishing trip. It opened my eyes more than any other to the incredible quality and inexhaustible range and potential of this Rocky Mountain region's fishing, which I now realize—probably like a million people before me—has started to obsess me and infiltrate my waking hours. It's always there, like a beckoning dream, an enticing allurement.

I've been spending an inordinate amount of time lately thinking about fishing destinations and scheming and planning future trips, or running over prior ones in my mind. This past summer, after Andrea and I married, we treated ourselves to a float trip (pricey at $250 for the day) on the B section of Utah's highly touted Green River. It was another eye-opening experience, as the red-rock canyon scenery below 500-foot-tall Flaming Gorge Dam is spectacularly wild—uninhabited and roadless—on a scale that can hardly be comprehended and is like nothing we Easterners had ever seen before in the way it dwarfs us puny humans, puts us in our place. Go there and you leave your baggage-ridden psychic domain for a while, is my advice to the lovelorn and world-weary.

Looking down into the Green River from the bow of a drift boat is like peering through a window into a parallel world. The water is so clear it's mesmerizing and even a bit spooky. Dark shapes abound: *was that a trout the size of my leg or an otter?* In that clear water it was a kick to see the take. Fishing was average, but we managed to catch some decent ones, nymphing as we went, including a 20-inch brown (nicely marked but skinny). At night,

back at the lodge, we looked up instead of down, and watched the constel-
lations whirl and dance overhead in a cloudless dome of sky and felt again,
even in our lovemaking, diminished in size to nearly nothing in the face of
that vast cosmogonical window. Trout and stars were our humbling wedding
presents to each other.

Yesterday, happy to say, more good stuff, thanks again to Rick Wollum,
who, in my estimation, is the best guide I've yet encountered, because he
imparts knowledge generously and makes his client part of the process of
discovery. As a teacher I understand that dynamic and how effective it is.
We hightailed it northwest out of Denver on Route 40 to a section of the
Colorado River near Kremmling. All new country to me.

Aspen leaves had almost all dropped, but the cottonwood foliage along
the river's edge was a brilliant yellow-going-gold and lit up like torches in
the bright sunlight and thin air. Every time a wind curried the trees, leaves
fell like gold dazzle to the river. I still see dazzly stuff filtering down as I
write this many hours later. Spotting a #20 Blue-winged Olive amid leafy
detritus and lengthening afternoon shadows became a challenge but was
worth an annoying case of eye strain. Half a dozen chunky 16-inch browns
and rainbows on that fly. One of the best dry-fly days I've had, thanks to
Rick's patient coaching during the *Baetis* hatch. A towering pile of student
papers faces me when I get home, but I'll call up the fishing yesterdays to
help me through the task.

Four Corners Faraway

28 March 1992

Spring break at Ohio University. Winter quarter over and done. Exams read, grades turned in. Two thirds of the school year complete. Starting a radical escape from the ivory tower and from the northern cold and snow, which has hung on this year almost beyond endurance. Even our normally reliable native redbud and forsythia haven't bloomed yet. Grouse season ended a month ago and the between-season empty space, the great yawning cavern of nothingness between hunting and fishing seasons, the dreaded Zero Time, is about to be over. Andrea's college is in session, so she's had to stay put. My father flew out with me to Albuquerque to tour the Four Corners area for some leisurely sightseeing and artsy reconnoitering. The painter Georgia O'Keeffe once called this region the "Faraway." I like that: faraway from constant professorial, left-brain head work.

I don't think D. H. Lawrence, Willa Cather, and O'Keeffe fished, but they made their marks with words and paint in compelling ways, and all left their mark on and/or drew inspiration from this part of the country. It's a fascination with the creative process that I can't shake. Dad enjoys these junkets, too. He's a great, open-minded travel companion who derives pleasure from brushes with greatness, like viewing Turner's paintings at the Tate in London, touring the Keats-Shelley house at the Spanish Steps in Rome, or visiting Faulkner's Rowan Oak in Oxford, Mississippi.

Geographical places have their own vibrations and polarities: "The spirit of place is a great reality," Lawrence says in *Studies in Classic American*

Literature. I'm teaching his book in a graduate seminar this coming fall quarter and wanted to get a feel for what he saw out here. Lawrence was right: the vibrancy of the Southwest's landscape is astonishing to the Eastern eye. Nothing here that disputes his claim; nothing like this in Ohio or Connecticut!

Driving Route 84 between O'Keeffe's Ghost Ranch and her little Abiquiu hacienda (which we found after some snooping and a bit of help from a pair of friendly women photographers) links between the scenes in her paintings and the corresponding desert landscape are immediately apparent and breathtaking. The varicolored tonal palette of earth and rock and geological strata is arresting. Forget the austere animal skulls that became her popular signature icons. She may not have fished per se, but I've heard that she liked rafting, and some of her dramatic landscapes show that riverine influence: to my eye they appear to flow like water. There is something very contemporary, very *now*, about her art. She died only six years ago at the age of ninety-eight, and I like to think she may have seen the San Juan River in its current iteration. And dead or alive she lends a presence, an extra level of engagement and perception, to this far part of the country. After her, it is impossible to look at a desert the same way again.

I've been hearing about the San Juan River for several years from guides and other fly fishers. Heard the fishing was reputed to be superb and in a category with the Bighorn in Montana and the Green in Utah. The current *Fly Rod & Reel* sports a piece by Paul McGurren called "New Mexico's Desert Rose," and in typical slick magazine *you've-got-to-try-this-place* formula, he makes it sound like a go-to destination, not to be missed if you value your life and time. One part of me is a sucker for his kind of hype. Live most of the year away from even marginal trout fishing, and the publicized high-profile rivers beyond my normal reach begin to seem not just desirable and beckoning but downright legendary.

These distant homemade US waters (all destinations seem remote from out-of-the-way Southeast Ohio) will have to feed my adventure appetite. I've been to the Bighorn and the Green with varying and mixed results, so part of me is also wary about the sure-fire promise of stupendous outcomes.

On these limited-budget travel junkets, one day is all there is to get right with the fish, which makes for a very narrow window indeed. I'm not sure what I expected. McGurren was awestruck by pods of twenty or thirty hefty fish cruising around. I did not see that, but two evenings ago, when Dad and I arrived in Navajo Dam and had checked into Abe's Motel, I walked down to the river and fished for a while. I caught nothing. But as I was wading in the dimming light, some wild things bumped my leg. Not muskrats as I first thought, but sizable rainbow trout. That seemed like a premonition.

But I admit there's something deeply intriguing about a fishery that springs up in a remote spot as a result of the Bureau of Reclamation plunking down a 400- to 500-foot-tall dam that in turn creates a fertile, cold tailwater river that snakes through the otherwise dry and sere desert country west of the 100th Meridian. The juxtaposition is startling, as true juxtapositions usually are. It delivers a surprise factor that's hard to wrap the mind around. An oasis, I guess it could be called, in otherwise rugged, arid, wild, remote country that at one time was someone else's homeland. In the global view, history is robbed, the past is held hostage, but the present and future are served even though they are compromised.

I've read Ed Abbey's *Desert Solitaire* and Marc Reisner's *Cadillac Desert*, and I know the dams don't simply store water in arid regions but are also symptomatic of cultural and governmental hubris run wild; I know human beings and native tribes were displaced for their construction, and miles of habitat erased and species threatened or obliterated; I know their reason for being is to serve the commerce of agriculture and power often in places miles distant from their location, and I wish it were otherwise. But the unexpected give-and-take of aridity and fecundity is metaphoric somehow, an example of a kind of ecological yin-yang in its most elemental configuration: arid earth versus fructifying water. Like an O'Keeffe painting.

No question but that environmentalists have the moral high ground regarding native purity and pristine ecological values. Abbey was right about that. I don't want to sound cynical or reactionary or hypocritical but we latecomers also play the hand we are dealt, though not without a guilty conscience, not without being aware that even an act so simple and innocent as fly fishing has troubling moral and ethical repercussions. The price of postmodern consciousness: everything fair game for deconstructors to unmask the hidden sin, expose the ugly backstory, the corrupting influence. The bottom line for wayfaring anglers: though completely artificial, even

down to the planting of alien species, the trout fishing possibilities these engineered places foster can be, in a word, *exceptional*, though whether the ends
justify the means is hotly debated and not likely to be conclusively solved.
Try to make sense of the binaries, ironies, paradoxes, I guess, is the lesson to
be learned here. Be large and contain multitudes.

Yesterday I arranged a full-day float trip for us. We woke to inclement conditions and an unexpected piece of winter: gray skies, hard wind blowing
from the north, and cold, bone-chilling rain. Dad passed on the trip, took
our rental car, and explored the Aztec ruins instead, a good thing, too, as
river conditions were tough. Not inclement for fish, though.

With rain gear on and a fly rod in hand, I found the weather didn't
matter and the fish were extremely cooperative on various nymphs and on
a red yarn pattern called a San Juan worm, which to my mind, anyway, really stretched the definition of an artificial fly. Trey, my young guide, was
a student at Fort Lewis College in Durango, Colorado, and we spent time
talking about Hemingway, who he was reading in one of his classes. I appre-
ciated that he understood the Hemingway ethic and showed me something
I'd never seen before: the unscrupulous "San Juan Shuffle" caused by kicking
the bottom-dwelling blood worms free and in effect salting the water with
instant fish food. He gave a couple of kicks on the bottom, and we could
see the worms dislodge from the substrate rock and drift downstream, to
be pounced on by waiting trout, like cats on unsuspecting mice. Cause and
effect in its most basic appetitive form. I was impressed when Trey made
me swear I'd never resort to that underhanded method. I agreed to being
drummed out of the fly-fisher's brotherhood if I ever did.

Drifting tandem nymphs below a gaudy indicator does wear thin, but it
killed time until later in the day when small olive mayflies showed on top and
the fish turned on. I managed a couple of very fat 18-inch and 19-inch rainbows
during the hatch (and lost a few others), and they were exciting, thick-bodied,
hard-fighting fish (but not aerial) in that cold, cold water, and I'm inclined to
think it was worth the trip to see them sip tiny *Cleons* on the surface.

The trout here have a blimpy football shape, which means because they
feed constantly year-round and put on pounds and inches the way I do at

Christmas holiday, they have impressive girth and poundage for their length. They look stocky and rotund, like pumped-up Technicolor potentates with keys to the steroid cabinet, and I confess that I'm not crazy about their disproportionately small heads. They look like caricatures of trout. But they are big, there are lots of them in perfect water conditions with ample food. Desert rose, indeed: the brilliant bloom in a sere background, ready to be plucked. Does that make me a soulless consumer and nothing more?

Even local chambers of commerce are placing ads in fishing magazines: "Catch your Rainbow on the San Juan." They tout the San Juan as a premier all-season, 365-day-a-year fishery. "World-class fly fishing and trophy-sized trout," one of the ads boasted. I think that helps explain the rabid appeal of this place, how it has become a kind of fly-fishing mecca, like so many other man-made tailwaters. Maybe that's all trout are—mere commodities to feed our acquisitive desires. Karl Marx probably thought so. But it strikes me that this is the kind of place that could be loved to death if capitalism and its discontents run amuck here without some reasonable restraint being exercised. Deconstruct the constructors. But tell that to the merchants hereabouts. Meanwhile, count me as part of the problem rather than the solution.

It is hard to think of the fly-fishing experience as unique or solitary here. I saw license plates from a dozen states in the parking lots today. A legion of other hopefuls hooked by the same desire to catch a big one that gripped me. I lost count of the number of cars, anglers on foot, and anglers shoehorned by twos and threes into guide boats. When I was a boy, the New York *Daily News* always ran a back-page photograph of opening day of trout season in New Jersey, with anglers standing elbow to elbow around a bathtub-sized pool awash with just-released trout. Even the staid *New Yorker* ran some covers back in the '50s satirizing that kind of mob scene. Seeing the elbow-to-elbow activity here reminded me of those frantic depictions. Nothing quite that exaggerated here, but still, despite my current complicity, it isn't a way I'd care to be for very long. I'm spoiled, I guess, and want it both ways.

Dinner at the Sportsman's Bar and Restaurant, the only happening joint in Navajo Dam, New Mexico, where the best thing to say about the food is that it's hearty and there's plenty of it, especially the fries. It will definitely do after a long day on the water. In the company of a lot of other hopefuls from all corners of the globe who were also just in from a long day on the water. Good cheer and salutations all around. Some guides being feted by their grateful clients. One guy went on and on about his fish of a lifetime, which, judging from his extended arms, looked to be at least two feet in length. He kept toasting his guide through a whole pitcher of beer and several shots. The guide did not seem to mind but looked a bit embarrassed as the night progressed and finally excused himself and slipped out the door into the chilly night.

We were a good audience for goings-on that were as entertaining as the fishing had been. We watched the finals of a pool tournament, which made Dad nostalgic for his youth. The television was tuned to a basketball game, with the audio silenced. No one seemed to be watching it anyway. The center ballroom was hopping, and couples, all no doubt the epitome of good country people, sashayed around the room to jukebox music. The poignant lyrics reminded me of another era and my long-ago grad student and hunting pal from Murfreesboro, Tennessee, John Paul Montgomery, one of the greatest good-time honky-tonk storytellers I've ever known. He'd be in his element here.

Anyway, one tall lanky guy looked like Richard Petty, down to the dark shades and big cowboy hat, feather in the band and all. Wide-brimmed hats much in evidence all over the joint, as were women with their own pool cue cases. Dad loved that. Everyone drank beer and smoked like chimneys; there was much laughing, singing, and general horseplay. The spirit of the place, unbridled, wide awake, joyous. "Men are only free when they are doing what the deepest self likes," D. H. Lawrence says. Women too. In one way or another, the great river outside the door carried us through the night as it had carried us through the day, and fed us all, whether we were anglers or not. Dad and I stayed out later than usual, drank more than was good for us. When we turned in, we slept the sleep of the deeply contented and thoroughly amused.

The View from
Staley Springs

25 July 1992

Andrea and I left Athens fifteen days ago. We camped most of the way out here, westward along Route 80, and we cooked our *al fresco* meals on my old trusty Coleman two-burner stove. We slept in our tent when the weather was good, otherwise we squeezed into the back of the 4Runner. Came into southern Wyoming where we camped a couple of nights near Saratoga, not far from where Bob Bertholf and I camped in 1969. We soaked in the Hobo Hot Springs (free and open to all), made love outside our tent under a meteor shower and a canopy of stars that went on forever. I fished a bit on the North Platte River where I broke out my latest indulgence, a new Orvis Madison rod. I shouldn't say indulgence, though, because I splurged for the rod when a windfall book advance check came in, so it was almost like being free, at least that's how I justified it to my frugal wife. Anyway, I fished without success, though it hardly mattered as my sense of fulfillment was elsewhere. Consolations of the flesh trump minor angling failures every time.

We stayed at Parade Rest last year, but since then discovered this truly funky Staley Springs Lodge on Henry's Lake. It's just inside Idaho but close to West Yellowstone in one direction and the Madison River in another. It's a famous lake. A childhood angling hero, Ted Trueblood, used to fish it. It was an old-time fishing camp that once hosted a cadre of Depression-era politicians, financiers, and even Hollywood types (*Gone with the Wind's*

Victor Jory) looking for a suitable drinking and fishing retreat. They found the right place, as the fishing is matched by the scenery. The lake is situated at 6,000 feet, partly flanked by the Centennial Mountains and brooded over by 10,000-foot Sawtelle Peak, whose prominence can be seen for miles in every direction. We have cabin #6 with its creaky screen door, smoky fireplace, and early Salvation Army furnishings. A portly groundhog lives in the crawlspace. The front deck looks out across Henry's Lake and on clear days we can see all the way to the western side of the Tetons, almost close enough to reach out and touch. But then such is the nature of illusion.

When I'm not fishing I can plop myself in a porch chair and pretend to read while I am actually watching people fishing from boats and float tubes for giant hybrid trout for which this place is renowned. Once in a while a happy angler will come up the path by our door with a stringer of eight-ten-twelve pounders. Eye-popping trout. It's amusing to see a gangly kid come by with a stringer of trout almost as long as he is tall. He could have posed for Norman Rockwell in all his folksy best.

Catch and release not their thing, but who can blame them? I've kept fish to eat over the years and have nothing constitutional against that. I've been in that acquisitive mindset myself. As a kid, fishing with my uncles and my cousin Phil, we used to slay (that's the appropriate word) those pale-skinned rubbery stockers with our spinning outfits and cart them home in a galvanized bucket to clean and freeze. The offal and remains went into our family gardens, so no part of the resource was wasted. We harvested them twice if the bounty of fruits and vegetables is considered in the tally as well. That was sound ecological practice, but I still can't help but think we were being piggy.

Or that time in 1958 on Cape Cod with Phil when we caught scads of Atlantic mackerel on lead jigs in the surf. A spinning rod venture that brought mindless indulgence. A 6-foot fiberglass rod, a Langley reel with one hundred yards of six-pound-test mono. The jigs were so heavy we could cast nearly the whole line each time. The lure would sail nearly out of sight. The fish hit everything we threw on nearly every cast, and fought way bigger than their foot-long size, exactly what you want in a game fish. To say it was exciting is an understatement. We pitched them behind us and cast again. I still hear those mackerel, flopping around on the sandy beach behind us, their brilliant blue iridescence already fading. By then an audience had gathered to cheer us on. I'm ashamed to say that those fish would have been wasted but for some kindly stranger who stepped up and bought every mack we had for ten cents apiece. No one told us to quit and we were too young to know otherwise. It wasn't fishing we were doing. It was catching. In every fly fisher's garage there is a galvanized pail and a spinning rod asleep in the corner. Drastic difference from then to now.

I tried Henry's Lake the other day with a legendary local guide named Bill Schiess, a high-school teacher with encyclopedic knowledge of this lake, the birds and animals, the native history. He's the Thoreau of Henry's Lake. In his outboard boat we drifted over the open channels in this large, shallow water. Threw big leech patterns on a sinking line. Cast out as far as you can, let the fly drop as deep as possible, then strip back six or eight inches at a time. Rod tip in or near the water. Conditions were horrible, mostly due to a gale-force wind. Andrea had a few hits, and I managed one 16-inch rainbow. No monster for either of us today. Wind was so fierce that Bill called it quits after a couple of hours and gave us a rain check for another day. Terrific gesture of goodwill. Relentless casting in that gale wind gave me a crick in my shoulder. We'll be around here long enough to take Bill up on his offer.

Today I drove up from the Staley Springs cabin and fished the Slide Inn area of the Madison, just inside the Montana border. I doubled down on nymphing the whole time with a variety of mayfly and caddis patterns but not before I spent plenty of time on my hands and knees seining the water, rummaging through my net, putting this and that little bugger into glass vials for later study. Trying to learn the intricate underwater game, the language of the biomass, which just seems to be harder and more difficult than I would have thought. Micro-invertebrates and their discontents.

Grrr! What's the big fucking deal? Fish live in the water, the bugs they love to eat live down there too. Predatory trout rule the watery domain and lord it over the tiny wiggly things, which exist by the zillions in these insect-rich rivers and are meant to do two things: (1) breed more tiny wiggly things, and (2) function as food for those thousands of hungry trout per mile (2,500 I think the Madison estimate is). And yet when I put my lovely, sexy, enticing flies down there in the watery bio-soup, expected outcome and directed control are out of the question, and all I can do is hope and pray for the best. And though I have advanced a little in the four consecutive summers I've been coming out here, confidence and a knowing air still eludes me.

Most nymphing, at least the way I've been doing it, is blind fishing. Beneath the river's glassine surface there are dark inchoate shapes moving around, like darting shadows in the unconscious mind. Hook one and it enters your daydream like an archetype rising to meet you in the upper air. But there is something surreal about the experience. I've read my Melville and my Hemingway: I'm never quite sure if it's a fish I've caught or a symbol. So I'm not sure which is more frustrating: being skunked and striking out entirely, or having success only sporadically? The latter at least keeps me on the hook and coming back for more.

On July 15 I got a deep-bodied, hook-jawed male brown of about 17 inches on a Pale Morning Dun Wulff. An exciting moment! There is nothing that compares to a decent trout taking a dry fly. Nothing in my angling world anyway, especially when it's a result of the step-by-cautious-step stalking of a rising fish. In religion, philosophy, metaphysics, the problem of the One and the Many is thought to be unresolvable. But solving the problem of the One and the Many in fly fishing, like duck or quail hunting, is easy if you keep your wits about you. Hone in on the one rising fish, not the flock; take deep breaths, exhale slowly, slow your heartbeat, keep your eye on the prize, then make accurate casts and let all the chips ride on your single-minded nerves-of-steel presentation. I've been a hunter so long that I have that part of the game down. It's all the other elements that throw me.

Anyway, flushed with success and pumped up by my newfound skill as an angler, I promptly lost two others in the same riffle. One step forward, two steps back! The story of my angling (mis)education, which ought to teach me not to pontificate or give myself airs. One change came out of my success, though. Once again, I could barely get that ample trout in my Lilliputian net (this happened to me last year as well), so next day I went into Madison River Outfitters in West Yellowstone and bought a larger net, twice the size of my old one. "I need a bigger net," I said. A glorious moment and one of the highlights of the trip so far. I like to think I earned it and that maybe it presages good things to come, a positive turn in my angling fate.

I'm bothered that I can't always identify what's going wrong in my fishing and so I'm unable to adjust the variables accordingly, the way guides and so many accomplished anglers do. I've frequented all the fly shops in West Yellowstone in an attempt to grease the local economy and to glean whatever knowledge I can, but lately I have been drawn more often to Blue Ribbon Flies, where I find my neophyte queries and amateur dilemmas are treated seriously and respectfully, even though I am but a face in the crowd. The shop is inviting and has an informal, clubby atmosphere that is appealing. Presided over by Craig Mathews, the affable owner, it's always busy with people buying gear, talking shop, telling stories, catching up on personal news, exchanging tips, even bringing gifts of vegetables from warmer climates. It's fun to stand in a corner and eavesdrop on the animated conversations and exchanges or watch Craig or one of the staff tie flies in the midst of the daily hubbub. I feel alive when I walk in there. It's a hive of fishing and extra-fishing activity and everyone who comes through the door is heartily welcomed and well met. Blue Ribbon Flies's co-owner, an entomologist named John Juracek, cheerfully identified insects that I had caught and put in vials: small Western green drake (*Drunella flavilinea*) and cinnamon caddis (*Hydropsyche*). All of a sudden I'm using Latin terms! Call things by their right names, Ezra Pound said. True words for our age of linguistic slippage.

But then Mathews and Juracek are the guys who wrote the books on fishing this part of the world. They stand behind their words. Hatch matching is still a puzzle for me. I came away last week with their *Fly Patterns of Yellowstone* and their just-released *Fishing Yellowstone Hatches*. These are already helping my learning curve. Five days ago, on 20 July, I stalked a couple of working fish on a blustery, rainy evening and after refusals on other dries, tied on a Western Green Drake Sparkle Dun and took two nice rainbows of 16 inches and 18 inches in a row. Happy day! Regarding *flavs*, the authors say, "Inclement weather always seems to prompt the heaviest emergences and the best rises of fish. . . . Ironically, these same conditions drive most anglers from the stream just when they should be starting." Damn straight on both counts: I had an entire section of the Madison to myself that evening. What a delicious turn of events, duly noted in the margin of the latter book.

Nothing shaking at all at Slide Inn today, which would have made for a very sparse, brief entry in this journal tonight, if an unpredictable, oddball thing hadn't happened. For almost three hours I fished hard with a tandem nymph setup and was about to go back to Staley Springs for a much needed thirst-slaking beer when I thought I was snagged on bottom again, for about the umpteenth time. I pulled hard, with an edge of impatience, and, totally without warning, a sizable brown trout leaped three feet in the air. Knock me over with a grizzly hackle! It took me a second to realize it wasn't being chased by an otter or shot out of a cannon but instead was by God fast to one of my flies and that it was headed downstream with the heavy current propelling it along and that I'd better hotfoot in pursuit. I sprinted like a maniac—weak ankle and all (from last night's stumble chasing a hooked fish that broke off)—in the water and on the bank, all the while reminding myself this time to keep my rod tip up and a tight line to the fish.

I finally caught up to it 150 feet down the river; every time I got near, the fish got a head of steam in the heavy current and whizzed away from my net. The 4X tippet held, though. I can't say which of us was more tired when I finally cradled it in the net bag. A gorgeous, thick-bodied brown trout with a #18 Pheasant Tail lodged in its jaw. Laid out tail to nose, it reached the RL Winston Co. decal at the 18-inch mark of my rod. I felt elated, but I also felt a weird quietude, as though I was watching my little drama unfold from a distance. Legs still wobbly from the sprint, I knelt down, unhooked the fly, worked the tired fish back and forth until it revived. And gave thanks.

Ethics demand that we do everything feasible to go as easy on our fish as possible. Barbless hooks help. So does keeping the fish in the water, and wetting hands before it is handled—those kinds of commonsense protocols. It's a bummer to think of what possible long-term damage we do to a tired or too-tired wild trout. We can't protect them from otters, mink, ospreys, and herons, which will have their share, but we probably do more harm ourselves than we imagine or care to admit. (I caught and released a Madison rainbow the other day that looked like it had been beaten by thugs.) We don't mean to harm them but because we can't see into the fish's future we never know for sure whether its fight with us, even after it has been released, will be its last. Maybe it's the way of the world, maybe it's inevitable that we kill the thing we love or hold it for ransom even when our intentions are otherwise. This remains one of the mystery components of fishing, though I admit that isn't an answer I've ever found completely comforting or satisfactory. Still, when a slowly revived fish gives that muscular kick, a deep-body head-to-tail shudder that signals it is ready to swim on its own, it's a cause for celebration. Every time I feel that kick, an orchestra plays in my heart.

So today's glorious trout makes me wonder if I'm not counting too much on the top-down approach. In other words, *loosen up.* "Schools and creeds in abeyance," Whitman says. Good advice. Maybe it isn't all skill, but there's luck involved too. *Fisherman's luck. You lucky bastard. Have any luck today? I see you had some luck.* Fishermen always say that luck plays a role and now I see why, though of course there must be lots of definitions and gradations of luck, some earned, and some unearned. Maybe it is a Zen kind of deal: give in to the fishing zone and be one with it, be happy with whatever happens. Zen and the art of fly fishing: what happens will happen, in a sort of unconscious, nonprogrammable, random, quantum way. Keep your camel tied, but trust in Allah. Learn the technical skills, but be ready for surprise.

A couple of days ago on another section of the Madison I watched someone catch four trout in a row (not without envy on my part), and from now on I will always associate that stretch of water with that man's success. Though he was unaware of it, he became part of that day's angling history, part of my moment of observation, optimism, and hope. He entered the private space of my angling mythology, the interior place stories spring from. So from now on I can always say of that spot that it is eminently fishable. *It's a good run,* I imagine telling whoever cares to listen. *I saw somebody catch four beauties in a row right there.* Such things happen on every body of water on Earth but when they are personally witnessed they matter most.

When I hotfooted after that brown earlier today I ran past a young guy fishing below me. He saw me coming and kindly moved out of the way. When I came back upstream toward my original spot, I thanked him for his courteousness (especially welcome as I have had brushes with some world-class territorial louts and egregious assholes on the Madison lately), and we had a brief chat. He had not caught any fish all day and asked me what I was using. I showed my #12 Prince/#18 Pheasant Tail rig. I doubt I will ever see him again. But then no stranger has ever asked me for advice before on a Western stream and I was flattered, a little like Nick Carraway giving directions to a stranger for the first time in *The Great Gatsby.* For a brief moment I felt like I somehow belonged to the time and the place, and it gave me a little swelling in the chest. Maybe it's the teacher in me, but it felt right and proper to give him what little hard-earned information I had. Perhaps he went on to catch some trout and I entered the mythology of his day. Maybe he's telling his story to someone already.

The Beaverhead Is a
Movable Feast

3 August 1992

$\mathbf{F}$ly fishing has a kind of loopy, backcasting, stop-and-start kind of flow. When I was a boy, I considered myself homely and awkward, which made me self-conscious and insecure in the world of adults or the society of my peers for that matter. I had an active physical life—I fished, hunted, swam, played basketball, football, soccer, and especially ice hockey, and was most at home in those bodily sporting realms where neither neatly pressed civilian dress code nor by-the-book table manners were required.

Yet as an only child, I also lived inside myself for long stretches, and except for extended family and the closest of friends, I preferred to frequent the public library or hide out in my attic room with all the volumes of Charles Sylvester's *Journeys Through Bookland*, companion to my errant thoughts and dreams. I did a lot of sullen scheming in those days, constantly wondering *what if* this or that could happen and my life would be instantly improved. What if I were taller, what if I were smarter, what if I had clearer skin and smaller ears? Those kinds of speculations that bedevil kids endlessly in the lonely precincts of their rooms, and for which they only realize years later were stupid things to worry about, mainly because there was no power on Earth that could change them.

But some of those adolescent moments, still sharply etched, stay with me and keep playing out. Few things, from the time I was nine or so until

I was fifteen, compared in vividness and intensity to waiting for the second Saturday of April, which was opening day of Connecticut's trout season. That was an annual event that put my private dream life and threshold of expectation into high gear. Anticipation is hardly the word to cover my emotions. Time slowed down to a crawl, school was unbearable torture, chores were completely neglected, girls totally lost their allure, and, in a kind of perverse logic that was completely unfathomable to me, the appointed day seemed to recede farther and farther into the future.

In an essay called "The Angler" that Washington Irving included in *The Sketch Book*, he speaks of having been "completely bitten by the angling mania." But mania seemed mild compared to my affliction. I was insane for trout season to begin. I was impossible to live with, and my parents, both loving and kindhearted people, grew weary of wondering aloud who the creature was their only child had turned into. For a week beforehand I could hardly sleep and the Friday night before opening day I was up all hours, checking tackle, reading fishing magazines and books, planning the day, playing out angling scenarios in my head, which of course became more and more elaborate and heroic as dawn approached.

I didn't get a wink of sleep, but by God, I was ready to go forth and do battle with the trout of the world, even if they were only recently released cookie-cutter hatchery fish. *A trout is a trout is a trout* was my thinking then. My mother got up before dawn to make oatmeal for me and to pack a small lunch of a ham or salami or meatball or tuna fish sandwich and piece of fruit in a paper bag. Sometimes one or the other of my parents obligingly drove me to the Saugatuck River in Weston and dropped me off at the Cartbridge Road area or upstream at the precipitous Devil's Den gorge area, then picked me up hours later. But more than likely I'd just strap my gear on my back and ride my bicycle to the Perkin-Elmer parking lot or the Kent Road bridge at the nearby urban Norwalk River and fish upstream or down as long as I pleased. It was Saturday after all, and there was no school to bother with, no tidy clothes to wear, no civil manners to obey, no piper to pay. One year, I upped the ante by making it to three successive trout openings: New York's, Connecticut's, and Vermont's. If I had died then I would have gone happily to the promised land.

Some anticipated days just seem to take longer to arrive. Yesterday was one of them. One hundred eighty-seven years ago, almost to the day, Lewis and Clark and the Corps of Discovery began exploring the Beaverhead Valley region on their westward trek. Now it's my turn, at long last. I've read about the Beaverhead and its trophy trout for years, and yesterday was my turn to taste its fruit. Many of my old opening-day jitters were in place. And why not? I've been dreaming about the trip for four years, ever since Rick Wollum told me about wrapping up a week of guiding in Colorado, then driving with his buddies 800 nonstop miles up to Dillon to float the Beaverhead for a day or two, then turning around and driving all night back to Denver to be ready to guide their clients in Colorado the next day. That's the kind of passion that makes converts; that's a story that enters our angling mythology.

The fishing passion. Epic road trip, a staple of Western fishing. Drive all night, fish all day. In *Remembrances of Rivers Past*, Ernest Schwiebert says that a typical pattern of fishing addiction starts first with the writing that was born on its waters. Well, Rick's anecdote and all the magazine articles I've read, especially "The Beaverhead" by John Holt a couple of years ago in *Fly Fisherman*, have fueled the fires of desire and need. At long last, a trip to the Beaverhead. River of Al Troth, originator of the Elk Hair Caddis, no less. "Trout hardball in bigtime-college fashion," Holt says.

But Holt's essay wasn't all peaches and cream, and in fact it was somewhat dire in its news that drought conditions and unusually low winter flows out of Clark Canyon Dam have had a negative impact on the trout population. Even at that, I figured, any day at all on the Beaverhead would be better than no day at all. Tennyson might have said it best: *better to have fished and lost on the Beaverhead than never to have fished the Beaverhead at all.* Simple fact: supposed to be more trout over 20 inches long per mile in the Beaverhead than any comparable Montana stream.

Andrea and I got up before dawn, were on the road by 5:45 a.m., and made it the 140 miles to Tollett's Frontier Angler in Dillon by 8:15, having passed for the first time in my life something I have seen countless times in photos: the iconic Beaverhead Rock, the fabled landmark Sacagawea recognized in early August 1805 as part of her original Shoshone homeland, the discovery of which was a shot in the arm to Meriwether Lewis and the Corps of Discovery and a boost to the westward voyage. Anyway, like so much out here, pictures don't do the rock justice.

Tollett's shop was busy and by the time we met our guide, Jay, got registered, paid the $275 bill, and trailed to the river it was 10 a.m. before we started fishing. Young Jay, who it turned out was stellar at spotting fish and reading water, was pretty much a pill in almost every other regard. He struck me as one of those people who got by on the bare minimum of effort and didn't much give a shit whether his clients liked that or not.

He'd been out partying the night before and reeked of booze, smoke, and sweat. He looked disheveled and unkempt, and admitted he had only gotten to bed a few hours earlier and slept in his clothes. When we put in at the access below Clark Canyon Dam, it was cloudy and coolish, but when the sun broke through, the sky cleared, Jay's barroom odor would hit us like a slap in the face. Every so often the wind would pick up and bring relief. He was completely ineffective in helping Andrea get on fish and was actually disdainful toward any pansy, myself included, who thought the Madison River was a good trout stream. I guess it was a class thing with him. Working-class guide versus the rest of the privileged upper-crust world. And though Jay admitted to never having fished the Madison, that did not stop him from bad-mouthing it. At lunch, when he put our unfinished potato salad and baked beans back in their original containers for his next day's clients, Andrea, the most patient and precise and nonconfrontational person I know, was so flabbergasted she quit fishing and never spoke another word to him the rest of the way. We came precariously close to scotching the whole day's outing.

I'll admit it: the Beaverhead is the most difficult fishing I've ever done. I felt like a complete novice in casting, presentation, hook set, all the important stuff. Maybe trout-bum Jay was right in being a zealous advocate for his local river. Maybe what I know of fishing the Madison cannot be applied to the Beaverhead, which exists in a technical category all its own. Like the Madison it too is a tailwater, but strikes me as being quite a different bottom-release type of river from the San Juan or Bighorn or Green, and on a much more intimate and less dramatic scale. Less patently artificial, somehow, if that makes sense. I can't quite explain what I mean, but the Beaverhead and the Madison both just have a different feel and ambience to them than the other three mega-rivers.

I never saw a river like it: narrower than the Madison, with very deep holes, crazy vortices, and deep swirling eddies where the fly is carried *backward* in the foam line, long undercut banks and braids that are the troutiest, looking lies I have ever seen, and don't forget those over-hanging willows that hamper casting as soon as you let your guard down. The higher flows needed to feed the agricultural beast had cranked down somewhat and the river was running around 700 cfs yesterday, so water was nice and cozy back up under the bank willows where it was tough to cast or even get a decent drift. Which means plenty of room for fish to hide in those trout condominiums.

Photos of the Beaverhead don't do it justice. The minute I laid eyes on it I thought, *this is the river that exists in the mind of the Great Maker of Trout Rivers.* This is a trout stream as it is meant to be: sinuous (Captain Clark said, "verry Crooked"), darkly enticing, mysterious in its braids and runs and undercuts, awash with flora and fauna and more insect life than seems at first imaginable, plus a sibilant song all its own. In its current form it may owe its inception to human engineering and cultural and economic progress, but I'd be hard-pressed to condemn or even criticize the environmental cornucopia it has become. Lewis and Clark never saw it *quite* this way. In fact, if I remember right, they thought the Beaverhead was an extension of the Jefferson. The dam that created Clark Canyon Reservoir only dates to less than thirty years ago, and the res itself covers the confluence of the Red Rock River and Horse Prairie Creek, the historical beginnings of the Beaverhead and a resting place the captains once mapped as Fortunate Camp.

So they never saw the Beaverhead this way, but I've seen it. I was there, and my fishing life will never be the same.

The Beav, as Jay called it, lived up to its traditional reputation as a chucking river, and though I never threw big streamers, per se, I did have about twenty-five hits on various colored #8 and #10 Girdle and Yuk bugs, hurled against the bank and stripped back. I think the trout take them for stonefly or crane fly larva and maybe even crayfish, but who knows for certain? I got several decent fish that way, the best a 17-inch brown that got into heavy current and required some quick rowing by otherwise desultory Jay to keep up. Browns seem to predominate, and the number of hits on those ugly flies and the butter-yellow flashes and swirlings that look like quick, sudden bursts of sunlight under water made it seem that action was almost nonstop all afternoon. I kept waiting for a behemoth to materialize out of the depths, but alas today that never happened. Just knowing some bruisers were down below us in the hidden depths and might have shown their mugs had they cared to was excitement all its own. So there was always something to rouse interest even if no hookup occurred, though despite adrenaline rushes, slinging homely stuff gets boring after a while.

But the Beaverhead is also increasingly known as a finesse river and to tell the truth, today's best stretch was a slow-moving, placid side channel where in about thirty minutes I took three browns between 15 inches and 20 inches in a row on top with a #18 Parachute Adams. The soft tip on my 6-weight Winston rod protects tippets pretty well most of the time. Sour Jay seemed pleased with that run of events and cracked a smile and even offered a tiny dollop of praise, a smidgen so small and low in volume that I had to ask him to repeat what he had said. A bit later, as we followed that side channel back around to the main stem, I missed a nice rainbow on top by striking too soon, and I followed that error shortly afterward by breaking off a hefty 20-inch brown that took my Adams with it. It would have been the fish of the day. My teeth gnashed and my stomach turned over when that trout broke off. I had reason to doubt my trusty shock-absorbing Winston, but then my folly put me back on Jay's shit list and he seemed pleased with that, as I guess all was right with his world again.

Sometimes I did what my wife did—stopped fishing, let the rod go lax, quit the acquisitive mindset, drifted along at the river's own purling tempo, and especially disregarded our guide's admonishments. For a brief wrinkle of time words were not just irrelevant but useless. Go silent and disappear into the beckoning spaces and you become part of the flow of Zen Master Dogen's 10,000 things, when the river becomes not just a place for fish to be lorded over, where humans practice their rod skills, such as they are, but a crucible of organic connections, layer on top of layer, strand upon strand, of pulsing purpose and fascinating presence.

The Beaverhead's entire riverine corridor is like a "nature strand," as the old-time naturalists used to call such places. Like the thawing railroad grade at the end of *Walden*: fecund, entangled, interlaced, organic, flowing, generative, foreign in the last analysis to us myopic humans. Remove one aspect of it and the entire place is diminished. Focus just on the fishing and you risk losing sight of the ecological whole, the fructifying cornucopia, from the swarms of miniscule midges and mayflies to big flapping ospreys and great blue herons. We fool ourselves when we think we can completely understand water's inner workings or its influence on us. Anyway, I felt privileged to be in that place and in that moment. And stymied, too, because I couldn't soak it all in fast enough or deeply enough. Forgetting even a single impression suddenly seemed a tragic prospect that might haunt me forever. Already, I'd bet, I've forgotten more particulars than is good for me.

We got off the river around 8 p.m. I don't know what to feel better about: catching a dozen decent fish or only losing four flies (none in the bushes!) all day on my first ever trip to the Beaverhead. A pat on the back for that. Maybe my presentation was better than I first thought. I gave Jay a modest tip, grudgingly, and did not tell Andrea, who was dead set against any extra reward. We teachers live our lives day in and day out performing our best and ensuring good service without ever expecting anything extra in the way of a tip in return, so the whole gratuity business is a bit mysterious to the likes of us. Jay grunted when I handed him the money and true to form I never heard anything remotely resembling a thanks.

We ate dinner at the Lion's Den Bar and Restaurant. Judging by how crowded it was, I guess it's a favorite in Dillon, which has a bit of a rough edge to it, as befits a cattle town. We liked that there was nothing pretentious about it. It didn't have that faux-California feel of Bozeman. Andrea made a few bucks playing mechanical poker and I drank another beer and shot the shit with a few locals. I get the impression that they think most visiting anglers come from California, a place they have decidedly vocal opinions about. They seemed both curious and respectful when I told them we hailed from Ohio. I don't think they meet too many Buckeyes.

We made it back to Staley Springs after midnight, but not before we stopped along Highway 41 between Dillon and Twin Bridges, pulled over across from Sacagawea's rock, and for a few minutes waited in silence while the stone monolith kept watch over the broad nighttime valley.

Next day afterword: I would not have missed this junket for anything. This *must* become an annual event. The anticipation prior to the trip, the concentrated casting work, the gratification when a good trout was hooked, the lush, arresting fluvial landscape, the solitude (unlike the San Juan, Bighorn, and Green, we did not see another boat all day, though it has its share of car and truck traffic noise). It was all great. No lunker five-pound browns the river is legendary for, but it was still all great. In bed, still jacked up even after that long drive over darkened highways, mind reeling in every direction at once, I relived the day. I looked up the John Holt article again. I had it back here at the cabin. He said the Beaverhead is "humbling, educational, and occasionally rewarding," and I can't dispute that.

When I finally slept, I felt the river moving darkly inside me, through me, around me, and I was borne without complaint on its current to a distant horizon I could neither identify nor resist. That's the thing about rivers, especially the great ones—they stay with you, mix in your blood, become part of your memory stream, flow through your dreams, enter your unconscious, and roll on without cessation, calling your name. "I love them," Ray Carver says in a poem, "the way some men love horses/or glamorous women." That's good, I think, and I am two out of three, but I have to guard against drowning in my own fishing tale.

Through a Looking Glass

11 October 1992

In Reno for another Western American Lit conference, which closed on the 9th. I stayed on and reserved a day on the eastern side of the Sierras on the East Walker River at the Rosachi Ranch inside Nevada. It was a perfect outing. Weather excellent, air and water suitably cool and comfortable for fish and man. River running at around 40 cfs with trout after trout stacked in lovely runs, riffles, and pools. Dale Rosaschi said I was the only person scheduled for the day, and he asked if I'd mind if he fished with me. No problem. We did the whole day on the "alpine" section together, leapfrogging as we went, netting fish for each other, blabbing about this and that, comparing notes, and trading flies along the way, all the while wading a drop-dead beauty of a river in drop-dead beautiful surroundings.

Not all that far, either, from downtown Reno, and the *other* West, the urbanized one, the one fishing tales and pundits rarely mention. Which is more real, I wonder? Paradise or the Land of Nod? Land of binaries and strange bedfellows, poker chips and brown trout, where, Steinbeck says in *East of Eden*, the church and the whorehouse arrived at the same time. During a lull in the conference I poked around behind Reno's main drag where all the pawn shops are tucked away in back of the casinos. The seedy places where all the dreams end up, sold short for an uncertain future and another shot at luck. One shop had a Leonard fly rod on the block. I'd have given anything to know the story behind that.

36

My secret weapon on the East Walker was an old wet-fly pattern called the Picket Pin, invented in Missoula, Montana, earlier in the century, but I got my stash at a fly shop near the Housatonic a couple of years ago. It's furry and busy and looks like a conglomeration of three or four different styles and materials, but now that I see it works like hell, wet or dry, I'm inclined to believe the Connecticut fly shop owner's hype. Suggestive rather than representational is my opinion. I gave a couple to Dale and am happy to say trout jumped on our offerings all afternoon. Not huge fish—15 inches or 16 inches was the upper limit—but they were perfectly configured and colored and strong, lively, vibrant. Mostly rainbows, but a few browns as well in the mix and not a mark on any of them. We lost count of numbers but it was nothing to get six or eight trout on ten or twelve casts in some of the abundant runs. Surprisingly fast, exciting action.

Then there was the dream of a giant. Dale said he's taken brown trout up to 27 inches on his stretch of the river, which I think he said is about seven miles. As far as he knew, rod maker Walton Powell's 32-inch brown is the hands-down winner. What the heck would I do if I hooked a brown that big? I don't know that my Winston 6-weight would handle it. Do it and find out, I guess. We quit about 6 p.m. Before I drove back to Reno, he told me he enjoyed the day so much he was refunding my $65 rod fee. Fine with me! I've thought about his generosity a great deal. The way fly fishing makes friends, even for a day, is truly refreshing, though I guess that could be said about many human recreations and pastimes. Still, I knew nothing of his life or his politics and he knew nothing of mine, but for a moment as the world turned we had fly fishing in common and that was enough.

This East Walker side trip is a punctuation mark, an exclamation point, on 1992, which has been my best so far, not necessarily in terms of fish numbers, but in terms of the learning curve, still incomplete and fraught with frustration, God knows, but a boost in regard to knowledge and maybe confidence, too.

Between prepping for my courses, plugging away at new poems in *News of Loss*, and starting research for the first of the Library of America's Steinbeck volumes, I studied Frank Sawyer's classic *Nymphs and the Trout* (the second edition of 1970, not the hard-to-find original from 1958) and his investigations and commonsense observations of trout and insect activity on the River Avon where he was river keeper. Sawyer drew me in because I love the clarity and humbleness of his prose style, which reminds me a bit of Steinbeck's, and I guess his spirit of inquiry got hold of me. If Sawyer hadn't exercised his curiosity we would never have had his Pheasant Tail Nymph, the crowning achievement of his entomological trials. It's the utter "simplicity" (his word) and sheer stripped-down minimalism that makes the original Pheasant Tail so brilliant, so "effective" (his word again). "Simplicity is an aim to be desired," he writes. Amen to that. Less is more, in angling as well as architecture.

If there's such a thing as reincarnation I'd like to come back as a river keeper. My fantasy of the riverine life: I can't imagine anything more satisfying than being involved in all the facets of nurturing a trout stream and its denizens. I'll never achieve anything remotely like that in my angling life and instead will have to be content to tread in the path of the giants, picking up what leftovers I can as I go along, like a bird pecking crumbs at a banquet.

I remember a silly story Thom Steinbeck told me about his father. It's suddenly relevant. When he was living in Los Gatos, John Steinbeck once put a mirror in a small stream in the California mountains so a trout, the single resident of the stream, wouldn't feel lonely. I've never done that, but once when I was a boy, I dug out a spring on a relative's property and made a lengthy pool and put in one each of bass, sunfish, and trout to see how they would get along with each other. In due course, the bass ate the sunfish and a heron got the trout, so my experiment took a bad turn and I learned to be wary about tampering with the natural order of things. But I also never got over the degree to which my curiosity spurred me on, especially watching for hours on end those fish go about their daily fishy business in that clear pool. It was a window into subaqueous intrigue and a language I was only beginning to apprehend but which took hold of me nonetheless.

So I spent three weeks this past summer on the Madison watching, collecting, recording notes, and only then fishing daily. The experience of seining the water, getting down on my hands and knees with a magnifying glass to observe minutia, like mayfly nymph gills and imago tails, made me wish I hadn't switched my major in college from biology to English. I felt like a scientist in a laboratory. Peer through a 10× glass at a living insect in its home environment and its true dimensions and qualities reveal themselves. I realized how imprecise the artificial imitations can be. I came to see rivers in a new way: as a cornucopia of dynamic and ever-changing information, impressions, vectors, actions, and hydraulics. I can understand why Gary La Fontaine put on snorkeling gear and dove into trout rivers to take their pulse. His monumental 1981 book, *Caddisflies*, is a testament to that kind of immersive research. There is a world of shadowy, spectral activity below deck that seems almost incomprehensible and certainly utterly surprising and maybe even alien to a person standing on a bank and viewing the goings-on from above, which is what most of us do most of the time.

Rainbows in Paradise Valley

2 September 1993

I've been lazy and remiss about journaling. Too busy with academic obligations, Library of America research, conference travel, and the old blackfish of personal doubts and private discontents. The day-to-day crap that intervenes and marks life as *right here, right now* in my face. Lots of daydreaming and reading about trout fishing, but not as many actual hours spent on fishy water as I'd have liked. No one's damn fault but my own.

I have scattered about me loose diary entries, scraps of facts, tatters of notes, undeveloped paragraphs and observations that need pulling together, shored against my inevitable ruination if I don't get this writing project going forward again as an antidote to the work-a-day shit storm. I'm getting ahead of myself here, but things ended up beautifully—more than beautifully, maybe even transcendentally—in Paradise Valley three days ago, but it was a zigzag road getting there. An oddball, hit-and-miss angling year so far: eight months in and a definite drop off in activity from 1992. There was a disappointing trip to the North Fork of the White River in the Ozarks where I hoovered up a couple dozen rainbows and cutthroats, all between 10 inches and 15 inches, half of them out of one long 150-yard run that must have been a trout hotel. Despite the number of fish, not one of them was memorable or different or unique or out of the ordinary. They all fought the same as though they had been turned out in a factory according to an unwavering cookie-cutter template, even down to the similarity of spots and stripes. I felt like G. E. M. Skues's fictional Mr. Theodore Castwell, who realizes he's been fishing in Hell because every fish he catches is exactly the same.

Back home, I found pleasure fishing with my grouse hunting pal Rod Lyndon at various local farm ponds around Athens and the old standby marshy inlets at the upper end of Dow Lake and Fox Lake. Fishing toward evening made the smothering blanket of Ohio Valley summer mugginess almost bearable. Throwing brightly colored popping bugs for panfish and largemouths as evening comes on is excellent fun, the sport reduced to its least complicated factors. They aren't trout, but they do more than fine in a pinch. Rod threw those big stiff-hair frog patterns he ties and landed some chunky three- and four-pound bass, and that was fun to see and I cheered him on from the sidelines, not without envy in my voice: *you lucky bastard.* But of course he knew and I knew it was not luck at all. He can throw a split-cane rod like nobody's business. If he handled his booze the way he handles a fly rod, he'd be way longer for this world. I keep my fingers crossed.

I met cousin-in-law Earl DuBack in Bozeman on August 25 for a self-organized highlight tour of some Blue Ribbon rivers. Waiting for the Bozeman connection in Salt Lake City, I ran into a movable throng from the four corners of the US who also had the fishing fix on their minds. Thousands of people passing through the terminal and its myriad gates, going who-knows-where, and yet that small group of anglers was instantly recognizable. No doubt that fly fishing has changed the dynamic of tourism in the West. All of us bound for Troutland, the hallowed Troutopia. Pilgrims with fly rod cases in hand, like the staffs of penitents of old, their aim set toward the Holy Land. I guess it isn't too far-fetched to say there's a certain tie to the spiritual life not to be taken lightly. Izaak Walton and Norman Maclean thought so. Brothers and sisters of the fly rod, wielding the travel staff of fishing disciples. Some unaffiliated isolatoes like myself standing around, watching and waiting, happy to soak up the convivial aura created by entertaining groups of two and three companionable fellow travelers—both men and women (a sign that times are changing for the better)—cut loose from their day jobs and daily routines, who carried on lively conversations.

Tall tales. Spirited banter. Much laughter. *Remember that time*, was in the air like an echo. It was the stage of our journey when anticipation, eager projection, is the name of the game. No one is yet disappointed, frustrated, tired out, fed up. Hopes were high, spirits even higher. Whether it was holding a Sage or Winston or Orvis fly rod case or donning straw or felt or wool Western-style hat, or wearing a fly-shop-emblazoned fishing shirt, each person carried or wore some kind of badge of the fishing avocation. I prefer to think those items are not signs of exclusion or signs of conspicuous brand consumption, but a way of showing that a thread of shared enthusiasm, instantly recognizable, runs between us, the way a river runs through us. *Behold us, we're off to have fun.* Entertaining, captivating mythology, but not to be entirely capitulated to either.

Reached Bozeman with the rest of the acolytes. Gathered gear, rented a car, and drove over to Museum of the Rockies to see again the Russell Chatham painting, *Headwaters of the Missouri River in April*, on permanent display. Worth the side trip. Very imposing 10' × 14' canvas that's so big if you stand too close you can't take it all in. Like the West itself, I guess. My father and I saw it at the thirty-year Chatham retrospective there a few years ago, when I bought a poster of *Evening Fishing*, the painting Chatham did for the sixtieth anniversary of Winston Rod Company: a single angler fishing a goodly-sized river. A man looking into the aqueous unknown; a solitary figure about to roll the dice. Chatham gets the inner heart of angling in ways that few do. That is, fishing not as an accomplished fact but as a perpetual question mark. I framed the poster and hung it in my study. Every time I look at it I get antsy to head west. It's the only Chatham art I'll probably ever be able to afford.

That and two books of essays he published with his Clark City Press: *Silent Seasons* and *Dark Waters*. Both handsome volumes, even in paperback. It seems he can't touch anything without turning it to gold. The mark of genius. Chatham, Tom McGuane, and Jim Harrison all made fishing an integral part of their lives, but not their lives exclusively, and none of them ever looked back. With all the narrow-gauge specialists and self-proclaimed angling experts nowadays, who does that anymore? They had the passion and the balls to follow their own roads and streams, but more than that they had the aesthetic style and the artistic talent to make life their way, and now the rest of the world is coming around and says *yes, yes, yes, give us more.*

DuBack the holy fishing pilgrim arrived. He never goes anywhere without his fly-tying kit and plastic bags of dressing material. He has a complex, restless mind and a visionary intelligence, not unusual for an engineer in the nuclear submarine industry. He has a different take on the world than most of us and works in a realm I could never enter even on my best day. But he's family, and we share the fishing passion and speak its common language.

First stop on our road trip was George Kelly's nifty lodge on the Bighorn. Fished first day with a friendly hardworking guide, Brent Downey, who hauled his drift boat behind a spiffy Cadillac coupe, the smoothest, most luxurious shuttle to a river I've ever had. Wide leather seats with room to stretch out, even in waders. I managed half a dozen decent browns and rainbows up to 20 inches. Can't complain about that. Earl caught a wonderful rainbow about three pounds on a black Elk Hair Caddis at dusk. He had a smile a mile wide when I came up the bank to see what the fuss was about. More material for his *Fishing West* booklet he's compiling for his group back east, and more research for his innovative fly-line and fly-rod designs.

Second day we fished on our own. Water was on the low side, which made walking and wading easy. We did not encounter any of the angler-on-angler nastiness that Kelly warned us can happen in that overcrowded pressure cooker of a river, so not having to throw any punches, or defend ourselves against abusive tongue lashings, we felt ahead of the game on that score. Nice mix of *Trico* activity in the morning and caddis in the afternoon. Earl got a 22-inch brown trout on one of his caddis emerger patterns, and that was our best fish on that busy river.

Fished the Madison below Slide Inn all day on the 28th. It was twenty-two degrees when we woke. Not exactly hopper weather! We should have slept in but instead, gluttons for punishment, we hit the water at 8 a.m. and fished hard until noon, when a bunch of us—half a dozen or so like-minded strangers—quit at the same time, broke out our sandwiches in the parking lot, and shared stories of angling woe. No one had gotten a fish that morning. No one. Not one. Not one of us had unlocked the river's secrets. Not one of us had any wisdom to impart, though we yearned to be enlightened. Many of the luncheoneers took off, but Earl and I were undaunted, which is what I like about fishing with him. After more helpings of zilch and elevated frustration levels, we quit, threw the day in the garbage can, and set our minds toward the Beaverhead, our next stop on the road, which required getting up at 4:30 a.m. to make the trip.

The Beaverhead should have been better than it was, given how I had been talking it up to Earl. In one of the new fly-fishing books I've been reading, *What the River Knows*, Wayne Fields says, "Rivers always become memory." Since last year the Beaverhead has been with me, part dream, part memory, and I wanted to share it. But things faltered when Frontier Anglers, despite instructions otherwise, aligned us with my old nemesis, Jay, who failed to show up at the shop at the appointed meeting time. Our day began this way: he wouldn't answer his phone, so someone at the fly shop had to go to his house and rouse him out of his hangover bed. Of course it was too late to be assigned another guide, and we probably should have pulled out and gone our own way. But we felt trapped by circumstances. When we finally put in an hour later at the bridge below Armstead Campground, Jay discovered he'd forgotten our lunches and had to drive back to Dillon.

Plus it was moss-dying time and after just about every cast flies needed cleaning, either by hand or by an energetic roundhouse whack on the water's surface. Flies couldn't float five feet without snagging moss. We fished through the obstacles, and downriver we managed some decent fish between 14 inches and 20 inches, then I lost a goliath rainbow when Jay was slow following the fish in the current and then dicked around too long to get the net under it. There was something antagonistic about his actions, something almost spiteful. At twilight we had some fast action over an evening rise of caddis while Jay lounged in the anchored boat and smoked, calling out directions now and then, but he coached me well on improving my reach mend. At least he had the good sense to extend the day and not rush us off the river.

Next day, after Earl tied more flies and I composed a letter full of deliciously righteous indignation to Frontier Anglers, we hit the Yellowstone River inside the Park and pounded the water until dark for very little reward. A couple of cutts on dries was the sum of my fortune; Earl was blanked. We walked out of the river and back to the car under a clear sky that went on forever and a rising full moon that made our little section of troutdom look awash in silver and our breath shimmer like smoke. Days like we've been having, when fishing is more like work than sport, are all part of the overall effort, the grand unified angling scheme. We can't have one without the other, so grumbling won't help.

Then on the 31st, our final day, the stars aligned and the whole tenor of our trip changed for the better. It seemed like the kind of staple common in popular sporting magazines: the good old redemption narrative, stock-in-trade for the past zillion years. It's funny, though, how one day can make a difference. But better late than never, says I.

We booked a guided day on DePuy's Spring Creek with John Greene from George Anderson's Yellowstone Angler. We had talked about this for a long time, and my own ardor was fueled exponentially by reading about the legendary Paradise Valley spring creeks. When I saw DePuy's for the first time a bell went off in my head, as it had with the Beaverhead. Plus this: the place is voluptuous and downright sexy in its abundance and bounteousness. "Oh, I had never in my life seen anything like that trout stream," Richard Brautigan says in his wacky goofball novel *Trout Fishing in America*. He used to fish this water upstream from DePuy's on Armstrong's section of the creek. That was before a rod fee had to be paid per angler. The good old days.

John Greene was a true expert and master teacher on fishing to super-fussy trout, the likes of which I have never seen before. Trout cruising around feeding and bulging and rolling like they didn't have a damn care in the world but to go on with their trouty business. For once I had a vivid sense of the allure of Vince Marinaro's LeTort, Frank Sawyer's Avon, and the other legendary British chalkstreams where Frederic Halford and G. E. M. Skues and Hugh Selwyn Marryat learned their exquisite skills. Watching those fish, some biggies among them, I literally started to drool! I turned my back on the stream to settle my nerves and rig up, though I could hardly stop shaking. I was close to becoming so excited that I could forget everything I'd ever learned about fly fishing.

In that rarefied spring creek theater, first-time personal instruction is paramount. I would not have gotten into the subtleties without Greene's tutelage. Not to put an elitist spin here, but in that place and at that moment a bamboo rod felt like the only way to go. I strung up my 7 1/2-foot, 5-weight Orvis Madison, then took a crash course from John on ephemera hatches, tiny flies, and super-fine tippet.

In my entire prior angling life I have never used anything lighter than 5X, but in DePuy's clear water and under mostly sunny (though very cool) conditions, 5X looked like ship's hawser and 6X wasn't much better.

Welcome to spring creek fishing! I went with the 6X all morning, mostly pitching a single Pheasant Tail nymph, and beyond my wildest expectations, I landed three rainbows and one cutthroat, all around 16 inches but each one solid and muscular as a welterweight boxer. If we had quit then I would have been completely satisfied.

But then the little lower layer: after lunch, angling shifted into an arcane technical register. It was the prolific emerging and hatching part of the day. Sulphurs were on the menu and came off all afternoon. Like the Beaverhead, DePuy's has that "nature strand" quality to it: organic life in unimaginable profusion. DePuy's was alive and at first it was hard to take it all in, hard to know what to focus on, or where to put my emphasis. Even the waving watercress, elodea, and weed forests were mesmerizing. Trout rose with abandon, the water dimpled with rise forms. Cedar waxwings, kingbirds, and barn swallows barnstormed over the stream to grab their share of the fluttering banquet. And I, with my cane rod, 7X tippet, and #22 dry fly, felt I was about to enter a realm from which there might be no going back. I went willingly without one iota of regret.

We spent all afternoon, five hours straight, fishing below the PhD Pool in Betty's Riffle, then below that in Annie's Run. It was a humbling experience. My jitters subsided, and I was pleased with myself for not flock shooting. My first fish was a 20-inch-plus rainbow that soon broke me off and introduced me to the spring creek paradox: to fool these selective fish requires extra-thin tippet and miniscule flies with tiny hook gaps, but on that super-refined gear either most fish will break the tippet or the hook will pull out.

That conundrum set the win-lose boundaries for the afternoon. I hooked eight more trout and lost seven of them. Four took the fly with them; the fly pulled out of three others. My ineptitude was galling. I didn't like the odds, I felt wasteful and profligate, and I wasn't alone. All up and down the stream the whoops and hollers and lamentations of other anglers coming unbuckled or missing a strike sounded like a funeral chorus. Our collective flubbing and our music of frustration were cold comfort.

John Greene never gave up on us. He'd go from Earl to me and back again with advice, instruction, and encouragement. Then, while I was on my own, I saw a dandy trout rising regularly to sulphur duns in a tight spot less than a foot from the bank across from me on the west side of Annie's Run. It was tucked into a small indented corner underneath an overhanging willow branch where the bank jogged a bit inward like a little dog leg.

Despite the difficult lie, and the promise of being tested to my meager limits, I wanted that fish as much as I've ever wanted anything. *Cast, cast, cast, rest the fish, dress the fly, watch the water and the birds, scribble some notes in vest pocket pad, take a deep breath, cast again,* over and over. I was standing mid-thigh in the creek and about thirty feet away. Some casts fell apart and I missed the mark by miles. Or I got the distance right but the angle wrong and drag set in. Or the pesky branch blocked my fly from getting into the feeding lane. Or I couldn't time the rises properly and when I did get a decent float, the fish was not looking up.

But after forty-five minutes of concentrated trial and error, when all thoughts of anything besides that fish had been blanked from my consciousness, when my entire world had shrunk to a spot the size of a dinner plate, I dropped the fly a foot or so above the trout just as it was about to rise for another natural. I don't mind admitting that luck was definitely part of my equation. I entered a zone not entirely of my own making, aided and abetted by a southerly breeze that put a right-hand curve in my cast, so the fly was ahead of the leader when it hit the trout's window. The drift was perfect and the compliant fish ate and ran. John came up with his net, and suddenly there it was, a gorgeous, thick-bodied rainbow of about 17 inches in the bag.

I saw and had bigger fish than that in DePuy's but none as gratifying. Except for the Saugatuck River brookie in 1956 that kick-started my fly fishing, and the hefty Madison rainbow two years ago during my first-ever full-blown caddis hatch, this DePuy's rainbow was the most satisfying trout I've ever gotten. Maybe it will put on pounds and inches over the years and I'll boast that it qualified for the Wall of Fame at Dan Bailey's Fly Shop, but right now it doesn't need any melodramatic enhancement.

A redemptive day such as Earl and I had can't be guaranteed. It fell in our laps, came to us like a gift when it was least expected and most needed. The trick of course is not

Hard-earned rainbow on DePuy's. Credit: Earl DuBack

only to be persistent but to make the most of such moments when they happen, which I think we were both able to do. "Happy to have these fish!" Ray Carver says in his poem "The Catch." Amen! Our spring creek trout fed a week's worth of hidden hunger, and more. So what if some were lost? Venerable Father Walton says nothing is lost that you never had in the first place. We sorted flies and tackle, stowed down, packed up, said our good-byes, and flew home yesterday to our blessed wives and our work-a-day lives, all the while vowing to repeat the trip next year.

In Praise of Small Streams

1 August 1994

Dramatic change this year and a ramping up: no more folding fishing entries into my daily journal, but from now on I devote a whole ledger book to the annual fly-fishing journey. I found the right book for the venture in a stationer's shop in Venice. The paper is made for a fountain pen, with just the right degree of texture for smooth absorption without running or smearing. The Italians excel at such handmade *oggetto d'arte*. Utterly functional but tactile in a lovely, come-hither way, too.

I left Ohio four days ago and made decent time across I-80 to Wyoming. Blasting ZZ Top's *Eliminator* album is good for an extra fifteen or twenty miles per hour on the truck speedometer, and besides jacking me up so that I feel temporarily and foolishly invincible, the low-down boogie beat rockets me into the Western night, that moment when the road trip becomes an end in itself, not just a means to getting somewhere else. Jack Kerouac understood that. On Nebraska's High Plains, sun dropping beneath the horizon, a glimmer of stars about to peek into view in the blue-black firmament behind me, windows open, and the blessed evening coolness blowing the hot breath of day away, I feel like I could drive forever, that is until I come back to myself or get stopped for speeding.

Then a swerve northwest, crossing the torrid Great Divide Basin that appears to go on forever. Those words from *Lawrence of Arabia* looping in my head: "the sun's anvil," a good name for that area, too, in whose scorching, sun-ravaged spaces time slows down and doubles back on itself. Easy to get lost in the enormous spaces, the vastness of semi-arid landscapes that stretch horizon to horizon. Running water becomes a quaint memory and in a kind of panic, you wonder whether you will ever see another trout or indeed whether there are any trout left.

Almost eight months into 1994 and again I'm ashamed to admit that there has been no fishing at all this year outside of this Western trip. Just too busy with the reality of a buttoned-up, academic, professorial life. Deadlines for this, deadlines for that. But I am out here now hoping to make up for lost time and enjoying every minute of it, results notwithstanding.

Yesterday, I fished a section of the upper Green River. It looks like a trickle of sweat compared to the Green down below Flaming Gorge Reservoir at Dutch John, Utah. Lost one trout on a flashback beadhead Pheasant Tail and got one whitefish on a red Serendipity, and that was the sum of the action. The upper Green is a pretty river, not awfully wide, and easy to wade. Excellent-looking pocket water that I just wasn't adept at picking. Face it, I felt rusty and out of sync. Can't get discouraged, though. I've got several weeks ahead of me that should improve my lot.

Today I left Pinedale and drove up Route 191 toward Jackson. Then hooked around down 189 intending to follow directions in Fothergill and Sterling's *Wyoming Angling Guide* to another fishable area on the upper Green. I pulled off in Daniel at the Wyoming Fish Hatchery road, but drove no more than a couple of hundred feet when I saw a pair of sandhill cranes in a field to my left. Then to my right a Swainson's hawk lit on a fence post to eat some scurrying little fur morsel it had caught. Maybe it was a vole. What difference is there between a mole and a vole, I wonder? But hawks have high regard for voles as food, or so the bird books all say, so who am I to doubt? Definitely not a catch-and-release thing for them. For the next twenty minutes I watched through binoculars. Then I spied a bunch of blue-winged teal on a roadside slough and they were good for another ten minutes.

Finally the cranes ambled off the edge of the world, and the hawk, his lunch done, took off to look for dessert. But those birds, that little random clutch of fowls, felt like an omen pointing me toward something good. I felt loose and open to what might come. Always a good mindset where fishing is concerned. I went on as far as the Daniel Fish Hatchery and stopped to talk to the resident manager and to tour the facility, which is supplied by three million gallons a day out of two separate springs. Quite impressive. Trout by the zillions in the tanks and runs.

I never made it to the Green River because I got waylaid by Forty Rod Creek, a svelte little meadow gem that runs near the hatchery, but which, the manager told me, is rarely fished because anglers are hell-bent to get down the road to the more famous Green. I probably would have too if I hadn't stopped on the bridge and seen trout rising downstream and decided to ignore Fothergill and Sterling and take a chance on the lesser-known water course. More sandhills showed up and I knew this had to be the place. Swallows skimmed the creek. I couldn't say no. Forty Rod Creek is a meadow stream with undercut banks and long runs, a spring creek type of stream, eight to twenty feet wide. I strung up my Orvis Madison bamboo and used my venerable LRH reel rigged with a brand new Scientific Angler double taper 5-weight line, which is just right for this rod.

Everywhere I stepped, the exquisite smell of wild mint wafted up. I stuck a handful in the top pocket of my vest, so every time I moved its fragrant odor moved with me. I spent the next four hours, from 11 a.m. to 3 p.m., in a blissful state fishing to my heart's content, landing and releasing at least fifteen of the twenty-five or so cooperative fish I encountered. Nothing arcane: they fell for an Adams Wulff in progressively smaller #14, #16, and #18 sizes as the day went on and the fish got pickier; I caught nearly all my fish on those, even during a pale morning dun hatch, which went on modestly from 1:30 p.m. until almost 3 p.m. and drove the swallows crazy.

The rainbows and cutthroats ran 8 inches to 11 inches, though I lost one rainbow about 15 inches that slipped the hook just as I slid it netward. It would be lovely to think they were stream-born fish, but more than likely, given their cooperativeness, they were escapees or perhaps plantings from the hatchery, or maybe they emigrated up from the Green, though in that moment of delight it hardly mattered where they came from. They were in my lap with their silvery sheen and rose-pink accents and that's what mattered.

My favorite trout-fishing scenario: small stream, willing fish rising to dry flies, and no one else around. It's not for nothing that among my favorite outdoor images are paintings of fishing small streams, and here I was with life imitating art. I might have been in an Arthur Shilstone painting. People drove right by, headed for the Green. *Go ahead, keep driving, move along,* I urged under my breath, *nothing to see here folks, nothing worth stopping for here.* It's not that I wanted to hog those fish, but that the occasion was quickly becoming more than itself, more than one solitary angler on an abandoned (for the moment) stretch of water. Archetypes were rising, resonances were coming into play, memories were flooding in, and as I plied the water, a pathway gradually opened to something deeper. It went on like that for a long time.

I had a twin thing going, a double haul of a backcast. The Orvis bamboo felt great in my hand, responsive and alive in the way only handmade cane can. I hadn't cast the rod in earnest since that marvelous day last August on DePuy's and had nearly forgotten its sweetness. Hefting it, swishing it back and forth, brought an early pleasure, a layer below my present moment. Back in the late 1950s, I bought my first split-bamboo fly rod, a used 2-piece, 7 1/2-foot Sewell N. Dunton "Angler's Choice," model 152. Duntons were a homegrown New England rod, made in Greenfield, Massachusetts. Mine was a bargain-basement, bottom-rung wand all the way, right down to its plastic reel seat. It's a shame Duntons have never been recognized as valuable or become collectible among aficionados. They're light in the hand and medium to medium-fast action, which makes them ideal for casting dries on small streams. Nothing fancy, nothing adorned, but an utterly serviceable rod for a greenhorn kid as I was then.

There was a backstory: Archer Huntington, head of the hunting and fishing department at Bob's Sports Store in New Canaan, where I spent countless hours drooling over equipment and gear I could never afford and asking a barrage of annoying questions, not only tolerated my persistent quizzings and curiosities, but took me briefly under his wing at a crucial juncture in my teenage life. Arch sold me that Dunton for $15, a price so ridiculously low even I could afford it with my meager caddying money. It took me many years, however, to figure out that the rod actually cost a good deal more and that Arch himself had put up the lion's share of money for it. He must have wanted to wean me from spin fishing and get serious with fly fishing, and he was willing to start the process with his own version of a fishing lie. Arch's deception worked, and of course it was the best money I had ever spent. It became my most prized possession: a lovely honey-brown lightning rod for conducting every angling dream and hope I had. Since then I have gone the fiberglass route, then the graphite and composite route, but I've owned one other Dunton (an 8-foot, 3-piece "Angler's Choice") and now this Orvis Madison, and can't say beyond a doubt which means more to me. In carrying me forward and serving me well, both bamboos have carried me back, too, toward an origin I only partially understand but cannot relinquish.

But the deeper thing is that in such odd ways our lives are touched by others—sometimes relative strangers, sometimes family—and deserving or not, we profit from their kindness. So mentorship, too, is part of that formative outdoor equation. Where would I be without elder guiding hands? Like a million other fledgling nimrods I was fortunate to be guided in my teens by a firm familial hand and no-nonsense attitude. Uncle Tony Ventrella, Mom's brother, is nobody's fool and possesses a case-hardened outlook at times chilling in its severity. "Let me tell you where you made your mistake," he'd begin his litany of criticisms. I took it—my cousins and I all took it—because we knew he was right, as much as it killed us to admit. Although he has a robust sense of humor, Uncle Tony is not much given to carnival-style frivolity (black and somber gray are his favorite color choices in clothes). He's not the kind of person to set your inner dreamer free because he's too practical for that, but he gave me an education in realism and straight talk I never would have had otherwise. He could be gruff, but I always felt completely safe and looked after in his presence.

Every spring we plied with spinning rods and later with fly rods the local rivers all over southwestern Connecticut—Norwalk, Saugatuck, Mianus, Rippowam, Silvermine, Aspetuck, and some tributaries whose names I never knew—as well as the Green Mountains' pristine yard-wide (and narrower) brook trout streams in summer. The five-hour car ride north on Route 7 from Wilton to Danby Four Corners, where our modest cabins were located, established a lifelong road-trip pattern that is ingrained in me. So is the sound of Uncle Tony's voice—I always hear it in my head—spinning one of his innumerable (and shape-shifting) stories, full of his artful and achingly funny malapropisms. He has always been a raconteur without peer.

No place, no stretch of river, no patch of upland woods existed without an attached corresponding human story and a cast of oddball characters—Old Man Abbott, Mrs. Hatchet Face, Scabnose Marietti—whose quirky exploits and legendary misdeeds were endlessly entertaining and instructive. Long before scholars made cultural geography popular, my uncle understood the intersection between narrative and place, and how place is always more than mere landscape. It's reassuring to know he's still active as an outdoorsman in his mid-eighties, and best of all, still passing on what he knows and loves to younger members of our family.

So in the matter of fly rods, fishing tales, and especially trout streams, small and off the beaten path can be better than anything else. Our American fascination for bigness, hugeness, enormousness, gigantism, is at best a conflicted path to travel, a last bastion of hubris, because the double-entendre phrase "size does matter" cuts more than one way. I learned that on small feeder tribs of the Norwalk and Saugatuck rivers, some of which, like Comstock Brook near the toney suburban Middlebrook Farm Road in Wilton, held some surprisingly beefy brown trout, probably unbeknownst to the privileged resident property owners, and no doubt were forgotten holdovers from the state's stocking program. Whatever: Uncles Tony and Bob knew about them and they certainly were worth the effort of sleathy stalking, roll casting, and occasional trespassing that they required. Nothing as outsized as Old One-eye, the bully, tackle-busting brown in William Humphrey's novella, *My Moby Dick* or Old George, the behemoth brown Ed Shenk quests after in *Fly Rod Trouting*, but now and then trout of 15 inches to 17 inches with heft and gravity that I can still feel.

But the small stream bug really got in my blood when I was newly married, and my first wife Michele, our daughter Liz, and I spent the summery part of each year in tiny, remote Danby Four Corners. Our cabin was cheek-by-jowl next to a little blue-line squiggle called Weatherby Brook. We were situated with no one above us at the edge of a couple thousand acres of never-to-be-developed private mountainside woodland owned by the ill-starred, recently deceased Currier family.

Weatherby Brook started in a rock-borne spring a few hundred feet up the mountain. It gave us fresh water to drink, cook, and bathe in, and as it widened and grew swifter in the decline behind our cabin, it provided soothing night music—we fell asleep to the sound of its gurgling every July and August evening. And as if that weren't enough, it held native brook trout that no one else knew about except us, or so I liked to believe. It has been a long time since I ate the fish I caught, but back then a few times during the summer I'd get up at dawn and angle a few brookies for breakfast, grilled over a wood fire in a wire-mesh basket to preserve and crisp the delectable skin, and then served with hash-brown potatoes and fried eggs. Breakfast on Olympus. I lived then in Paradise but didn't always know it.

Other times, when Liz was a bit older, we'd canoe on Emerald Lake hunting for northern pike, and when she became more adept at traversing jungly places, she and I would follow Weatherby Brook down across Danby Mountain Road to the broad meadow where, beneath the shade of overarching alders, Mill Brook wound its way through surprisingly deep undercut banks and waist-deep pools on its way down the mountain to Danby proper and across Route 7 to north-flowing Otter Creek. Mill Brook meandered and switchbacked so willfully that it would take the better part of a day to fish it from beginning to end, from the beaver pond to the south all the way to the Benefiel's cabin to the north. On rare hot Vermont summer days, under the arching corridor of alders, it was the coolest, best, most delicious place in the world to be.

In those days, for those close quarters, I used a fiberglass spinning rod

rigged with my LRH fly reel, and Liz, just learning the rudiments of fishing, threw small lures on a light spinning outfit. I taught her to stay low, creeping and crawling on hands and knees where necessary in tight quarters and throwing a side-arm cast or jigging a spoon or a worm on a hook in a kind of dapping motion. Her first trout was an 8-inch brown, a bigger catch than one might expect in that reclusive water, though on occasion I encountered browns up to 13 inches.

Liz DeMott with a Mill Brook brown trout.
Credit: Michele DeMott

That size thing again. Big is a relative term. John Gierach got it right in *Fly Fishing Small Streams*: "Maybe your stature as a . . . fisherman isn't determined by how big a trout you can catch, but by how *small* a trout you can catch without being disappointed. . . ." That's as good a lesson as any fishing parent can teach a child. Even after life and age and time intervene in their various and sometimes-nefarious guises, one hopes the metaphor as well as the reality holds true.

Then and now I came out of both streams the way I went in: thankful for their presence. *I praise small streams*, a voice inside me kept repeating. *First, last, and always, I praise small streams and their abundant virtues.*

The Myth of Fishyfus

11 August 1994

Yesterday Earl closed out the weeklong Western trip that he'd been planning since the day we got off DePuy's last year. We fished every day all day since August 3 when I picked him up in Jackson. This year we've fished Madison, Big Hole, Slough Creek, Henry's Lake, and Henry's Fork. Long days, fish into the night, drive countless miles, eat and sleep on the fly, cover as much ground as possible.

We were guided on a Big Hole River float by John Sampson, who owns Four Rivers Fishing Company in Twin Bridges. His congenial attitude, expert guidance, and friendly demeanor opened new avenues for us into the glorious Big Hole, a sizable river with many moods and conditions, but surely one of the most desirable rivers on the planet. Everything about it is spectacular: scenery, wildlife (bighorn sheep, golden eagles), and don't forget fishing. We liked it so much that instead of going back to the Madison as planned, we fished the Big Hole around Maiden Rock on our own on foot the two following days. Despite some setbacks—broken flies, snapped tippets, lost fish—the fishing was memorable in many ways, especially when we fished under overcast skies and our quarry, some truly gorgeous browns, shed their inhibitions and gave us a taste of dry-fly heaven. We encountered only a couple other walk-and-wade fishermen and felt privileged to have the canyon mostly to ourselves.

Last evening, we hightailed it down Route 20 to Last Chance and fished the evening at the Railroad Ranch on the Henry's Fork to get Earl's last fishing licks in. We parked across from the Mailbox, then walked the mile west to Stock Bridge, accompanied part of the way by a contingent of entertaining Japanese fly fishers who were eager to share their news and fly selections with us. And though none of us understood the other's national tongue, we had the language of fly fishing to help our communication.

Quite a fabulous place—wide, wide river, very placid and slow moving, with abundant bug hatches now. But the only fish we saw rising were small. Easy to see how this place got to be the most famous dry-fly section in the world, though. Unfortunately that's not the case so much anymore, due to many harmful reversals of late—ridiculously low winter flows, anchor ice, influx of trumpeter swans, silt in the river flushed down from Island Park reservoir, and so on through a laundry list of river disasters. At least that's what the scuttlebutt has been hereabouts.

It's a shame because the Railroad Ranch on a clear summer evening is really a glorious place—*serene* is the best way to describe it. There is a quietness over and around the water where the only sound is that of wind moving across huge unobstructed spaces and the water itself—implacable, moving with a rush. It's a very wide river with lush weed growth and crystal-clear water, and overall gives me the sense of being in the presence of something that dwarfs me—not overwhelmingly, but with perspective and a sense of continuousness. It goes on without us, but needs our help too. Which is what the Henry's Fork Foundation plans to do. Anyway, a lovely place—a sacred spot, some might say—but a hard place to fish and figure out. I doubt I'll ever get it right here.

And to prove that, we got nothing again last night. Wind was blowing hard when we started, so casting was tricky. I worked a very long undercut bank by standing out in the current and casting toward shore. The shifting wind, occasionally at my back, helped. I got three scattered hits (better than nothing) on various dries, and my heart leaped into my throat for a nanosecond with each strike, but I caught zilch. My plan was to work up the edge as methodically as possible, hoping there would be a goodly fish lurking along the bank (as they were on the Big Hole)—but no such luck. A good plan in theory but not in reality.

We joked about the Myth of Fishyfus—the ancient Greek tale of Sisyphus applied to trout fishing. Constant casting into the unknown is our version of pushing the boulder uphill. Casting repeatedly to insouciant trout in the face of hard wind and the blank visage of chance, unpredictability, futility, nothingness. Yet, we tell ourselves, there is dignity in trying, futile or not. The human situation, the angler's condition. It's in a moment like this that persistence becomes a virtue and reward in itself and maybe even a form of penance.

We reached the truck after dark. The mile-long hike back felt a good deal drearier and more challenging than the walk in. Doggedly putting one foot in front of the other was all we could do. We unhitched our gear and entered the zone that marks the ceremonial end of each day's fishing. It's that moment when fishing is done for the day, and you haven't yet had time to sort out the jumble of experiences—fish caught or not caught, fish hooked and landed or hooked and lost—and there is a deliberate slowing of time as you put up tackle one item at a time. Unstring the rod and wind up the line and leader, stow the reel, break the rod down, wipe it off and pack it in its tube, put the fly boxes away, checking vest pockets and judging what's where and what might be needed next day, and making another mental note of whereabouts so items can be found without too much rummaging in the morning when the ceremony starts again in the opposite direction. I don't amass gear for its own sake, but I realize that without the bedrock reality of our stuff, our traps, our paraphernalia, all the accoutrements and gizmos that give fly fishing its variety, texture, and particularity, the whole venture might be less appealing. Kept within bounds, using the right tool for the right job is a sensible way to proceed.

Next comes climbing out of waders and wading boots, putting on driving shoes, flip-flops, sandals, whatever, and perhaps changing shirts for the ride home. Then a dive into the cooler for a beer, a soda, a water, hoping whatever you grab is still reasonably cold even though the ice melted hours ago. And maybe more if the time is right, like a joint. I doubt everyone else goes about this process in the same way or in the same order, but no matter how effected, the procedure is a transition between fishing and the reflection that follows. A savory, toothful moment when elation or frustration are let go, and the day itself begins to become another page in a long, ongoing narrative of one vital part of your life, no different perhaps in the final analysis than all the other fishing days before it or those yet to come. But all yours nonetheless and a distinct pleasure no matter the outcome.

When each thing was in its appointed place for the time being, we drove over the mountains to Jackson Hole. Arrived about 11:30 p.m. to find that our *guaranteed* reserved room at Teton Gables Motel had been given away an hour earlier. That led to a run-in with a greedy owner who got our reservation money as well as the squatter's and refused to refund our fee. Amid curses and lamentations and self-righteous indignation, we retreated to Lejay's Sportsman's Café, open all night, and killed several hours over a late, late dinner or maybe an early, early breakfast. Drove to Jackson Airport and slept in the truck—fitfully—until 5:30 a.m.

Earl got off on an early flight back to Connecticut and I, with the rest of the day to kill, putzed around the tourist-trap town square a while, considered registering a complaint with the Better Business Bureau, thought better of it, got an oil change for the truck, browsed in fly shops, then drove over the Tetons and up to West Yellowstone, where I stopped at the Post Office to contact Tom Heyes, a college pal, who is now Assistant Postmaster. I have not seen him since we graduated from college in 1965, so we agreed to have dinner later this week and begin catching up. I'm delighted we're on each other's radar again.

Left West Yellowstone and went to the pay fishing spot at Cliff and Wade Lake Access of the Madison and fished several hours, though few risers were seen in that beautiful piece of water. A hint of sun hit the mountains to the east and a quarter moon rose like a bright ceramic fingernail in the darkening sky behind me. Nighthawks, sounding their Whitmanian bar-baric yawps, yapped overhead as they hunted for insects, and at near dark a majestic solitary great blue heron, carrying the evening on its back, floated almost ghostlike across the river to roost in a standing tree. I flailed the water in futile hope of bringing up a trout—*any size will do*—from the bottom.

Fishing-wise it's been a frustrating end of day—my first skunking of the entire trip—and by that I mean, not even a hit or refusal, let alone a hooked fish. There were moments in this stretch of pocket water and side ed-dies in recent years at around dusk when the cosmic switch was thrown and suddenly twenty-five or thirty rainbows materialized out of the depths like living treasure to rise and porpoise to hatching caddis. When their crimson sides broke water, each fish shone like a newly minted copper penny bur-nished to the nth degree in the last portions of daylight. Those jaw-dropping sights have been among the strongest, most indelible angling images I've ever experienced. At first nothing to be seen, then something, then everything. The game's amiss this year and nothing like that has occurred. I fear for the future.

Angling legend Charles Ritz claims in his classic *A Fly Fisher's Life* that the "charm of fly fishing lies in one's numerous failures and the unforeseen circumstances that must be overcome." That's humility at work. I get that. Yet after six years of Western fishing it grieves me to think that I'm not a more skilled angler, capable of making something happen on any given day. But what's the myth here? That we are in control of our destinies, or that the fish are? Most of the time I think it is the latter, with those rare moments when the window opens and we are allowed to see into a secret chamber—when that happens, all the casts are good, the fly floats without drag, and the trout rise willingly. But such perfection is the exception rather than the norm. Nothing in fly fishing happens as you think it will, and overall, for an average practitioner like myself, it is decidedly a hit-and-miss proposition. I despair of ever mastering the discipline. Good thing that compensation and satisfaction aren't always dependent on net count.

Got back way after dark to cabin #1 at Staley Springs to find a package from Library of America on the doorstep. The first volume of the Steinbeck series: *Novels and Stories 1932–1937*. A couple of years in the making, and a publishing job beautifully, handsomely, gorgeously done. Fruits of the other life, which, thankfully, is never far away.

Nick Nicklas Instructs

27 July 1995

"Man," poet Wallace Stevens says in his aphoristic "Adagia," "is an eternal sophomore." By which I think he means we men and women are perpetually in a learning posture, moving toward some vaster knowledge or increased level of skill without hope of ever fully attaining it, but despite that, undaunted, we keep forging ahead anyway. In other words, we are always underclass students and might never graduate. A year older but who knows if any smarter?

I've fished every day for the past ten days since arriving at Staley Springs. On a couple of float tube outings on Henry's Lake I've tangled with hybrid cuttbows big enough to pull me around at will. My own version of an old-time whaler's Nantucket sleigh ride. Cumulative impression thus far: river fishing has been slower than I'd like, in part due to what the folks at Blue Ribbon Flies call "roller coaster weather patterns" and cool temperatures that have slowed hatches. Everyone I talk with seems to agree on that score, which is what I find so convenient and reassuring about anecdotal evidence. It tends to fit whatever view of the world you happen to have. There has been talk about whirling disease in the Madison impacting the rainbow population, but no one knows for certain what the outcome will be. Too early to tell. All fingers crossed and breaths held, until more factual data is known. The impact on the fishery here and the area's allied economies would be catastrophic. On the plus side, water flow in the Madison looks to be as good as I have seen it in many years. Plenty of places for the trout to feel comfortable.

Anyway, thankfully my learning curve is aided and abetted by more accomplished souls. Like today. Up early to get into West Yellowstone by 8 a.m. to meet Nick Nicklas at Blue Ribbon Flies for a full day of guided fishing. He's one of the most respected guides and innovative fly tiers in this area and I've been hearing about him for several years. On the road by 8:20 a.m. to the Madison River at Raynolds Pass Bridge. Parked and walked downstream along the south bank of Madison and fished a new way by casting a dry fly *downstream* with a halt-action cast and a wiggle of the rod tip at the last moment that (1) pulled the fly line back toward me and (2) put plenty of slack line on the water. The goal: fly is the first thing that enters the trout's window. Great in theory but I had a tough time getting the hang of that and thought I was in for a long, trying day. I felt badly that I would be a disappointment to myself (nothing new in that) and to Nicklas, whose prodigious reputation as a master guide, I admit, intimidated me and set a bar that might be too high for me to reach, given my questionable skills. Anyway, we were prepared for all comers and I fished two rods all day—9-foot, 4-weight Orvis Power Matrix for drys; and my shorter 6-weight Winston IM6 for wets.

I was slow learning that downstream cast effectively, getting the timing right to put S-curves in the line so the fly would not drag, but after a while with Nick's instruction, happy to say, I began to improve. That's what a great guide does—makes you a better angler. We saw half a dozen feeding fish and around 10:50 a.m. to be precise (according to scribbled stats in my vest pocket notebook), I made a downstream approach to a rising fish and got it on an Iris Caddis. Nice 16-inch rainbow that appeared unscathed by disease. A good sign all around. A confidence booster, and earned words of encouragement from Nick. But action slowed down again—I couldn't get a couple more fish to take, and in one case after a successful downstream cast, I responded too quickly for my own good and pulled the fly out of the trout's mouth. Embarrassing scenario realized: the duffer factor on full display! Nick rolled his eyes at that one. I can only guess that he wondered what he'd gotten himself into.

We drove to the Cliff and Wade Lake Access, which Nick told me is locally referred to as "$3 Bridge" and which I should have known, as I have willingly put money in the iron safe in the upper parking lot for years. From now on, I promise to refer to it by its local name. We walked downstream to several likely looking spots along the way. Gangs of fishermen here today—counted sixteen cars at the parking areas. The height of popularity: July on the Madison River. After lunch, I got a 17-inch rainbow on a brown Serendipity, one of Nick's signature patterns, trailed behind one of his elegant, sexy soft hackles. Another healthy looking fish, followed a few minutes later by a sobering sight—a rainbow that looked as though it had been mugged with a blackjack, broken jaw and all. Not a whirling disease victim, but probably a treble hook casualty.

Then nothing for more than an hour as we weaved around other fishermen, intent on the same goals as us. We spotted fish working both upstream and down but the difficulty was targeting a fish that hadn't already attracted the attention of other anglers. We zigged and zagged, ducked and juked, bobbed and weaved, and at mid-afternoon I got a dandy 18-inch rainbow on an Elk Hair Caddis. Wonderful top-water take. Fifteen minutes later I got another like fish—a 17-inch rainbow—on the Elk Hair again. We were suddenly the envy of two other groups of fishers and one guy dressed all in camo came over to ask us what we were using. Caddis activity not strong but apparent and a blessed good call by Nick, who offered his selection to the stranger. Both fish in fine fettle and robust.

Next, on the way back upstream toward the bridge, we watched a nice fish working in a quiet slick right next to the shore—in fact almost all today's fishing was in close to the bank in soft water that most people, myself included on occasion, would walk right through. Earlier today as I was about to wade merrily into bankside water, Nick put a firm hand on my shoulder and stopped me. He didn't say a lot but when he did it was effective coaching and worth heeding. "The best fish are often in the calm slicks next to the bank. Stomp through there and they'll be gone." Big lesson relearned today and it set the tone for the rest of the outing. Attitude adjustment, I guess it could be called, though I did not mind being corrected. Anyway I kept casting upstream to that riser and finally hooked up on a dead drift. Turned out to be an 18-inch brown. The kind of fish I love to see on the Madison. This one took a PMD Sparkle Dun.

Around 4 p.m., we drove back to Raynolds Pass and fished upstream from the bridge, hoping for a pale morning dun hatch and a thinning of the angling crowd. No such luck, however, on either count. Few bugs on the wing and more people started showing up to get their licks in. I alternated both rods up and down the bank, and eventually we found a few fish working, but woe, woe, woe, again I took the fly right out of one trout's mouth by striking too soon. The duffer factor again rearing its ugly head. My guide was silent.

Later, on the way toward Nick's truck, we watched a lovely fish working steadily against the bank in a difficult lie, a narrow chute between the bank on the right and a boulder on the left. Trick was to drop flies on the inside of the rock for a decent drift but not to hang up on the rock. In the wind, that was easier said than done, but Nick had been schooling me on sharpening my cross-body casting stroke that made it possible to punch through the turbulence. On the third cast I got it right and hooked a 20-inch brown on a generic pmd emerger trailed on two feet of 5X tippet behind a Sparkle Dun. This tickled me plenty because it was a deft technical piece of work, way better than my usual offering. Without a backhanded, cross-chest, off-shoulder casting technique, which let me place tandem flies above feeding fish, I would not have caught the last three trout today. I had no photos of our earlier prizes—I forgot my camera in Nick's truck—but this one came to the net and smiled for its photo. Not just a nice fish, but a superlative one and my candidate for fish of the day.

So a long day on the water, but worth the price for being tutored by such an experienced guide and capable instructor. I doubt I will ever look at Madison River water in quite the same way.

Desert Places

18 August 1995

Blazing hot! Ninety-five degrees again today along the Bighorn River. My next-to-last stop before trekking back to Ohio. The landscape here looks baked: heat devils rising in shimmering spires everywhere. Squint or cock your eye just right and the whole world looks like an optical illusion. Even casting a fly rod is a tiring chore in these oven-ish conditions. After the slow fishing today, maybe I'm in hell after all. It's 10 p.m. Cooling down but still too warm to get into my tent. I'm writing this at the picnic table with a flashlight in my left hand. Coleman lantern is hissing away. Gives plenty of light but creates weird shadows and shapes on the page and pulls in every pain-in-the-ass insect in this part of Montana, most of them flying up my nose or in my eyes. They look like flecks of pepper on this page. Their final resting place, like it or not. Tiny fossils buried in inky tombs.

There's that uncanny thing the other night that haunts me. I've dreamed it vividly so often I can't tell if it really happened or not, or what part of it was real and what part imagined. A little of both, I guess. Something similar happened to me years ago on a fishing junket to Ontario with some grad school pals when I felt as though I had been reduced to nothing by an intimidating landscape. There must be a clinical term for such peculiar cranial confusion, but damned if I know what it is. I was in my float tube on Earthquake Lake pitching streamers. I fish evenings on the Madison, but this was different. I began to doubt whether it was a good idea as soon as I got in the water and started kicking around in the graveyard of standing dead timber at the end of the lake. Cloudy night without much light and the darker it got, the more ominous and eerie the trees looked. Flashlight not much help. Every once in a while a cormorant would squawk or fly off its roost and startle the shit out of me. Or there would be a commotion in the water that I couldn't see but the noise hung in the night air like a threat. I shrunk to nothing in all that vastness. I felt disembodied, untethered, a kite without string. The hair on the back of my neck stood up. Samuel Barber's "Adagia for Strings" played in my head.

I got a hit. At first I thought I snagged a submerged tree, but then it moved and shook and took some line and then it was gone. Maybe it was the fish of a lifetime, maybe it was something else. The darkness distorted everything, threw a strange wrinkle in reality. Whatever: it was something large enough and strong enough to break off a big flouncy streamer on stout leader. I came in. There was no one else around. Then I woke up, all questions unanswered, suspended between two enormous realms of darkness, deep calling to deep. I'll leave it at that except that Robert Frost was right. Wimp that I am, I have it in me to "scare myself with my own desert places."

But the heat, the dryness, the wind, the Quake Lake fiasco, and that spectral *Heliobatas* ray I saw at Fossil Butte in Wyoming last month all lodged in my head and launched some lines toward a new poem: "this ancient ray, sun-spiked, petrified behind glass,/remembers only the *now* of its passing,/a long exhalation under waves,/a voice on this tearing wind." A start toward my next book of poems down a darker road than this year's *News of Loss*, with less chat and more existential starkness to come if the floodgates stay open. All of a sudden there's a *noir* side to trouting. Twenty-eight people died in the 1959 earthquake that dammed the Madison Canyon and formed Quake Lake, so I should not be surprised that vibrations linger. Beneath the beauty and grace a glimpse into the terrible Sublime à la Edmund Burke.

The yin and yang of fly fishing. Good one day, meager pickings the next. Plenty of both the last several weeks. Plenty of ups and downs on Henry's Lake (from very good to awful), the Harriman Ranch section of the Henry's Fork (bust as usual), numerous outings on the Madison (from very good to okay), Red Rock Creek (bust), and on a Big Hole float trip from Divide to Melrose with John Sampson (very good). My fishing education and casting ability raised a couple of notches after being guided by Nick Nicklas on the Madison last month. But in such ways do we expand our repertoire, enlarge our palette, satisfy our angling curiosity hunger. That's a wonderful thing about fly fishing—there are always new waters to entice us, so many, in fact, that they can't all be fished in a lifetime. Depending on one's point of view, that's either exhilarating or depressing.

And now here I am camped on the Bighorn. Been fishing since 7 a.m. at Three Mile Access where I walked to the main section of river across a couple of shallow side channels. Between dodging gangs of other anglers, I watched for rising fish but few to be seen, and nothing compared to the stupendous *Trico* and caddis activity I encountered two days ago with George Kelly's guide Adam Wagner when the trout seemed to throw themselves at my flies. A thirty-fish day with many uniformly gorgeous brown trout and even some rambunctious goldeneye shad in the mix. It was almost too easy, but Jesus it was fun! But that's what I shelled out the $300 for, to be on hand when this bounteous river gives up its treasure.

Anyway, a guided trip, like the three I took this summer, has to be considered a luxury after the normal routine of grind-it-out, work-a-day fishing that is my stock-in-trade. A guided trip is a treat but it's also an anomaly— helpful as it otherwise is, a good day with a guide can be misleading because it prods me to thinking that I'm a good fisherman, when in fact all it really means is that I have refined a few basic skills. The real test, the thing not to be lost sight of, is what I do on my own. Like today when I managed only two decent fish on *Trico* spinners, roused some passing interest with ants and beetles in a few fish (one stopped my heart when I saw how big it was) but could not connect, then at twilight a 14-inch brown on a Hemingway Caddis and a 16-inch brown on an Elk Hair Caddis. Enough cool light on the water from a waxing moon above the tree line to see the takes. Despite the low numbers, I can't say these weren't satisfying fish, hellish conditions aside. Arthur Ransome says in *Rod and Line* that there is no such thing as a "blank fishing day" because something always comes along to save it. I think I feel saved.

For Whom Big Wood River Tolls

26 July 1996

Six days on the road, Ohio to Idaho. This year's Western trip kicks off with a conference, "Hemingway and the Natural World," put on by the Hemingway Society, a group of like-minded men and women scholars, teachers, writers, and aficionados, at the toney Sun Valley Resort. Hem left his stamp on this area from the late 1930s and then on again and off again for the next two decades. He wrote part of *For Whom the Bell Tolls* in 1939 in room 206 of the Sun Valley Lodge, where he hobnobbed with wealthy and famous guests (Gary Cooper, Ingrid Bergman, Howard Hawks) at the Lodge, hunted ducks (but didn't fish) on Silver Creek, bought a house in 1959 in nearby Ketchum, and was buried in the Ketchum Cemetery.

Yesterday I did my part by moderating a panel of experts on "Nature as Metaphor and Reality" that featured four specialists from different universities illuminating personal and literary aspects of Hemingway's considerable involvement in the natural world. I suspect that for a number of conference attendees Hemingway's outdoor achievements, which often clearly smack of testosterone-fueled machismo, must seem obscene. Such pursuits fall outside the pale of routine ivory-tower existence. But grow up interested in hunting and fishing, and Ernest Hemingway is bound to be on the personal radar screen.

He died by his own hand thirty-five years ago this month, less than a month after I graduated from high school back in 1961, and his passing touched me deeply, even though at that time I had read only a few of his writings and at that the standard fare, *The Old Man and the Sea* and a few short stories, though I thought then, as I do now, "Big Two-Hearted River" was one of the finest of its kind ever written. It's signature Hemingway, from its painterly Cezanne-inspired tonality to its backcountry setting in the Upper Peninsula. Nothing happens to young Nick Adams in the story, Hemingway admitted to Gertrude Stein, and yet everything happens, if that makes sense. Happens, I mean, below the surface, where the true meanings are. It has always been a touchstone for a certain kind of restrained prose style. Not the sensibility usually on display in popular fishing stories but one we no doubt could use more of.

Hemingway's not for everybody's taste, but he was the face of hunting and fishing, for good or bad, in this century. Part of my conference prep work was reading his friend Lloyd Arnold's photo-laden *High on the Wild with Hemingway*, S. Kip Farrington's *Fishing with Hemingway and Glassell*, and H. Lea Lawrence's *Prowling Papa's Waters*, where many of his celebrated sporting activities are on display. Snapshots of the strenuous outdoor life: I'd wager he is the most photographed writer of the twentieth century and became something of an instantly recognizable brand rather than a mere flesh-and-blood individual. He harkens back to Twain and Teddy Roosevelt and Zane Grey in that regard. I can't think of anyone who's his equal for publicity in our time.

Writing aside, manner of death aside, his outdoor exploits were legendary and formed part of a masculine sporting tradition every wannabe nimrod grew up wanting to emulate. The Hemingway Mystique, I guess it could be called. Whatever it was, authentic or manufactured, it was in the air we breathed and formed a model for the way some amateurs imagined themselves to be in the field or on the water. Even those lone wolves Jim Harrison and Tom McGuane are in his shadow by dint of their sporting subject matter and tough masculine orientations. What chance would a lesser person, impressionable me for example, have in not being starstruck or escaping Hem's gravitational pull? None.

Conference organizers made special arrangements with the Nature Conservancy to make Hemingway's Ketchum house, now off limits to the public, available for a visit. The house is set on a dozen acres on a bluff overlooking the Big Wood River. The setting is knockout beautiful with great views and ought to have served as a soul-saving buffer between himself and his demons. But not so. Here's the sobering part, the lowdown skinny, the true gen: I stood in the foyer of the house at the exact spot where he pulled the shotgun's trigger, did the deed, and entered a prolonged silence of his own making. Nothing—neither all the many biographers' suppositions nor the many psychoanalysts' mumbo jumbo—adequately explains suicide. Words falter, then fail. I felt chilled and angry and helpless too to unravel the enigma of his late years' decline and death. If it could happen to him, it could happen to anyone. I could go on a long time in this morbid vein, but what's the fucking use?

The talk among the house visitors grew quiet as we continued our bus tour toward Hemingway's gravesite, a simple granite slab beneath tall pines in the Ketchum Cemetery. People leave all kinds of stuff—pilgrimage gifts—at Hemingway's grave. I was no different: mine was a plain plastic box with a couple of Coch-y-Bondhu wet flies I bought at the Hardy store in London several years ago. Along with the Professor and Hardy's shrimp fly, it's a pattern Hemingway used often on Western trout when he was fishing his favorite setup, a three-cast wet fly leader rig, which was, according to some unpublished fishing diaries that I inspected at the Kennedy Library in Boston, one of Papa's go-to flies when he fished the Clark's Fork of the Yellowstone River at Lawrence Nordquist's L-T Ranch in Wyoming in the 1930s. Fly choices confirmed by his son, Jack, a world-class angler himself, according to *Misadventures of a Fly Fisherman*. Praise the fly, honor the man, that part of him anyway that I love. Maybe a small gift will go a long way.

Then there wasn't much else to do but to go fishing. I took out twelve-year-old Ian Wilson, son of a conference colleague, for a few hours on the Big Wood River south of Ketchum toward Bellevue. I'm not sure it's the best stretch of the river, but time was short and access was easy along Route 75. I'd heard Hemingway fished the Lower Cottonwood section of the river, but I could not find that area, and so our dream of fishing in his wake went unrealized.

I haven't been on any stream since March when I fished a couple of afternoons with modest success on the LeTort and Big Spring in Pennsylvania, old haunts of limestone creek impresarios Charlie Fox and Vince Marinaro. I felt rusty myself, having been ensconced too often in libraries lately. I mentioned that to Ian, so he wouldn't get his hopes too high, and mostly I lent a hand to his endeavors. He's an accomplished caster, has enormous enthusiasm for fly fishing, and is a quick learner, so it was an easy afternoon. Pale morning duns trickled off, danced in the shafts of sunlight, and in one short stretch Ian had three strikes on his dry fly in fairly rapid succession, but could not connect. I kept cheering him on and I think I felt worse than he did for coming up empty. But just being out there on that historic stream, passing something of value on to a beginner, wiped the slate clean, or almost clean, because it will always be haunting to realize that nothing in nature's glories could keep Hemingway from killing himself.

At the conference farewell dinner on the lawn of Sun Valley Opera House last night, food, booze, good cheer, and stories prevailed. Times like these the sum total of Hemingway seems to be much larger than his final deed. Hilarity reigned. Professors and students, guests and spouses alike raised glasses. We toasted. We toasted again. We quoted Hemingway. Mine was this from his story "The Three Day Blow": "'Fishing,' Nick said, 'That's what we drink to.'"

Brown Trout after Dark

4 August 1997

In certain light conditions—say during late afternoon and into early evening—look downstream from the Raynolds Pass Bridge on Route 87 in Cameron, Montana, and the Madison River does not appear to be aquamarine or cobalt blue in color, as some sources say, but an iridescent darkish silver in the waning, slanting summer sunlight. The river shimmers like a long ribbon of Mylar against the creamy pale green-going-blue of acres of sage brush and the somber tan-going-brown of fading high summer benchland grasses.

When I squint my eyes the whole scene down the Missouri Flats looks like a vibrant Impressionist painting—a tapestry of vivid colors subtly bleeding into each other—and through it all, like a vein pumping blood, that brilliant wide ribbon of freestone trout water, with its myriad riffles, runs, and pockets, carrying my eye all the way to the horizon, flanked on the west by the Gravelly Range and on the east by the Madison Range, and last but not least extending in my imagination well beyond the line of sight. Often what registers on my inner eye is what stays with me longest. That's the way it has been here every summer since I first discovered the seductive appeal of the Madison River Valley.

I don't live here, except for several weeks each summer, don't own land here, don't winter over here like a true native, yet in another, looser sense, I *do* live here, if home can be said to be the heart's residence. I have nearly a decade of personal history with the Madison and consider these journal jottings to be my love song to it, which, like any fickle lover, only now and then returns the favor. No matter, the river here has furnished its part toward my soul.

The Madison is "the definition of Paradise," Ed Gray says in *Flashes in the River,* but in its popularity and attractiveness it's also "a place without secrets." Gray and I part company there. The Madison does have secrets and I've stumbled on one that has lit me up. I've turned a corner into a small alley of my own, a little side-channel byway less traveled by the throngs from all over the world who have been coming here day in and day out with visions of angling glory in their heads.

Long story short: The Madison takes a pounding every day, relentlessly, by anglers casting nymphs, dry flies, streamers, terrestrial patterns—every conceivable form of floating and sinking fur and feather concoction imaginable to fool trout, especially rainbows, which historically numbered in the thousands per river mile, though that figure is open to debate, given the devastating impact of whirling disease in the past four years. Now the population is so low it's numbered in the hundreds per river mile. Among the fly shops that talk openly and honestly about it there is an unprecedented level of concern, frustration, consternation, and teeth gnashing. "People are tearing their hair out," Craig Mathews told me recently.

Word of the decline has hit the world's news media, and fly fishers are reportedly staying away and spending their money elsewhere, so fewer anglers here than in the past means that "rod days," the admittedly imperfect quantitative measure of intense river usage, have dropped off, with predictable and lamentable economic results for area businesses. Like the stay-aways, I nearly wept when I heard the news about whirling disease; like them I was tempted to do the same. The Madison's pull on me was too strong to refuse, even though I know now what happened to those glorious evening rises of rainbows I found so captivating in the early '90s—those fish were cut down by an insidious killer, a juggernaut mowing down trout ranks like a medieval pestilence.

I've had people tell me that the fishing is kaput on the Madison and have ridiculed my plan to keep fishing here rather than try other rivers. But here's the hard-earned secret that I started to puzzle out last year: into the interstices left by declining rainbows, brown trout have filled the empty holes in spades. None of the principals in this drama can be said to be native to the Madison. One invader extirpated by another invader and replaced, partly anyway, by a third invader. It has the makings of a crazy little eco-morality tale. Whether there is irony, tragedy, or symmetry in that equation, proclamations trumpeting the Madison's death strike me as being premature but not necessarily for reasons others claim.

I'm not a callous person, but the upshot of this cataclysmic upheaval is that anyone who irrationally loves the brown trout, as I do, is smiling, more or less. Not because of what has been lost, but because of what has been gained. Last week, when I was at Blue Ribbon Flies to pick up my weekly fishing report I showed another customer photos of recent browns I'd caught. When I said I got them in the Madison, he was so incredulous that he accused me of lying. He was certain the stricken Madison no longer had fish of that quality. I understood his disbelief. The Madison has gone from being a river where, according to fisheries experts, a competent angler can average three or four rainbows an hour in broad daylight, to a river where nighttime is the right time to encounter the naturally warier and harder-to-fool browns that cruise into the soft water near the bank looking for dinner. Around 5 p.m. anglers pack up and head home for their own dinner. I've done that too, in my early years here, until Juracek and Mathews advised me rather pointedly that I was leaving the river too soon. So now when I arrive I find long stretches of it abandoned, especially my favorite spot, which takes about fifteen minutes of brisk walking to reach. I rub my eyes, count my blessings, say a small prayer of thanks to the river spirits, dance a little loose-limbed jig. Then I sit on the bank and watch and wait before I string up my outfit.

Leave it to the French to coin a nifty phrase for dusk: *entre chien et loup,* "between the dog and the wolf," the transition zone between day and night, between furry family pet Fido and dagger-toothed predator. It's my hands-down absolute favorite time to be on the river. A sense of mystery hangs over the whole scene. As the sun lowers toward the horizon both water and air cool, the wind often dies down to make casting easier, the day's commotion and bullshit quotient lessens, the mind's white noise subsides, and as evening moves inexorably toward dark, inward sensations heighten when the palette of colors the eye is heir to deepens, darkens, becomes less expansive and familiar. Technicolor fades to *chiaroscuro.* If Baudelaire had been a fly fisherman he might have discovered his belief in the "derangement of the senses" after angling at night.

Start fishing in the morning and the whole day, with its clear, dazzling sunlit shapes, opens out before you like a welcome greeting. Step in the Madison in the evening and the opposite is true. Perception changes. It's like looking down the wrong end of a telescope, or like crossing a border into some foreign territory, some twilight-edged zone, where spookiness and a warped sense of time reign.

Some of the fastest, most furious, and most memorable action comes in the transitional period as dusk morphs into dark when my favorite bugs, the under-valued *Hydropsyche* caddis—spotted sedge, cinnamon caddis, call it whatever—and the *Lepidostoma* caddis—little brown sedge—ramp up their wild emergence and bring acrobatic trout up to the surface in sizable numbers. To be in the midst of a full-blown emergence of these supremely important insects is magical. The later it gets, the heavier the hatch, the more aggressive the trout become. Once hatched, caddis don't ride the currents like mayflies, but pop out and are quickly gone, headed for their sex-starved rendezvous. Trout of the Madison have to be contortionists themselves, willing at times to go airborne like missiles to capture a meal. Dimples, rings, swirls, splashes, and watery commotion mark their efforts. As light fades, caddis land on my hands, crawl on my face, my glasses, my vest, my arms. I pop one in my mouth to see what all the hubbub is about. As bugs go, this one doesn't taste like much more than dust. But the trout love them and that's what counts.

Brown trout, with their fixed-iris eyes, are best suited to low-light, night-hunting conditions. They are "negatively phototropic," Cecil Heacox says in his elegant study, *The Compleat Brown Trout.* But what's preferred by them is alien to me. After 9 p.m. and for the next couple of hours, I'm a stranger in a strange world, urged on by some inchoate stirring in me that has no name. That and the chance at a goodly fish.

Orientation, my sense of how and where I am positioned in a darkening riverine world, grows more tenuous minute by minute. There is a Zen-like quality to post-twilight fishing, because, almost blind, I have to grope my way forward, let go of linearity, trust in faith and my latent senses, rely on the unseen. The approach is indirect compared to daytime's routine. Nothing can be taken for granted. Wading is difficult and must be done slowly; it feels more like prowling than walking. For a brief span of time I too become a night predator. I'm an owl or a mink, though I don't see as well. A small Petzl headlamp and a compact gooseneck light in my vest help illumine close, minute work, but even they are limited in wide-range usefulness. I keep them shut off most of the time, but at the ready. Having fished a place numerous times in daylight helps get the lay of the river bottom fixed in my internal compass. But no matter what, this is fishing with my inner eye.

Hook a fish after dark in one of the slick areas near the bank, and most of the time it will head directly for heavy mid-river current to escape. With luck and steady pressure it can be turned quickly, but more than likely requires a sprint that ends up twenty-five to fifty yards or more downstream from where I started. In darkness, that gives new meaning to hanging on for dear life. Precariousness keeps me alert and guarded.

There is an odd, even eerie, sensuousness to hooking then fighting a fish you can't really see, but can only feel through its pumping, surging motion. The imagination runs wild in the inky darkness. The effect is jolting, electric, like you've just touched a live wire, or peeped into a forbidden room. Trying to net a fish in the dark, even with a headlamp shining at that crucial moment, is a hit-and-miss affair as though the nighttime world is tilted off-center, pitched at an unaccustomed angle. It isn't always possible to see the whole arc of action, from hand and arm to rod and to line and leader and hooked trout. The trout's only a rod length away just under the surface. It is frothing the water with desperate lunges and hell-bent surges, but is difficult to see in its entirety, so it's best to look for the glint of the leader and follow it downward. Stabbing with the net at the spectral form is like trying to corral a ghost or an idea. Margins for angler error increase exponentially. *Here now, there now.*

Around 8 p.m. last night below Raynolds Pass Bridge I found numerous fish working in one of my most treasured slicks, a wide indent behind several boulders where the heavy current is shunted away and leaves a relatively placid and smooth window of water. I got outside and downstream of them and cast a short manageable line slightly over and across the riseforms using a modified dead drift with a modest upstream mend. When these trout are on their game, as they were last night, not much will put them down. It's possible to get fairly close without spooking them. Better that than a long flailing cast across several kinds of current and flies tumbling and dragging willy-nilly. Started with #17 olive Iris Caddis as dry top fly and an antron Caddis Pupa as a wet dropper. Second cast a goodly fish took the dropper and broke me off. Lesson learned: I re-rigged, this time with 4X tippet instead of 5X.

As it got darker, more fish cruised to the feeding grounds, and I counted at least a dozen working and rolling regularly on the surface. Changed again, this time to a tan #17 Iris Caddis on top and a #18 tan X-Caddis as dropper, both dressed and fished dry. Took a healthy-looking 14-inch rainbow on the X, a welcome surprise, then a 17-inch brown, an even nicer surprise, then lost a third fish, way bigger, when it threw the barbless hook. That's the thing about fighting fish in those conditions—you can't see them but you learn to feel their size, sent up in a series of seismic shocks and head shakes through the rod and into your hand and arm.

The dark also compounds terminal tackle fuck-ups. Don't know why, but the lost fish caused a ridiculous tangle. Even with my two small lights blazing away, re-rigging was slow for these old eyes. Then disaster struck:

when I had my two flies retied and redressed I clipped what I thought was a tag end but it turned out to be the main tippet. Curses and lamentations. Back to square one to get it all straightened out and redeem my ineptitude.

Trout were still active at 9:30 p.m., and under a clear half-moon there was enough residue of light to make out some enticing wakes and phosphorescent splashes,

Typical Madison River night-time brown trout.
Credit: Robert DeMott

but not enough light to see my flies or the take. Even the white zelon wing loop on the Iris Caddis disappears in these conditions. I have to *imagine* the fly on the water. This is Hail Mary fishing. Make an offering, say a prayer, hope for the best. Discretion says *reel up and head home, you've had enough*; adrenaline says *stay where you are, fool, and keep fishing.*

I cast the same short amount of line each time so I have at least a vague sense of where my fly is in relation to the risers. I squint into the gloaming and strain my eyes to look for any aberrant movement in the water or some little out-of-the-ordinary twinkle or refraction that signals a feeding trout. I know fish are down there, and the later it gets, the bigger, more wolflike the trout that swim into range in the placid side pockets.

At a certain point it is impossible to distinguish between movement on the surface made by a feeding fish and that caused by river hydraulics. By then I have no choice but to go to my wing-and-prayer method: short cast of twenty feet or so, track line as best I can, then as the flies drift downstream, count a silent *1001, 1002, 1003, 1004,* then lift the rod tip. It's an exercise in uncanniness, extrasensoriness. It's a crap shoot, too, because the take can't be seen, though by my reckoning six out of ten times there's a fish on when I lift. Often, the later it is the bigger the trout is. Face it: my life would be a lot simpler, my fishing a lot more streamlined, if I threw big meat-hook streamers or mouse patterns after dark to draw explosive strikes that telegraph a trout's location, but somehow, given my small-fly fascination, that would be cribbing.

Last night it was a brilliant hen brown, solidly hooked, on the little X-Caddis. As soon as she hit I knew I was onto a special fish. I had to scramble downstream before I could steer her close, and even at that I missed her twice with my net. She taped out around 22 inches and I guessed her weight at four pounds, and her age at five years or more. She was a bit smaller than the bruiser I got last year under similar conditions, and a bit bigger than some 20-inch beauts—two browns and one rainbow—I got last week. She was so girthy I could hardly get my wet hands around her when I slipped her back into the river. Holding her rear section, her tail wrist, in my left hand and cradling her forward body in my right, I gently swam her back and forth in the current. Then her entire body shuddered, like a single flexed muscle, and she rocketed away. It's another kind of magical moment, strange and eerie and humbling, too, to be in command of such an elusive wild creature, such a dream fish, even for a few seconds while it regains its *mojo*. It's only an illusion that I'm in charge. Who says it ain't *love 'em, then leave 'em?*

I reeled up and walked out. The moon drifted in and out of the clouds. Ever-present amber mercury lamp in the front yard of a vacation cabin near the bridge led me out along the bluff path toward the road. It was nearly 11 p.m. when I crossed the cattle guard near the highway. Except for a few swooping nighthawks, the parking area was empty. My truck thermometer read fifty-four degrees, almost twenty degrees cooler than when I started. Until I reached the truck I hadn't noticed the change. I shed my vest and waders, stowed gear, and put on an extra shirt. I could hear the great river rushing on in the darkness, implacable, as it had rushed on for millennia.

I was home, then, for now.

Western Rivers Guide School

7 July 1998

Today is writing and catch-up day. In cabin #8 at Staley Springs Lodge since yesterday, after a two-week-long guide-school adventure in Wyoming and Montana. I wrote every day during the guide school, but still have loose ends to tie up. A couple of years ago when I began daydreaming about retiring from full-time teaching (maybe as early as next year), I decided that in my next life I'd like to be a fly-fishing guide. I didn't consider that a romantic dream of escape to the wilderness, a vainglorious attempt to recapture a youthful ambition, or a last-ditch effort to enter a burgeoning world of trendy commercial enterprise, but rather as a natural extension of a lifelong career in teaching, at which I had achieved modest recognition and an immodest amount of satisfaction.

It would be a neat thing to establish a fly-fishing program geared toward seniors or retirees. I think it would be not only a unique proposition (in a sport tyrannized by youth appeal), but also an extremely challenging and gratifying endeavor on all counts. Fly fishing for the fifty-five- to eighty-year-old set as a gateway to physical exercise, mental therapy, environmental awareness, and appreciation for nature. Basic stuff. And though I never underestimated the sheer hard work and long hours that would require, it's also possible to say that guiding and instructing anglers—old or young—doesn't strike me as being that much different from guiding and instructing literature students. Both jobs require patience, understanding, generosity, tact, enthusiasm, and the sharing of a certain kind and degree of special knowledge.

Believing I could make the leap from classroom to trout stream, I enrolled, at the cost of a couple thousand bucks, in outfitter Joe Bressler's Western Rivers Professional Guide School. Going to guide school, I reasoned, would at best be a mixed blessing, for truthfully speaking, how much could one learn in fourteen days? Some self-taught veteran guides I'd met on the Bighorn and the Beaverhead showed healthy criticism, even downright contempt, for such a quick fix. And I understand that, but if my expectations were realistic and my attitude was respectful toward the craft, I told myself, maybe I'd learn enough to come out okay. Certainly I'd get a better handle on whether guiding suited me. And if not, whatever new skills I acquired could help my private angling life. Anyway, curiosity got the upper hand.

Two weeks ago, five veteran instructors and ten students of varied backgrounds and angling skills from around the United States gathered in Alta, Wyoming, on the west side of the Tetons, for a curriculum of intensive classroom sessions on nuts-and-bolts aspects of guiding, including etymology, knot tying, ethical behavior, etiquette, protocols, role-playing, business advice, CPR training, and boat packing, because, after all, the drift boat becomes your mobile office and floating work station. It was a barrage of facts, information, attitudes, personalities, opinions, skills, requirements. Some of it I knew and recognized, some of it was utterly new to me; I entered with an open mind and willingness to listen, watch, learn, and contribute what I could. The students all seemed eager and attentive; our instructors, all thorough-going professionals in more than one sport, were effective teachers. Two in particular—Gary Beebe and Dave Miller—had that added element of charisma.

Then last week, after classroom work wrapped up, our whole tribe caravanned to the Big Hole River near Melrose, where we pitched our tents and set up fishing camp. That was my favorite part of school. From then on it was practical, hands-on experience rowing drift boats and trout fishing to our hearts' content. Each day two students took turns guiding an instructor on a morning-to-evening, eight- to ten-mile-long float trip. While one student rowed, the instructor and the other student fished like there was no tomorrow. There was friendly bantering and a few competitive casting games along the way. But it was all good fun, spirited and sociable. I learned something valuable every day. Gary Beebe's insistence on proper rowing technique: back straight, roll wrists with each stroke, keep oars at the same length and distance. Watching Pete Erickson handle a nymph rod like a fine concert instrument and Mike Jannsen rapid-firing bright yellow-and-copper Tequeely streamers to within inches of the bank was worth the whole week's tuition. They set the skill bar high. It was more than that, too, more than demonstrating a set of physical skills: they had knowledgeable explanations and plausible reasons for everything they did. Even the *al fresco* camp meals were excellent, and I'm not sure cold beer ever tasted better.

Overall, river week was demanding physical work for me, the oldest of ten students, used to a life in the ivory tower, but extremely gratifying nonetheless. Even as my shoulders and hands ached from rowing and casting, and tennis elbow and carpal tunnel syndrome woke me up with their fiery pitchforkings every morning at 4 a.m., there were still times in that superb setting, adrift on a broad river of possibility, when I felt I had gone directly to heaven. Like four days ago, on a stretch of the upper river near Wisdom, where I was handed a gift: several grayling on a #16 tan Elk Hair Caddis. My first encounter with that rare, legendary native fish that I'd read about since I was a boy. They were more splendid than I had imagined.

Not all gravy, though. Later on we went from idyllic, bluebird day to a lashing hailstorm that was so fierce it smashed the lids of our plastic fly cups. Storm so violent that Beebe, a master of river craft, took over the rowing from me and got us safely under a protected bank of willows. Even in waders and a Gore-Tex fishing jacket, the chill blew through us and we shivered in our boots. The storm came up in a blink of an eye and proved the greatest object lesson I could have had about the necessity of being prepared for a day on a Western river. Hope for the best but pack for the worst. By such extremes we are both humbled and chastened.

At the end of our course, Bressler and his staff held graduation ceremonies (complete with suitably uplifting speeches) in the gravel parking lot of a bar and carryout in Glen. Graduating from a guide school, one instructor said, "is worth more than just a feather in the cap." I wasn't sure what that "more" would be, but I was pleased with my efforts anyway. I couldn't speak for the future plans of my pals John Adams, Jon Lancaster, Chad Plumly, and Paul Swan, but I'll always be an amateur, because despite my original intention, there was no scenario I could envision where I'd ever be supporting myself, that is, making my regular paycheck, by full-time guiding. Ad hoc maybe, part-time maybe, but not sole occupation. Anyway, I won't give myself airs, and I knew that on my best day I would never reach the skill level of my instructors, but even before we went inside and downed our congratulatory beers, I knew I would be wacky enough to prize my graduation certificate from Western Rivers nearly as much as my PhD diploma thirty years ago.

Querencia

11 July 1998

Fishing on the Madison has been excellent. Some of the juice from guide school is still with me, so I fished from morning until night. I surprised myself with my intensity, my zest for the game. Fishing wrapped itself around me like a cloak.

In his indispensable little gem, *Fly Fishing*, Lord Grey found the "evening rise" worth the effort and "perfectly fair fishing." But he had reservations about fishing after dark. Hook a trout then, and you rely more on force than skill to land it, and "much of the pleasure," he says, is lost. I honor fly-angling traditions and history, and I love Grey's brilliant book, which is small and compact enough to carry streamside in my vest, as I've done this week so I could dip into it during lulls in fishing, but I swerve away from the good viscount on the subject of fishing in the dark, which I consider not just immensely pleasurable, but needful. Not fishing through until dawn, but fishing past dusk into the first inky part of night when the world draws inward and distances collapse.

My life must be way more ho-hum and boring than Lord Grey's, because I find the after-dark gambit an exciting pursuit. Or maybe it's just that the era of the genteel angler is over, and a century later I wonder if I am an avatar of moral and ethical declension, a barbarian at the gate? Dispense with protocol, break down restrictions, go for broke, let the ends justify the means? Outlaw that I am, I could hardly wait to resume my night-fishing routine.

My current fascination started several years ago more or less innocently when I walked into the first prolonged caddis hatch on the Madison I had ever seen without really knowing what it was. That was before whirling disease hit and I could hardly believe the number of trout I saw rising in the waning light. I can still visualize the broad-backed rainbow that porpoised on my Elk Hair fly and hooked itself on its downward arc. Suddenly I was sprinting after a leaping fish that ran me one hundred feet downstream. It came out of a side pocket above the Slide Inn in water so shallow I didn't think it could harbor a minnow much less an 18-inch trout.

My hands trembled when I removed the hook, for it was the most substantial and picturesque rainbow I'd ever gotten, right down to its rose-pink lateral stripe and constellation of black spots. It was a mind-blowing, adrenaline-buzzed moment when I realized a path had opened for me and that I had not just the inclination but the compulsion to follow it. From that moment I was a convert, though it would be a long time before I could approach the game with nuance and finesse. That single trout was as influential to the plot of my angling life as the very first one I caught on a fly on the Saugatuck back in 1956, or that hard-won rainbow from DePuy's in 1993. Interesting that we catch many fish in a lifetime but only a few of them reach mythic, paradigm-shifting proportions.

Now I think this day's-end preoccupation is as close as I will ever come to any sort of angling A-game. It is delusional to think any part of fishing is a sure thing, but these outings are among the few times in my life that I sense success is a possibility if self and world align rather than collide. What I most love about evening-to-dark fishing is the way it dissolves accustomed barriers and expectations, puts me in a hybrid place where angling mysteries and variables are compounded, and the sense of the unknown, of *who-knows-what's-to-come?* is ratcheted up. It's solitary, lone-wolf fishing, an intrusion of wild uncertainty into my normally straitlaced, linear academic existence. So what if visibility declines as evening goes on? Intuition, interior sight, inner meaning heightens during the darking period and I meet myself coming and going.

Last night and the night before, for the third year in a row, I had wonderful outings downstream of Raynolds Pass Bridge. My *querencia*, my sweet spot of angling topography, rarely disappoints. I gloat a bit about this because only a couple of times over the past decade have I ever seen anyone fishing it. People walk by it on their way to some other fancied honey hole, which is fine with me. Perhaps it looks nondescript or has a reputation as a waste of time. Again, fine with me. Nothing could be further from the truth. I've come to know it well enough that I can fish it with modest familiarity and confidence after dark. Some large boulders, a downed tree trunk, a small island, and a quiet side channel nearby are points of reference I can rely on when darkness prevails. Each spot has its quality, its character, its functionality, its history, its place in the angling chain of events. There's something unchanging and stable about the place, too. In the past decade it has been impervious to high water and the shape-shifting power of runoff.

Two nights ago the action was hot and heavy. Trout working everywhere in that flat-pocket water below the boulders. Some rocketed straight out of the water to chase caddis pupa, their bodies exposed three quarters of the way; others were rolling and tailing and porpoising and having what I could only imagine was a high old time. *Good for them; good for me.* A mix of caddis, too, as nearly as I could determine, with *Hydropsyche* and those little *Glossosoma*, I think they are. Both kinds landed on my vest. Emergence conditions perfect: still, clear, warm evening with little or no wind. A textbook scenario. An astonishing number of big fish gorging on caddis. I think it might have been as large a number as I've ever seen there at once and reminded me of the halcyon pre-whirling disease days.

As it grew darker, activity ramped up. There were spinners as usual in the mix, as well, but once again in an utterly perverse move I was riding the Caddis Express and ignoring the mayflies. I felt as though I had something yet to prove. After several switcheroos following fumbled knots, tangled tippets, and bent hooks, a single #18 tan X-Caddis was the hot fly. For the next two hours, until well past dark, I had on at least ten hefty fish, some of which I lost or broke off when I couldn't keep them from mid-river current. It was like being hooked to a Buick. Even a mad dash downstream was futile. Amid all that bounty, when my own heart beats like a trip hammer, things can and do go wrong, but adversity is part of the game and can't be avoided. Wind gusts create an errant cast, the small hook pulls out, or an abraded tippet snaps, and there's nothing short of shooting the fish with a gun that can be done to stem the evil tide. Cursing helps. So does insane laughing.

It's fishing in the moment, fishing in the midst and thick of things, when I feel life on my pulse and in my blood, below rationality and reason, beneath the brain's wiring, in a way I have never known before and might never know again. Atavistic fishing. With luck, though, and a suitable number of pleas to the fish gods, I landed several fat foot-long rainbows, then two eye-popping browns, both between 21 inches and 22 inches. It's the bully browns I come for. They are part and parcel of the darkness. Their allure is narcotic and I'm a junkie looking for his connection in the mean streams of Montana. *Savor this*, a voice says, *for all it's worth.*

Last night, in the same spot, conditions were different. Windier and cooler. In the fading light tunnel between 8:45 p.m. and 9:25 p.m. I hooked three more 12-inch to 14-inch rainbows, which suggests there's a whole age-class of healthy trout in the river defying whirling disease. This bodes well for the future. One broke the hook at the bend; the other two came to net. Fish kept rising in the pool but nothing like the previous night. Still pretty damn good.

Around 10 p.m. I heard the jaw-smacking *plop, plop, plop* of a feeding fish working the seam between the slick area and the choppier outside water. I guessed its position, made short cadence-count casts into the murk, and tied into a strong fish that wheeled off yards of line before I got tight on the reel. "I've got a brown on," Richard Hugo writes in his poem "Langaig." "My line is writing a song."

After inching backward in the dark, feeling my way around submerged boulders, I eased it into the quiet side channel. In the wash of my headlamp, a glorious brown trout, a rhapsody-inducing fish, a symphonic beauty nearly 23 inches long, almost too big for my net. An arresting pale-colored fish, with unusually small red spots, whose flanks gradually shaded from tan to pewter, set off by a huge black tail as large and wide as my spread hand. A brilliant fish forged in liquid metal. A joyous trout to feed all my desire. If I were an artist I'd have painted that fish. I had never seen one quite like it and took a photo instead while it was in the water, then slowly revived it, for it was too great and honorable a creature to spoil or demean by careless handling. I held my breath until it kicked its farewell. Part of my heart went with it.

Trout were still rising at 10:30 p.m., but I resisted their siren call and quit, already humbled by my exquisite fortune, and spent emotionally too by its ecstatic demands. It couldn't have gotten any better even if I stayed until dawn.

Millennial Trout

23 December 1999

Starting the 112th page of this year's angling journal. Thirty full fishing days in all so far. Not exactly trout-bum totals but then that's not an identity I ever cared to assume. It's been a varied year, a hit-and-miss year from a mid-March spring-break trip in New Mexico to today's holiday-season outing in suburban Connecticut. There were many other high points along the way this year and no end of memories, reflections, images rising out of this personal record book, all fodder for late-night ruminations, especially tonight as it approaches midnight. And yet the auspiciousness of the historical moment, with our feet poised to enter a new *thousands* century, makes *all* narrative seem glib.

Of course, end of year/decade/century breeds retrospection and ubiquitous top-ten lists. I'll keep mine to two favorites. (1) a leisurely fishing hike into Nez Perce Creek in Yellowstone Park where the only sounds were the creek itself sliding along, hoppers whirring and clicking their castanets in the sere grasses, an occasional lodgepole pine rubbing its back against its neighbor, and ravens and magpies—now comical, now deadly serious—telling their secrets to the wind. And (2) a day on John Sampson's Ruby Springs Lodge water where sizable brown trout swam 15 feet or more from undercut banks and deep pools to smash a hopper. If they missed the hopper, they took a trailing beadhead. Even impaling the fleshy part of my left index finger with a #8 hook couldn't dampen the occasion.

I learned it's possible to operate on myself and keep fishing. It's that couple of thousand dollars' worth of guide-school training! Keep fishing, no matter what, even when there's blood on the cork.

The daily accounts are all here, even the nuts-and-bolts expenses—my four-day spring jaunt to New Mexico cost $1,300 for travel, lodging, meals, a guided day on the San Juan River, equipment, flies, and license, reminding me that such ventures, as refreshing and soul-enhancing as they are, also have a cold-cash bottom line that keeps me tethered to reality and leavens the mystification quotient of fly fishing. Makes me wonder how many days of teaching I need to complete to pay the fishing expenses. Best to keep both sides of the ledger in balance. All relevant facts and figures recorded as usual in this companionable fishing book, this extended epistle to myself, this autobiography of my fishing heart.

I've just read through the entire year again, though I'm not sure to what purpose, except to indulge my dawdling and to lament not having fished more in 1999. Given this moment in history when Y2K fears about technological collapse and computer Armageddon seem imminent but as-yet unproven, the whole year, indeed, the whole century, comes down to this afternoon's outing in Wilton on the Cannondale section of the Norwalk River.

"To revisit a river is like trying to redeem a dream," Bliss Perry claims in *Pools and Ripples,* and like much of what the good professor wrote about literature and culture and teaching in his distinguished career, that too is on the mark. Sometimes it all works as it's supposed to. I carved out a couple of hours away from holiday shopping and preparations for tomorrow night's traditional family Christmas Eve dinner. I pulled myself away from one more cup of coffee and the savory odors of my mother's kitchen, dressed myself warmly in fleece jacket, wool ski cap, fingerless gloves, and my heaviest waders (it never got above thirty-six degrees today under a weak northern sun and a light breeze), and drove to my accustomed spot about five minutes from my parents' house. I wrote my first fly-fishing journal entry here ten years ago, so the place has from the outset been part of my fishing-writing destiny.

I parked at the Cannondale Grange Hall and set up a 4-weight rod. A gaggle of huffy Canada geese watched me. Judging by the amount of shit on the lawn, they own that part of the stream, so I placated them with half a dozen Oreo cookies I had stashed in the back of my truck. That got them out of the water. I rigged a #14 Rainbow Prince fronted with a single BB shot on a 4X leader, and as a dropper, I alternated a #20 Pheasant Tail and a #22 Brassie on 5X tippet. The holographic Prince is a new fly to me. All riotous neon and flash, like a disco ball light or a Christmas tree decoration. And it has sexy rubber legs, too. I discovered it at the Orvis shop in Ridgefield the other day. It looked like it was put on Earth to catch fish. Or me.

The river is not very wide, though it does have decent pools and long runs and glides. I fished adjacent to the grange parking area all the way up under the bridge, where, because the girders are so low, it's like fishing in a cave, and only a side-arm cast works to keep the tip-top from scraping the roof. I waded upstream along the stone retaining wall and on farther toward the spillway. That took a while but I was in no hurry. To my left, the specialty stores at Cannondale Crossing were busy with shoppers, and every so often one would catch sight of me flogging the water, then shout a hearty "Merry Christmas" that could be heard over the purl and gurgle of the current. I kept my inner Scrooge in check, waved back, and continued fishing past the traffic.

Evening comes early here this time of year. A muffled, greasy light draped across the stream. The water looked almost ebony, and I had to stare at it long and hard to make out bottom structure and now and then a fish moving among winter shadows. I caught three rainbows, all about a foot long, with the new-fangled Prince accounting for two of them. Stockers certainly, but well-acclimated and healthy. Out of the cold, dark river each present came forth gaily decked in brilliant colors and ornate hues, the silver of their lower bodies set off lengthwise with a glistening crimson sash. The final fishes of an era, each a palimpsest, a hieroglyph of a mysterious alien world. How trout see a fly the size of an eyelash, or sliver, or grain of sand, or speck of dust in the sunless firmament is beyond me.

Christmas trout, trout of the century, millennial trout: our quarry in one way or another for most of the past twenty centuries—give or take a few hundred years—since human beings in ancient Macedonia figured out that tying fur and feather to a hook might fool such finny creatures. Details change, materials improve, mythology expands, techniques sharpen, history marches forward, but the basic angling paradigm remains constant and humbles me with its size and scope, its presence and continuity, its pleasure and purpose. It's a process that's been there before me and will be there after me. Mastery is out of the question, an illusion for egoists to entertain. Perhaps it's true, as Ecclesiastes claims, that nothing is new under the sun, but as the year turns toward another century, here's hoping the pleasures and gifts that angling brings never end.

Elk River Trout Ranch

15 May 2000

Color me surprised. Color me more than surprised. Color me astonished. I'm getting ahead of myself, but I feel as though I have had a mind-blowing experience not too much different than seeing Bob Dylan go electric at Newport in 1965. You had to have been there for full effect.

Two days ago I drove the 215 miles or so over to out-of-the-way Monterville, West Virginia. The country's elevation and its look and feel reminds me of the Green Mountains and the Taconic Range of southern Vermont. I fished the catch-and-release section of the Elk River at the Elk Springs Trout Ranch, on the site of an old private trout hatchery no longer in full use. It was the first time I've fished in West Virginia since the spring of 1971 when life-long pal John Mitchell and I spent a weekend camping on the Cranberry River. We caught dozens of trout, including genetically mutated, hatchery-concocted palomino trout shaped like rainbows but colored like pet-store goldfish. I found them so distasteful that for thirty years I never returned. But a brief piece a few weeks ago in the *Orvis News* extolling the upper Elk River as a unique trout stream intrigued me so much that I followed up to investigate. The story was accurate.

I fished a couple of hours in the evening on the 13th, then a good part of yesterday, and again today, all within walking distance of the funky little Orvis shop/snack shack near the old trout hatchery. Bug action abundant with March browns, sulphurs, blue-winged olives, and Hendricksons coming off in the mix. The latter were especially prevalent, which made using Red Quills and a pinkish Comparadun excellent choices and made me think I actually knew something about fly fishing. I consider Art Flick's Catskill-style Red Quill the most elegant and beautiful dry fly ever tied. But until two days ago I had never in my life experienced a Hendrickson hatch, so at long last I was able to use my iconic Red Quills, buried down deep in one of my fly boxes. Fly hoarder that I am, I'd been saving them for years, maybe even decades, *just in case*. Who says the angling gods don't smile on us now and then? And to think, I was ready when the call came!

As nearly as I can tell, the Elk issues primarily out of an underground river and enormous subsurface limestone springs that create perfect alkaline-enriched habitat for a smorgasbord of insect food. One guy I met the other night said the river has everything except *Tricos*. Grannoms, quill Gordons, green drakes, yellow sallies are also here at certain times. I was flabbergasted. I had no idea such a blessedly endowed river existed within a relatively easy drive from home. The locals here call this river "The Lady" and from what I have seen we all have to be on our best behavior in courting her. No question it is a special place. I'm already obsessed by her. Who knows what the future holds, but I'm salivating over a long courtship, steep learning curve be damned. A side note: on the drive over I saw a brilliant male indigo bunting, my first ever, and I take it as a fortuitous sign.

More of the same good tidings yesterday. Rigged my Orvis Trident TL 4-weight for nymphing with #12 Gold-ribbed Hare's Ear as top fly trailed by a selection of small midge offerings—WD-40s, Zebra Midges, Brassies. This brought some chunky rainbows and browns to hand, three or four of them in the 18-inch range, truly wondrous fish, as good in quality as last month's fish on the Green and Provo in Utah. On one of Carl Richards's V-Duns I landed several brook trout, the first of those lovelies I've gotten in a long time.

Today another pleasant spring day with air temps in the mid-sixties, and the water itself at a fish-friendly fifty-six degrees. Fished my limber 3-weight St. Croix today. Played around some more with my British flies and actually caught a trout on the dry Red Tag that I bought at Hardy's in London, but the Tups Indispensable still goes begging for a hookup. Switched to a double nymph rig with Hare's Ear on top and miniscule Brassie or WD-40 as trailer. I lost a couple of trout that got by me in heavy current and pulled off, and then I lost three pairs of nymphs—that's six flies—in about thirty minutes when I stupidly kept hanging up in the same deep chute. I must have been half asleep because I kept casting back to the same spot without realizing that the snag would occur again and again. But it was the fishiness of the run that seduced me and kept me expecting a different outcome. Stupidity on display! I ran out of 6X tippet and went to 7X, a bit extreme for this early in the season, but the changeup worked and as I fished back toward the parking area, I took a nice brown on a #22 Disco Midge, confirming what I'd heard from some of the Trout Ranch regulars the last couple of evenings, that the Elk is a river that rewards sparsely tied patterns and small flies. I can live with that. And not a palomino trout in sight. I can definitely live with that.

Success Is Counted Sweetest

15 August 2000

After a stretch of doldrums on the Henry's Fork (again!) and Red Rock, and being handed some slim pickings with *Tricos* at Baker's Hole on the Madison, I've had intense, rewarding fishing these past four or five days, from the Madison in Cameron to Poindexter Slough and the Beaverhead in Dillon. All very good, especially yesterday on a High Bridge to Henneberry float on the Beaverhead with Dan Curtis, a guide out of Watershed Fly Shop. Numerous 20-inch-plus fish on infinitesimal #20 nymphs, including a 23-inch brown that weighed about five pounds and had a head that looked like an alligator's. Stupendous, thick-necked, broad-shouldered fish. My best ever on the Beaverhead. My knees felt rubbery when it came to net. Also hectic sprints of late-night journaling these last four days to keep this year's angling plot going. Plus time squeezed away from both fishing and scribbling to be tested for casting ability. I passed my FFF casting certification. This is as welcome as it is surprising, given my dismal past record of failure.

Guide school two years ago rubbed in my face what a makeshift, seat-of-my-pants caster I am, so I got it in mind that my chances for landing a post–Ohio

University job with a Western outfitter or lodge or fly shop would be greatly enhanced if I was sanctioned by the Federation of Fly Fishers as a basic level Casting Instructor. This would amount to added value—not absolutely necessary for a guiding job, but a helpful addition to making future applications more attractive. So I started on the FFF certification route, which became an *idée fixe*, an obsession. I enlisted the aid of a master in casting arts, to whose house in western Ohio I trekked on several occasions to enhance my skills, which, as we both realized, were full of quirky habits.

I read the FFF's bible, *The Essentials of Fly Casting,* a zillion times, and with images of straight-line paths dancing in my head, practiced loop control daily by casting at the hula hoops scattered on my lawn and dangling from tree branches in my yard. I also watched educational videos by superstars Joan Wulff, Doug Swisher, Mel Krieger, and Lefty Kreh, whose tape I watched so often that it wore out. After my cram sessions, I signed up to be tested. The FFF exam is a two-parter: a thirty-six question multiple-choice and true/false test; followed by a physical performance test. Eleven people took the exam and nine failed. I was one of the nine. Other examinees complained bitterly about their treatment, but I knew I deserved to flunk.

It wasn't exceeding the limit of wrong answers on the written exam that bothered me most—additional boning up on technical aspects of rod mechanics would help me improve that part. Neither was it the inconsistent showing I made on the performance test: thoroughly rattled by then, I followed a pinpoint accuracy cast with a botched double haul, the latter ending in a dreaded tailing loop that is as unwelcome as writing a sentence fragment or a dangling modifier is in a formal composition—it happens but it shouldn't be done, and you'd better know how to correct it. That I had double hauled perfectly fifty times earlier in the week was suddenly immaterial and irrelevant, proving, I guess, that you're only as good as your last cast, and that when things go wrong, they go colossally wrong.

The most disappointing aspect of my showing was that I did not have the proper spiel to contain or shape what I knew, and therefore I could neither explain to my two eagle-eyed examiners what I was supposed to be doing on each cast, nor could I say why the desired effect did or did not occur.

Words abandoned me, language failed me, or worse yet, I failed language: I hesitated, I hemmed and hawed, I stammered, I stumbled over what should have been a delivery "accomplished quickly and easily" according to the FFF instructional brochure. It was a moment not so much of embarrassment as of horror. My examiners knew that I was a complete fraud—I proved that every step of the way—but they could not have known how bitterly I understood myself to be a hypocrite of the first order. My only recompense was that no former student of mine was present to witness my meltdown. Sometimes shame is best kept private.

My approach had been overly determined. I had tried to colonize certain aspects of the instructional process from the top down rather than approach it naturally from the bottom up by slow, patient, organic learning. I was in too much of a hurry to get where I thought I wanted to go. I had sold short the most important part of education, had bypassed the place where all explanatory narratives come from—my own experimentation and observation.

I also realized that I would need a regular mentor. So last summer, as soon as I made it to Montana for my annual summer angling foray, I introduced myself to Bob Jacklin, proposing that I might hire him for private instruction and tutoring. Besides owning and operating one of the oldest fly shops in West Yellowstone, he's considered by many experts to be one of the best casters alive and is on the FFF's Board of Governors.

Jacklin conducts a free casting clinic near his tackle shop every summer Sunday evening at 7:30 p.m., and once I confessed my tale of FFF woe and asked for his advice, instead of taking me on as a private student, he generously invited me to attend his weekly clinics and "help out." He believes teaching others is a way of learning. I was dumbstruck that he would show that much faith in a total stranger, and a failure at that, but I came to admire that despite his somewhat gruff exterior and no-nonsense demeanor befitting an ex-military man, he is thoughtful and compassionate.

Over many weeks last summer and again this summer I drove the thirty-five miles from my rental cabin on the Madison into West Yellowstone and lent a hand every Sunday night for the privilege of listening to Jacklin's delivery as he introduced the complexities of fly casting to a group of neophytes. Bob made it remarkably simple and accessible, yet his presentation was engaging, informative, and both humorous and anecdotal. Following twenty minutes of opening comments, every student—sometimes as many as fifteen or twenty—was handed a rigged fly rod and reel and set

Assisting at Jacklin's weekly fly-casting program. Credit: Robert DeMott

into action around the rectangular casting pool behind the old Union Pacific building in West Yellowstone. Jacklin and his ad hoc group of instructors, myself included, made the rounds giving hands-on directions, advice, correction, and encouragement to the students.

Adding an informal teaching dimension to my apprenticeship was just what I needed because it put my education on familiar footing and boosted my confidence. Jacklin must have sensed that because last week, knowing I'd be heading back to Ohio soon, he asked me if I'd like to take the test again, which as an FFF Governor he was empowered to administer on his own. Flabbergasted by his generosity, I leaped at the chance.

So, on the 10th, I sat on some boxes in the cluttered back room of his fly shop and took the written examination, trying not to eavesdrop on his conversation with Joan Wulff, who was in and out of the shop. When I finished, Bob graded it on the spot. And he did what a good teacher would do: he patiently reviewed each answer with me (thankfully, for both of us, I got all but one correct), and we had a lively back-and-forth dialogue about fly casting's physical and metaphysical dimensions.

We broke for lunch, then reconvened at the casting pool where I took the Basic Fly Casting Instructor Performance Test (as it is officially designated) and moved through its requirements pretty smoothly. Next came my nemesis, the Instructing Ability section, which concludes the ordeal, and which requires explaining the whys and wherefores of the casting process. Apparently I marshalled my stories well enough to get past the final hurdle without embarrassing either of us. The upshot: I passed! Jacklin could not have been kinder or more generous in his mentoring.

In one of her most famous poems, Emily Dickinson writes, "Success is counted sweetest/By those who ne'er succeed." Even if flunking happens rarely in one's life, Dickinson is correct in suggesting that setbacks enrich our sense of success by giving sharper definition to our eventual achievements, no matter how grand or minuscule they are. There's something appealing, even liberating, about realizing—against the grain of masculine bravado—that failure *is* an option in everything we undertake. So, until we can tell a meaningful story of our preferred discipline, we haven't got it down pat, and as a result, rather than the discipline—the body of knowledge—failing us, which is the glib and cynical excuse, we fail it. For anyone committed to a life in learning, nothing could be more horrifying than not being able to interpret what we know, or not being worthy to share what we love.

I fished the Madison that evening, as I have done so often during the previous five weeks. Fishing was so-so and seemed more like work than sport. This late in a very warm and dry and smoke-filled August, the once prolific hatching caddis are now a trickle (a few stray small browns came on various caddis imitations), but the windy night was lit up by a nearly full moon that hung like a cotton ball in the cloud-strewn sky. Around 9:20 p.m. I brought to net a lovely rainbow on an Iris Caddis, and the fish was resplendent and almost glowing in the late evening dimness. I thought of a dazzling line from Hart Crane's epic poem *The Bridge*, which I taught in my American literature seminars many times, but never before quite understood: "I learned to catch the trout's moon whisper." I had done just that. I went away relieved and happy, though cautioning myself against being too smug or overly confident, as who can ever predict when the next shoe will fall?

Spring Creek
Tantalizations

11 August 2001

I've been hanging around Livingston for a few days. The place has a pulse, a vibe. Hard not to like its qualities. Annual Federation of Fly Fishers Conclave is on, dubbed this year "In the Spirit of Angling Tradition." Some nifty exhibits and vendor displays to view and dally over. Watching fly-dressing demonstrations I rued having given up tying years ago, though I realized that, with my blunt fingers, even on my best day I'd never come close to the skill of some of these men and women artists. I also signed up for a workshop on "Instruction for Instructors" with master casting guru John Van Dalen. Typical mixed bag with two or three enrollees monopolizing the time and putting the rest of us on short fuses. Listening to strident know-it-alls I realize what a solid, competent, *quiet* job Dennis Hess and I do in teaching our Trout Unlimited chapter's fly-fishing school. Is it immodest to say we both deserve a pat on the back for that?

Meantime, I haunted the book stalls and bagged two copies of Ernest Schwiebert's pioneering 1955 *Matching the Hatch,* the essence of the American fly-angling tradition, all the more so as he was only in his mid-twenties when he published it. My copies were far from pristine—both had copious interlinear comments, marginal notations, and underlinings in ink and pencil by their previous owners. The book vendor sold them cheap because he said they were "disfigured orphans," but proof of their concentrated use was exactly why I wanted them so badly. I love marginalia, the tangible evidence of someone else's handprints through a text: Schwiebert's authoritative text and muted color plates with his perfectly elegant drawings of delicate insects, and the rougher skein of interlarded amateur commentary and earnest backtalk scribbled throughout the pages. The conversational byplay, the interlinear give-and-take, symbolizes fly fishing's process of evolution. The Quill Gordon, known by the apt name of *Iron fraudator* to Schwiebert and his sub-rosa commentators, is now *Epeorus pleuralis*, so whether it's taxonomy or rod-making materials, nothing in our sport is etched in stone.

Yesterday over to Milesnick Recreation Company in Belgrade to once again try my luck at Benhart and Thompson Spring Creeks. MZ Ranch is a poster property for sound, ecologically balanced agricultural practices. Bravo to Tom and Mary Milesnick for an enlightened stewardship that proves cattle and trout can coexist on the same turf. The West needs more landowners like them. I also appreciate their honesty: they make no apologies for the rarefied quality of their fishing.

MZ's super-picky trout love their *Tricos*, those tiny white-winged blacks, which hatch abundantly on these glorious spring creeks, and fall by the zillions as spinners in mid-morning. They float down the stream on a conveyor belt and into the mouths of more sipping browns and rainbows than I can count. It gets the juices flowing because there are few things better than fishing with tiny flies over freely rising trout in the sibilant, sliding water of a spring creek. With that many naturals on the water, the old dilemma is getting a fish to look at your artificial. As a last resort, as Huck Finn discovered, praying for what you want doesn't help.

I fished hard from 9:30 a.m. until after 6 p.m. on Benhart. Never made it to Thompson. Caught one brown and two rainbows, missed a couple of others, all lovely specimens of trout with PhDs. Good to fool at least a few nice smart-ass fish. They put memorable bends in my Orvis Madison rod. Trout rose eagerly all day in midstream current seams, out-of-the-way lies beneath overhanging grasses, and hard-to-reach marshy inlets. I lost count of the number that refused me with impunity. Slap of the DT line on the water, the tiniest micro drag on the fly, the flash of the rod in the air, the waves caused by pulling my feet out of the muck—all were enough to put trout off. Even at thirty or forty feet away these fish spotted me attempting to stand and they blew up. Their V-wakes tell the sad tale of flight, so much of the time I crawled along the bank on my hands and knees keeping a low profile until my joints and back ached. Hunched down that low, and keeping backcasts above the bank-side grasses is no sure thing. I caught vegetation on just about every fourth or fifth cast. And yet, kneeling was about as tall as I dared get. And the damn trout still went AWOL. Then after a lull they would start rising again, tantalizing me at the margins beyond comfortable casting range. *Come and get us if you can.*

Fishing here is a test of character, and the gambit is to face rejection, humiliation, and frustration without wimping out and abandoning the creeks altogether in favor of easier fishing on the MZ's miles of freestone East Gallatin River, as many daily rod payees do. Forget the sure thing. Put it out of mind. No whining allowed. Take your punishment straight and your booze unwatered is the lesson here. Even so, *three fish in nine hours of casting.* That's one trout every three hours. Scarcity in the midst of plenty.

I'm not complaining about the low catch rate, which is par for the course on hyper-technical MZ Ranch water, but what I mean is that my feverish mind drifts to absurd lengths in those long empty hallways where the echoes are louder than the footfalls, and the weirdest stuff begins to seem plausible and possible. I don't wish to imbue my fishing plots with excess intellectual baggage, but I'm coming to think that perhaps Harold Blaisdell was leaning in the right metaphoric direction when he theorized about reaching a "third dimension" of understanding in *The Philosophical Fisherman*: considerations, strategies, habits of mind that are beyond mere fishing itself, but that illumine the fishing act.

Case in point: I bought *Upstream: Fly Fishing in the American West* by Charles Lindsay and Thomas McGuane. It's pricey at $45, but I've never seen anything quite like it. Paging through it, I knew I had to have it. It was published last year in New York by Aperture, the well-known photography-book publisher. Such an imposing, sweeping title promises much for those who aren't hung up exclusively on by-the-book instructional value or the orthodox history of angling literature. *Upstream* strikes me as an alternative—maybe even an antidote—to some (but not all) of the regulatory, buttoned-up elements of Angling Officialdom, the way watching Lefty Kreh, or Joan Wulff, or Mel Krieger demonstrate fly casting at the FFF Conclave is in a class all its own. *Unique. Different. Better.* They make nearly everyone else a pretender.

Most of fishing is an exercise in meager offerings, not buxom lollapaloozers. McGuane's prose commentary, all about the quotidian aspects of angling that are often ignored or taken for granted by more refined and elegant authors, has its own stop-and-start trajectory. Lindsay's moody, quirky black-and-white photos have their own random gravity. And yet, as with my marked-up copies of *Matching the Hatch*, at the edge between word and image there is a relational dance, a dialogic concert, which defamiliarizes fly-fishing rituals and scenes, and reorders expectations in such a way that each reader must navigate the borders between words and photos or competing voices by angling for the right connections.

As with many similarly hybrid collaborative texts, meaning lies as much in the alternate spaces, in the unseen and unsaid, as in the obvious and apparent. A world of activity goes on in the liminal places, or below the surface. River as text, text as river: "reading the water" to determine where the trout are most likely to be, which is our fly-fishing *modus operandi*, has particular relevance for streams and books. Both require being attentive to a process of discovery. There is no sure thing; so you learn as you go.

Meditating on *Upstream* makes me wonder if a fee trout stream, with its marked boundaries and economic protocols, can't be considered an example of a similarly alternate space. The spring creek as a hybrid zone, both real and symbolic, a buffer zone, where learning, play, discipline, pleasure, and skill keep company with nature in different ways and complicate notions of normalcy and success. In other words, a place of sporting deportment, cognitive process, and cultural practice. No disputing that entering the spring creek domain, like reading *Upstream,* brings us into an interruptive realm that puts life in perspective or on hold for the time being. Can a pay-to-play spring creek ever be considered a sacred space or is it always already a privileged consumer product? Is *Upstream* a symbol of a new way of viewing the angling passion *or* just a collection of one-off, odd-ball pictures? Am I spouting claptrap?

Yes and no, I guess, depending on point of view. In his excellent *The Fly and the Fish*, painter, writer, angler John Atherton says that "thinking and fishing go well together," which I take to be a modern twist on Melville's "meditation and water are wedded forever." I agree with both formulations and I'm comforted by their seriousness, their prevailing assumptions that water instigates philosophical inquiry, though there are also times, I admit, when too much cerebration gums up the works. Still, I'm less concerned with the conundrum itself, than with the context that brought the conundrum about. Perhaps it is enough to say that these are the kinds of maddeningly unresolvable meta-piscatorial tantalizations that rise to the surface during long stretches of abject fishlessness, of which over the years I have had more than my share.

I quit then, reeled up, went to my truck, got a beer and a sandwich out of the cooler, and thought about my next move. Like reading the Lindsay/McGuane book, fishing a spring creek doesn't suit everyone's tastes, but I could have stayed there, knelt low in the bank-side water, bowing to those imperious fish forever. Such places teach us a long view: humiliation aside, every refusal taught me something valuable, something to build on. Reasonable $50 rod fee at MZ Ranch, too, compared to the Paradise Valley creeks and worth every penny when curiosity, rumination, and learning are part of the deal.

Part II (2002–2015)

"Fishing is casting a petition into the unknown, and the eternal wonder of it is that almost anything could be down there ready to bite: your heart's desire; your worst fear; even something big enough to . . . catch *you*."

—Charles Gaines, *The Next Valley Over: An Angler's Progress* (2000)

Marryat's Fly Box

9–10 July 2002

After several years of dreaming and months of planning: two days of fishing on England's River Test, with a day on wild trout tributary Wallop Brook at the Nine Mile beat and a day at Compton Manor on the Test's main stem, both easily accessible from lodgings in Winchester, where I was collected by Simon J. Ward, my guide (from London-based outfitter Fishing Breaks) for the once-in-a-lifetime adventure. Simon is an angler *extraordinaire*, river keeper, angling historian, photographer, and generally speaking, a man of many parts, as the old-timers used to say.

Fishing in Hampshire was SLOW. I arrived shortly after a period of such torrential rain that even the normally clear-running chalk streams were murky. Yesterday at the Nine Mile Water beat, Wallop Brook, we stood around for several hours waiting for water to clear so that fish might go on the fin. No blind fishing over here. You're dealt a hand by weather and climate and expected to play your appropriate part. No whining allowed. No casting for the sake of casting. Okay, but for a Yank who has dreamed of and read about this legendary water for years, it was the most excruciating four hours I've ever spent, worse than waiting for the football coach to put me in my first varsity game in high school. (He never did.)

Finally, after lunch and a spot of tea, water clarity improved enough so that, from the stone bridge that spans the narrow stream, we were able to target half-a-dozen rising trout and in a manner of speaking give chase.

Actually it's *wait, wait, wait, cast a few times, then wait again.* All under the watchful eyes of curious cows in an adjoining meadow, and a couple of brilliant male common kingfishers that lit up the gray sky with their iridescent neon colors, each one leaving "a rainbow splinter sticking in your eye," according to a Ted Hughes poem.

Between intermittent rain showers, I had four hits on an olive floater but lost every one for various reasons of ineptitude. Thankfully my bovine gallery never uttered a word, though the kingfishers, vocal to the end, were clearly rooting for the fish. *Less for you, more for us,* I guess was what they were saying. By that time Ward and I had spent a great part of the day talking about British fly-fishing history, and our mutual enthusiasm and exchange helped soften my miserable failures. So did a couple of Cobra ales and a plate of tandoori chicken at Gandhi Restaurant when I got back to town last evening and reflected on the day.

Rich threads of memory rise here as I dally over this experience. Two years ago, on an early spring visit to England with Andrea, we spent the better part of a cold, blustery day bundled up in fleece and slickers, heads bowed into the wind and occasional spitting snow, carrying out a modest literary pilgrimage to Winchester Cathedral to visit the grave of Izaak Walton, patron saint of all anglers.

His memorial ledger stone is laid in the floor of the tiny Chapel of St. John the Evangelist, on the fourteenth-century cathedral's east side. It reads in part:

HERE RESTETH THE BODY OF
MR ISAAC WALTON
WHO DYED THE 15TH OF
DECEMBER 1683.

Walton died thirty years after publishing the first edition of *The Compleat Angler,* one of those rare books that, thankfully, has never been out of print. Equally intriguing are the two stained-glass windows. They are late additions, having been added in 1914 in honor of Walton. Shameless plagiarist or not, we owe Walton a great deal, as a fisherman as well as a bookman, for as nearly as I can tell he was the first notable angler who read and fished in both rivers and books. My kind of old-school role model.

One of the windows shows the old master at ease on a bank of the River Itchen, his rod and angling traps stowed at his side, while he reads a book. He's the picture of peacefulness and tranquility. The inscription beneath his feet, "Study to be quiet," is from the New Testament, 1 Thessalonians 4:11. Walton used that allusion as the final words of *The Compleat Angler.* No wonder fly fishing is called the "quiet sport."

From the cathedral, Andrea and I walked along the River Itchen near another fourteenth-century edifice, Winchester College, where we watched a brown trout set up along the close bank and begin rising to midges. The fish hung in the current, suspended, the way trout on the fin do, so that in watching it I felt all that old tightening, as Hemingway said. It rose near the route toward St. Cross Hospital that John Keats followed in the fall of 1819 during his two-month stay in Winchester and where he wrote one of his most famous poems, "Ode to Autumn," after ambling those pathways. It's a wonderful, teachable poem, full of signature Keatsian passion and insight. But part of me as angler rather than educator always preferred Keats's comment in a letter to his sister, Fanny, where he extols the area around Winchester and says of the Itchen: "There are the most beautiful streams about I ever saw—full of Trout." Amen!

Today before Simon Ward and I headed to our appointed Test beat, we detoured (at my request) to look at the Abbotts Barton section of the River Itchen, where another of my angling heroes, G. E. M. Skues, had rod rights for more than five decades and where he first discovered nymphs in a trout and had his *aha* moment that continues to influence us a century later. It is a fair amount of fishable water: a couple of miles of the main Itchen, plus a couple of miles of side streams and irrigation carriers that date back to Roman times. I walked up and down one carrier stretch, soaking it in, then sat for a while on the Skues commemorative stone bench, thinking about the man and his incomparable books, *Minor Tactics of the Chalk Stream* in 1910 and *The Way of a Trout with a Fly* in 1921, his masterpiece.

I bought those books two years ago when Andrea and I wandered into the Winchester Bookshop, a rambling old place that had a fine collection of secondhand and antiquarian angling books, a number of which I had never seen nor heard of before, including Skues's *Itchen Memories,* which I would have bought except that at eighty pounds it was a bit dear. His other two books and a copy of Dr. E. A. Barton's *An Album of the Chalk Streams* and Bernard Venables's *Guide to Angling Waters* were my booking catches that day, keepers, I guess it is fair to say, because they were reasonably priced.

But those two Skues books: forget the technical stuff, the many natural history observations and angling and fly-dressing breakthroughs Skues made. What's most important, to me, anyway, in my bench-sitting ruminative moment today, was his tone and attitude toward the body of material he worked with. We know Skues now as a giant of angling theory and practice. He was by some accounts the greatest fly fisherman who ever lived, though Simon Ward says that honor should go to George Selwyn Marryat.

What I love is that Skues disavowed "authority" because it tends to "darken counsel," as he famously said. An expert should stimulate original thinking, not paralyze it. The simple plaque on the bench reads:

IN MEMORY OF G. E. M. SKUES
WHO FISHED THESE WATERS FROM 1883–1936
A MAN WHO HAD A WAY WITH A TROUT.

Wear your learning lightly and the world will come to your beat. Dr. Barton's book concludes with a photo of Skues on the Abbotts Barton water: "It was an education to fish with him, for he seemed to know instinctively the most likely fly to use," the good doctor writes. We should all be so prescient.

Simon regaled me with tales of Skues's expertise and also times the master was unable to catch fish at all. (*So, what's he preparing me for, abject defeat or comforting solace?*) Best of all, we weren't done with the magical history tour. We stopped at the venerable Houghton Mill in Stockbridge, once home of the legendary Houghton Fly Fishers, among whose members was Frederic Halford, towering proponent of the dry-fly revolution in the late nineteenth century, and a man whose purist adamancy propelled Skues to differ. Say what we will about the contested cultural and ethical schism between fishing wet and fishing dry, my life is richer for having made the pilgrimage to both legendary sites.

At last to the main Test at Compton Manor, complete with thatched-roof fishing hut, mowed lawns, and lush paradisical setting. I expected a Walton or Cotton look-alike or maybe even a milkmaid to pop up any moment to complete the pastoral picture. Or at the very least, an angler dressed in tweeds and necktie as seen in earlier black-and-white fishing photographs, such as Dr. Barton captures in his chalk stream book. The day turned windy—too windy—for the 3-weight rod I was using. For a right-handed caster like myself, fishing upstream on the Test's left-hand bank was at worst frustrating and at best challenging, but I managed a couple of small browns on top, which pleased me mightily. Elation was short lived, though, as I repeatedly struck out trying to fool a husky 20-inch brown. Sprawled on our stomachs on the Test's bank rifling through Simon's fly collection comparing notes and seeking a pattern that would spark interest in our finicky prize was a moment of conspiratorial fellow feeling and good humor. Of such moments angling memories are made.

My two trout cost about a thousand dollars apiece, undoubtedly the priciest fish I have ever caught. But expense aside, the rarest part of the journey, the part that made the trip utterly worthwhile, took place in another register. At lunch today, Ward, who had spent years researching Marryat's pioneering angling career and publicly advocating his profound influence on Frederic Halford and the dry-fly revolution, had a surprise to show me. With a flourish he drew out of a velvet bag Marryat's chalk stream fly box. He had taken it out of his bank vault to show me. It was thought to have been lost, but after considerable detective work Ward traced it to Marryat's descendants in South Africa, who graciously turned it over to him, he said, on "permanent loan."

The black metal box, six inches long by four inches wide, looked like a modern Wheatley, with two dozen inch-square compartments, each with its own spring-loaded transparent glassine lid. Each compartment was divided in two, effectively doubling its capacity. But Richard Wheatley did not produce that kind of box until 1908, and the box Ward showed me, no doubt engineered scrupulously by hand (perhaps as a prototype) if not by Marryat then probably at his instruction, dated from the mid-1880s.

Each lid was hand lettered with the name of the fly therein. Inside there were more than 150 small split-wing dry flies tied on those "Snecky Limerick" up-eyed hooks, each one, especially the Ginger Quills, a wondrous little piece of art. They were tied, Ward was certain, by Marryat himself, who had perfected the upright split-wing, quill-bodied dressing. They were the most beautiful flies I had ever seen, and put me in mind of the opening line of William Blake's poem "Auguries of Innocence": "To see the world in a grain of sand." Each fly was an exquisite small universe of its own, each a marvelous, crafted curiosity in its own right. Taken together, of course, the effect was transcendent. Eventually, after I stopped drooling, Simon told me the only other person to whom he had shown the box was Datus Proper, so I felt doubly blessed by his generosity.

I'm tempted to say that Marryat's fly box provided the most arresting part of this trip, proving once again, I guess, that the best fishing isn't always in water. The experience allowed me to glimpse firsthand the differences—loosely put—between American and British fly-angling sensibilities. We don't honor our forebears as much as we should, and we sometimes lean toward an extreme take-no-prisoners approach. This is good and bad. As far as I could tell, the British aren't extreme in that same gonzo way, but they are obsessive about their history and fanatical in the single-mindedness of their pursuits, though a bit more conservative in taste. Depending on one's orientation, this too can be considered good or bad. These are generalizations, I know, but useful as far as they go in demonstrating that no proposition is free from irony or paradox, no authority without its darkening shades.

We trout fishers are miniaturists. We might cast 9-foot fly rods, 105-foot lines, 9-foot or 12-foot or 15-foot leaders, stuff ourselves into oversized chest waders, and ply rivers in capacious drift boats, but the coin of our realm is tiny enough to fit in Lilliputian boxes that in many cases are compulsively organized or indexed according to size, pattern, color, usage, seasons, rivers, and so on. Which is to say, we are all sons and daughters of Marryat. When each thing is in its properly ordered place, we feel comforted, and, dare I say, maybe even a bit smug. We rummage through our boxes looking for clues to fishy mysteries; we sift through them as though we are reading the latest whodunit novel, hoping for a revealing climax, a breath-taking *aha* moment, even if the pattern we choose is based on its appeal to us rather than to the fish. How else to say this? The box is the thing: it contains our currency; it houses our hope; it circumscribes the dimensions of our world; it says volumes about our ambitions as well as our limits. Long live the box!

On the North Tongue

6–7 August 2002

North Tongue River, Wyoming. Big Horn Mountains near Burgess Junction. It's after 9 p.m. and I'm writing this in deepening twilight, which my little headlamp keeps at bay so I can see what I'm doing, more or less, anyway, because my handwriting is looking more like the scratchings of a blind man.

I'm worlds away from the bucolic setting on River Test a month ago. Yesterday, to get here, I drove my 4Runner more than a mile in low range down an unimproved Forest Service road, dodging large boulders, opening and closing four barbed-wire cattle gates as I went, parked at the last clearing, then packed tent, sleeping bag, and fishing gear by hand the rest of the way to this flat spot a couple of hundred feet above the stream. I'm several miles as the crow flies from the highway, fifteen or so from Dayton, the nearest sizable town. The only sounds the last two days have been an ineluctable part of this place and moment: wind high in the pines, marmots whistling their ceremonial warnings, two belted kingfishers rattling sabers upstream. With my tent flap opened last night I could hear the river gurgling its delightful backdrop music. Not another man-made sound, except one jet high overhead. And no ambient light, either, just stars like a million light pricks in the dark firmament.

Everything appears perfect, and yet it isn't. Context is necessary: Before leaving Ohio last week I heard from Jim Harrison that Louis Owens had killed himself, shot himself in the heart with a 9 mm pistol. Impossible to make sense of this news. A moody depressive myself, given to the infernal blackfish, the ironies, paradoxes, and improbabilities surrounding Louis's deed are too many and excruciating to grasp or even to detail. He was blessed by outsized talent, movie-star good looks, wit, intelligence (he was going to be a visiting professor at Harvard this fall). He was the next big thing in Native American fiction, right up there with Gerald Vizenor and James Welch. He's the last person in the world I ever imagined committing suicide. But just when we think we know a person, they are most apt to surprise us.

Only a few weeks ago Louis (he was touchy about being called Lou) sent me a copy of his newest essay collection, *I Hear the Train*, and I had been pulled up short by a teasing photograph of him (he's part Cherokee) in a Lone Ranger mask. I guess he was less about the sure thing than about re-drawing boundaries, instigating challenges, and, in the last analysis, morbid enigmas that will never be fathomed.

Louis inscribed his copy of *I Hear the Train*, "To Bob, Long Friendship," which delighted me, but to be more accurate, he and I were academic colleagues at large, which is to say we were occasional acquaintances to whom vast areas of each other's life were likely to remain unknown. But we shared a serious scholarly interest in John Steinbeck, reviewed each other's books, quoted each other's writings, attended conferences, and served on panels together—those kinds of things. And we obsessed over running water and the creatures that live in and near it. He told me once that Cherokees have a strong medicine called "Going to Water." I thought, *yes, that fits.* Which perhaps explains nothing in the big picture, except that it brought me to this place, this moment of solitude and reflection tonight. Healing water for whom?

Sometimes, it helps to remember a person as he was. Fly fishing can be an intricate figure in the carpet, a thread that illuminates other corners of life (and in Louis's case, his fiction as well), for whatever that is temporarily worth. Cole McCurtain, protagonist of *Bone Game*, says at one point, all he wants to do is "go fly fishing." I could hear Louis saying that, and certainly could hear myself saying it a thousand times over in recent years when the general bullshit quotient endemic to universities seemed to rise exponentially.

Sorry to say, our talked-about fishing trip never happened. Yesterday afternoon as I knelt in the North Tongue River trying to sort out the language of the stream, I felt the full force of loss—the triple gut-punch of betrayal, anger, and grief. I always believed that Louis had beaten those odds—father (he left a wife and two children), teacher, scholar, creative writer and novelist, outdoorsman—he was a star who did so many things so remarkably well that he was the exception to the general rule that governs most of us. But envy and well-meaning sentiment aside, the tragic fact is that nothing saves us when we pass a certain point of despair. Look at Hemingway. Look at Richard Brautigan. I only hope sometime along the way Owens, who had once been all about survivance, knew how esteemed he was—and continues to be—in the world.

The last couple of days I caught many rainbow, brook, and cutthroat trout here. The North Tongue River cuts through limestone-rich geology, optimal for all riverine life. The water is pH-perfect, plus it's sixty degrees and flows down a moderate gradient and so is not at all difficult to wade. I am lucky enough to be in the right place at the right time. In fact, it's been one of those rare moments when the fishing is so good that it's almost too easy. A few weeks before Louis's death, we had promised each other reports on our summer fishing, and this is mine, such as it is, though he will never read it, which won't stop me: *get it down, get it down, get it down*, I can imagine him saying.

As nearly as I can guess, he would have had a similar reaction to so many gullible fish: too much success is a kind of failure, too, because when everything is going well, you aren't learning the intricacies, the complexities, the challenging lies as much as you should be. When trout rise readily to the gaudiest of artificials, a Royal Coachman, or a Madame X, or a Trude, or a brushy White Wulff, there is no need to tie on a more somber, realistic pattern, no need to match the hatch or find the proper key. Identifying the subaqueous smorgasbord narrows the odds considerably, though fly fishing for trout, like so many other pursuits, is still a crapshoot, a mystery whose failures and successes we blunder toward rather than fully uncover. When things are too easy, we let our guard down, take for granted what Owens once called "dazzling artifice."

Still, who looks a gift trout in the mouth? They gave me so much pleasure, these fish. Rainbows, some only 9 inches or 10 inches long, leaped three feet out of the water when hooked, the red stripe on their sides as sudden as "apples in a fog," as Richard Hugo said in his poem, "Trout," in *Making Certain It Goes On*. Their vigor astonished me, and they put an arc and a throb in my 3-weight rod worthy of larger fish. Trout of the North Tongue River: I salute you, I kiss your fins, I stroke your backs. I returned you all gently to the water; even now I cannot adequately say thanks for your presences.

Red Run Brookies

≋

10 October 2003

Met my West Virginia angling pal Dennis Hess at his camp in Bowden this morning, and we cruised over to Red Run of Dry Fork River via the Canaan Valley. Red Run is the small fly-fishing-only mountain stream that our Blennerhassett Trout Unlimited chapter has brought back to health over the past six or seven years by judiciously adding limestone at its upper reaches to drastically reduce acidity and the devastating range-wide effects of acid rain, the result of rampant uncontrolled burning of high-sulphur coal. The limestone solution: a commonsense, low-tech fix that has been heralded for its simplicity and effectiveness. The mound of sand leaches into the stream over time and does its buffering act gradually to the benefit of all animate beings. The project is considered a major success story regarding reclamation of a native trout fishery, and a few years ago our Trout Unlimited group won the West Virginia DNR's "Sportsmen of the Year" award.

Dennis, chapter president in those crucial years, has an intimate history with Red Run and has been trying nearly as long to get me on it. And at last, our schedules fell out in such a way that there we were. We parked at the upper gate, then hiked down into Red Run itself. We could hear it cascading below as we walked down a Forest Service lane. Then we dropped straight down a hillside to the stream. I mean a precipitous, straight-down clamber that took about thirty minutes.

But once down the stairs, it's a glorious, picturesque setting. The gradient is steep, the stream is narrow and cuts through imposing limestone boulders, but one or two strides will carry you across it in most places. To hit the many deep plunge pools requires some gymnastic contortions and acrobatic leaps from rock to rock. Because of the high forest canopy, even on a sunny day, as today was, it is gloomy beneath the overarching caverns of trees, so tread carefully is the advice of the day. I slipped once on slick rock and nearly ended my fishing for the year. Cast carefully, too, as the quarters are tight and some sections are hedged in and make even a 7 1/2-foot fly rod cumbersome. But it's the kind of stream that requires no extra frills and doodads. A 2- or 3-weight rod and reel, 6X-tippet spool, fly grease, a pair of hemostats, a nipper, one small fly box, a sandwich, and a bottle of water, and you have all that's needed to pass the time. No net. No wading staff. None of the normal encumbrances, none of the welter of gizmos we fly anglers inevitably accumulate in our quests for glory, even though we know in our hearts that less is more.

Red Run moves fast on its way to Dry Fork and carries a tannic stain because of its origin among peat bogs; and the fish themselves, ever adaptable, are darkish and hard to see in the stream. Attractor patterns are all that's needed, and I went with a #14 Mr. Rapidan, a bushy tan-and-yellow dry fly made for this kind of water. Even the wildly gesticulating rapids and crazy, choppy currents of plunge pools could hardly drown the thing and it remained visible among flotillas of brilliant hardwood leaves.

Dennis thought fishing was slow, and he was a bit dismayed that rumors he'd heard about poaching and overfishing on this little gem might in fact be true. The old story: news of success in stream reclamation breeds acquisitive, rapacious attention, evidenced by Styrofoam bait cups we found here and there. Not everyone loves a stream the way we do.

We did manage a few fish, an added bonus amid such stunning scenery. One of mine was a dark-mantled, almost black, male brookie about 8 inches long, decked out in the most vibrant spawning reds and oranges and yellows I have ever seen. The leaping brookie in the frontispiece of Louis Rhead's 1902 collection *The Speckled Brook Trout* has nothing on today's fish. I know the photo I took will not do it justice, for it was the most beautiful, striking brook trout I have ever caught, and it opened a pathway to memories of days sneaking along Vermont's tiny creeks and trickles around Danby, Dorset, and Mt. Tabor for native trout years ago. "No fish affords as much sport to the angler as the Brook Trout," venerated Thaddeus Norris says in his pioneering *American Angler's Book.* Nothing against the zillions of introduced rainbows and browns since then—God love 'em—but just saying that fishing for speckled trout is primordial, back-to-the-past fishing. It's simple, bare-bones angling for the true native that has swum these waters for millennia, from the southern Appalachians to the Adirondacks and north to the hinterlands of Maine.

For us Easterners brook trout are signature American fish. They are part of the nation's wild, cold-water heritage. The diminutive, parti-colored prince of mountain fish, the most companionable, gorgeously dressed, and affecting of salmonids. But the indigenous char Thoreau likened to "bright fluviatile flowers" in *The Maine Woods* is also the most beleaguered, given current rates of decline over its original range. Bravo to Trout Unlimited for getting behind the brookie's resurgence, not just for us, but for the generations to come.

Fishing for brookies the way Dennis and I did today—hopscotching each other upstream—is like going back to the origins of our trouting pursuits. Fishing toward the headwaters brings us closer to the fountain of our angling passion. Mine was a single brook trout caught on a streamer in the Saugatuck River in 1956. My life has never been quite the same since, and like Thoreau I too have dreamed in the night of fishing for those trouty "jewels."

A Fox Barked on the Hiwassee

28 March 2004

Inaugural fishing outing of the year, and a road trip at that. Romilly Fedden says in *Golden Days*, that "always before us lie further fields yet to explore." Sign me up! After a long winter with bouts of seasonal affective disorder, this excursion afield is especially welcome. Recently, my early-March, opening-season fishing licks have been on the Elk in West Virginia, but this year, I'm taking part in Western Carolina University's spring literary festival with Ron Rash, Sonia Sanchez, Robert Morgan, Linda Nieman, and Jim Harrison, and I'm slated to pick up Harrison at the Asheville Airport and get us both to the festival at Cullowhee by tomorrow afternoon. We're all giving readings and talks. Until then I'm on my own.

Weather improved drastically as I drove south from Ohio, and I could feel my spirits lifting when I reached the Cherokee Inn in Reliance, Tennessee. Mom-and-Pop setup, low-key, but rustic and remote. The kind of funky place I love. TV has three channels and the room has no phone. But it's blessedly sheltered and quiet, aided by its elevation, and the clear night sky, under which I can get some thinking and writing done interrupted only by the pleasantest natural sounds: spring peepers squeaking in a marsh nearby, then just before I went to bed, a lone fox barking its *here-I-am* somewhere in the Hiwassee River valley below me. I wonder what that fox was up to? I'll never know, but I don't think I'll ever forget the thin, wild sound of its yapping carried through starlit darkness to the doorstep of my room. Connected me to something more vast and cosmogonical than my paltry self. I was ready to turn in then, the day having found a memorable and satisfying conclusion.

Yesterday I splurged on a guided day with Dane Law's Southeastern Anglers on the scenic Hiwassee River. All new country to me, though I've been reading about these southern Appalachian TVA tailwaters for many years, always with an increasing promise to myself that I must check them out before I croak. So here I am.

Most of my fishing was with my 9-foot, 4-weight Winston rigged with a dry-dropper setup: Elk Hair Caddis on top and one of Dane's beadhead soft hackles as point fly. That was a fine combination that accounted for many trout. Easy, no-stress angling. The fish beat the crap out of a couple of Dane's flies. I'll paste one of his ravaged soft hackles into this journal when I get some clear tape. The year's first entry into the Museum of Twisted Flies. I've pasted in quite a number of mangled oddities over the years. It's interesting to see what havoc a trout can wreak on a small fly. Bend hooks out of shape, break off barbs and eyes, unravel feather, fur, yarn, tinsel, too.

Yesterday's rainbows were cookie-cutter size—all about 8 inches to 10 inches long—that were good little fighters but also uninspiring in the aggregate. I found myself having to fight off boredom as we drifted along, not something that should befall any human being on a trout stream. My head was elsewhere, though, and as we floated along I was paying attention to my fishing only in a half-assed way because behind my angling mask I was imagining what it was like here when the great naturalist and Sierra Club founder John Muir came on foot through this country 135 years ago and meandered along the Hiwassee and wrote about it glowingly in *A Thousand-Mile Walk to the Gulf*. "How fine the songs it sings," he said. Muir was not a fisherman, but he caught the spirit of water in that line. In his time there were no rainbow trout here.

Now lots of rainbows in Hiwassee's "sparkling" (Muir's word) waters, and we encountered them all through the system. They were fairly concentrated in a number of places—both the slow, flat, shallow pools and a few of the deeper, more aerated runs. I used my 9-foot Thomas and Thomas Vector 5-weight to throw nymphs with a big Prince beadhead, Dane's favorite, leading the charge, though a black Flashback Hare's Ear pulled up four or five fish later in the afternoon when a few Hendricksons were coming off.

I should not whine, but all the trout were small, though brightly colored. The biggest I saw—maybe 14 inches—rose to my strike indicator! Twice that happened and I wondered why we never threw a Stimulator or a big Wulff dry. Dane preferred one or two basic patterns all day. Fishing in the simplest register possible, I guess. No fuss, no muss. Anyway, we had lots of action, though also a two-hour stretch in early afternoon when it was slow, which was when I traded the Elk Hair Caddis on my dry fly rod for a tan Iris Caddis and quickly hit three better-sized fish on top. (I gave Dane the fly when we were done as he had never seen one before.)

Was it worth $300 plus tip for the trip? That's a high price for this water and destination, but I don't begrudge the payout for giving access to a new-to-me river. Is it the same as a day on the Beaverhead? Not at all, though everything I've read lately about the Hiwassee says it can be an excellent river at certain times and during certain hatches. Realistic assessment or hyperbole? Pay your money and take your chance, which is the name of the game, when a single day on an unfamiliar river is scheduled. "One of the country's best tailwaters," one popular magazine claimed; "one of the premier rivers in the eastern United States" with "some of the finest rainbow and brown-trout water to be found anywhere," crows another. Perhaps. But I didn't see that. I am not sure I'd come back here so this might be my only shot ever at this river. I think the Elk is better in many regards and is way closer to home. My discovery of it a few years ago still burns in me.

Nearly dark when I got off the river about 7 p.m. Had to drive down Route 411 to get a cell-phone signal to call Harrison. All is in readiness for tomorrow at Western Carolina University. Drove a few miles to Etowah and chowed down on the pizza-and-salad buffet at Tony's Italian Restaurant. One of those off-the-beaten-path places that made me feel like family.

Fishing with Jim Harrison

18 August 2005

At loose ends lately, and have taken some knocks, what with married life on the skids. Andrea and I have decided on a mutual hiatus for sanity's sake. Getting out of Dodge was exactly what the proverbial doctor ordered. Only view of home I wanted two weeks ago was in the rearview mirror with the Rolling Stones' "You Can't Always Get What You Want" blasting on the stereo. Traveling music. My vote for the greatest rock song ever recorded. Immortal words, as good as any I can think of right now. Plus these from Jim Harrison: "Come out and stay with us. It's probably easier for you to stay here, so we can chat and also if we have to make early morning moves to the river. I booked Danny for three days of fishing."

I lit out for the Ruby, Beaverhead, Big Hole, and new-to-me Big Sheep Creek south of Dillon, a surprisingly fine little river for eager brown trout. No river was quite uplifting enough to cure my anxiety but each was a start down the right path. Then up to Livingston where I've been hiding out at the Harrisons'. "Your room is ready," Jim said when I showed up. Last three days we've been fishing on the Yellowstone River with Danny Lahren, his regular guide, then gathering in the evening for bouts of unparalleled dining, convivial talk, and low-down gossip.

Last evening a tremendous windstorm blew through here and knocked out power for nearly two hours. Jim and I finished cooking a lamb shoulder on a charcoal fire, each of us taking turns holding the grill down so it wouldn't blow away in the tempest with the dogs, lawn chairs, croquet mallets, and cottonwood limbs. Turned out to be the best lamb I've ever eaten, but then how many times have I said that about the food he and wife Linda serve: fresh chile verde, spicy Thai chicken, Florentine veal chops, and that sautéed fresh abalone Dan shucked last year? All transcendent, off-the-chart dishes to a foodie like me. Visiting Jim is an exercise in outsized appetite and feats of gastronomical derring-do.

Woke up early this morning in the upstairs corner bedroom to find a great horned owl sitting on a vent pipe looking in the window at me! Linda said at breakfast it's their resident owl. An intrusion of the marvelous into my raggedy life. Its piercing yellow eyes took my measure. I know it won't give me away, won't broadcast my secrets to the stars. I take its presence as a good sign, a welcome symbol of goodwill to kick-start the day on an upswing. So is Jim's pre-fishing ritual of walking the dogs, especially if they flush a few resident Huns as they did today. Puts all concerned in a positive frame of mind.

There is a *tsk-tsk, you-should-know-better* school of academic thought that would label any cut-and-run sentiment as childish escapism, "a pattern of flight from the world," as novelist Wright Morris called it in *The Territory Ahead*. Mark Twain: "I reckon I got to light out for the Territory ahead of the rest," Huck Finn famously concludes his narrative, before his Aunt Sally can "sivilize" him. In *The Sporting Road*, Jim Fergus says outdoor sporting pursuits prove we are just "great big kids." I see his point, though I never thought Peter Pan was a suitable role model. But puerile or not, sometimes heading for the river *is* the best antidote and redress against the blackfish of personal dissolution, work day ennui, and wit's-end mania. Sometimes it's a flight *to* reality, to the incalculable, unmovable presence of mountains and rivers without end. No one knows about recuperative panic holes, thickets, hideouts, and road trips better than Jim. "Yeh. You don't think about anything else," he said the first morning we drove to the river. "Fishing erases everything impossible in your life. Every shit storm, every sling and arrow to the balls."

Jim enjoys acting as guide, dispensing angling wisdom and gists and quips from his decades of experience, which, as with every novelist, is a delightful admixture of fiction and truths, though often I'm not sure which is which. Danny balances Jim's self-confessed fibs and stretchers with practical, no-nonsense advice, and when I fail to heed his pointers on handling hot fish, I end up losing a couple of decent trout. Dan's one of the most competent people I've ever met, the kind of guy you want on your team when things go wrong because he can fix anything. Between them I get a proper schooling every year.

We had slow periods, as usual, when nothing could brighten the fishless gloom, and our curses and entreaties and laments to the heavens went unheeded. But then we had fast action, too, on very nice browns and rainbows, some on top with hoppers and big luscious attractors like the Madame X, Bugmeister, and Turk's Tarantula, and some subsurface on sleek black Wooly Buggers, olive conehead streamers, or a heavily weighted black marabou feather streamer concoction tied by Dan on a #2 hook that Jim calls the "Dead Bat," and that accounted for the biggest browns. Jim only has one eye, so matching the hatch with tiny mincing flies is not in the cards. He's a powerful caster who prefers big patterns that he can see with his impaired vision, or can feel with a jolt from an underwater take. He and Dan disdain fishing tourist style with a couple of nymphs under a fluffy strike indicator. "It's cheating," Jim says. "Real men don't nymph, son." End of discussion.

Although he has long affiliations with Orvis and is quoted and pictured now and then in its catalogs, and has his share of their high-end gear, he has no desire to accumulate the sexiest fishing equipment and outdoor clothing, no matter what the brand. Harrison's the poster guy for an utterly pragmatic, serviceable, unglamorous angling-wear style, "Early Carhartt." He looks like the grizzled guy who handles the trash, mows lawns, ranches for a living.

Today, under overcast sky and cool front, we met a bonanza, with a couple dozen trout making us feel like we were reasonably accomplished anglers. A couple of times Dan and I, then Jim and I, had fish on at the same time. One rainbow I hooked had the heebie-jeebies and jumped six times and tired us out just watching its acrobatics. "What the fuck got into him?" Jim asked.

Years before I met Harrison, I had been teaching his fiction in graduate seminars and had directed a couple of theses on it. *Working Days,* my edition of Steinbeck's *Grapes of Wrath* journal, had come out in paperback and I sent a copy to him in Michigan, not knowing if I had the proper address or whether it would ever reach him. I knew he admired Steinbeck and had taken potshots at high-toned critics who disparaged Steinbeck (people Jim said couldn't even write *The Grapes of Goofy*). In a note I said something to the effect that I was glad to know that he was alive and writing in the world and that his writing made a difference in my life that I could hardly calculate. Typical fan-letter stuff, sent out blindly into the blue. A few years after I met him and we became increasingly friendly, he told me that copy of *Working Days* was one of the few books he kept handy at his writing cabin in the Upper Peninsula. He dipped into it on occasions when his own writing stalled. Bless his heart, he reminded me of that again today.

But the truth is that three days of fishing the Yellowstone is really the least part of our yearly visit. For me the heart of it is elsewhere in nonstop gab fests about books and writing, lively banter, and running commentary—mostly sardonic, humorous, and ribald—on the foibles and fiddle-faddle of the usual suspect male topics, which is to say, politics, culture, food, and especially sex, sex, more sex, and, because Harrison is a master raconteur and hypnotic talker with a trapdoor memory, a barrage of animated yarns and stories, often about his bawdy and excessive Hollywood screen-writing days, full of so many digressions and tangents, that I have to be on top of my game just to keep up with him. Jim has a way of completely filling the space he inhabits and sweeping me into it, ready or not. "Bobby, did I ever tell you that thing about . . ." he'd start in his raspy voice, between puffs of the ever-present American Spirit cigarette, and from the bow of the drift boat I turn my head to catch his

Jim Harrison with Yellowstone River rainbow trout.
Credit: Robert DeMott

words before the wind blows them away like smoke over water, or a trout on the line hijacks his attention and his story trails off.

Anchored at river's edge east of Livingston, with our *al fresco* lunch of soppressata, Manchego cheese, crusty bread, fried chicken, hot sauce, and spicy peppers, laid out without fanfare or hoity-toity pretentiousness on top of Danny's well-traveled portable cooler, we watched the great undammed Yellowstone roll by, listened to wind in the cottonwoods carrying the *yucka-yucka-yucka* of a red-shafted flicker and the sharp cry of a circling osprey, and rehashed the tale of some of our day's best trout. Hard to inflate the ego or salt the wounds in the presence of so much natural grandeur.

Tonight, jotting this after too much wine at dinner, I've started feeling that life has regained color and vibrancy and urgency, as well. Maybe it's the wine and high spirits talking, but I'd almost forgotten that it's impossible to be depressed in Jim's company. In a world of hemophiliacs he's a blood transfusion. Something positive has started that I hope will improve, as I intend to stay on the lam for a couple more weeks of fishing. From here I go to the Madison to meet up with Dennis again, then on to the North Platte before I drive home to face whatever it is needs to be faced. I like to think I'll be ready, fishing and friends having aided and abetted a turnaround.

In the Driftless Region

〜〜〜

29 April 2007

Sometimes fishing is about gain, like a trout in hand. The sensory experience of a day on the water, with its symphony of sights, sounds, and scents, is a gain that can't be explained precisely or quantified accurately, but is part of the fabric of experience, the utopian moment of recognizable pleasure that stays with us. It works the other way, too, and sometimes fishing can be all about loss. The accident on stream, the missed strike, the one that got away, the poorly handled trout that doesn't survive, or worse. All are part of the darker side of our horizon of expectation, the dystopian sphere of our quiet sport. I've had my share of both lately.

Much of 2006 was a blur, following a divorce from Andrea and my father's protracted illness. Even my fishing journal, which covered March through October last year and ran to about 100 pages, had a stop-and-start jitteriness to it. In the midst of recent upheavals I resigned from full-time teaching at Ohio University after almost thirty-nine years in the saddle, because, well, enough is enough. From now on I'll teach one term a year until 2013 and won't have to perform the obligatory stuff that goes with a full-time tenure-track position.

I've come to terms with divorce but not yet the loss of my father, who died in January after successfully fighting cancer for nine months last year, then going under after an ill-advised aneurysm surgery that he never should have had and from which he did not recover. He was a pillar in my life, a profound influence, whose character and integrity and love and support were

129

unwavering. I was blessed to be his son. *Father, the debts I owe you can never be repaid, only acknowledged.*

Last week I gave talks on *The Grapes of Wrath* in Galesburg, Illinois, as part of a new Big Read Program, funded by the National Endowment for the Arts, in which a whole community reads and discusses a single book. The NEA uses my Penguin edition of Steinbeck's novel, so I get invited to lecture about it around the country. Anyway, Galesburg put me within striking distance of a long-intended goal: Southwest Wisconsin's unglaciated Driftless area. I have been itching to check out its many streams ever since I read Ted Leeson's *Jerusalem Creek: Journeys into Driftless Country*, which is so good that it makes me want to quit writing because nothing I say could ever come near it in quality. He's left a considerable footprint up here, though humble as he is, I can't imagine he'd consider his achievement quite that way. My head is stocked with finny images and watery promises, and I'm hoping not to have my angling heart broken any more than usual.

Southwest of the Wisconsin River and the city of Boscobel, the whole uplifted region, unleveled by Ice Age juggernauts, is interlaced with interesting coulees and surprising draws and myriad small spring creeks laced like so many lucent ribbons throughout the area. Turn a corner, come around a bend, look left past this scenic barn, look right beyond that gang of Holsteins, and there's a creek wending its way through the landscape. They seem to wink back at me. I can't throw a rock and not hit one. Best of all, many streams are accessible to the public from the road. They exist in a zone that scholars call "democratic space," the public space in front of our faces, that is, or should be, traversable by all. Populist Steinbeck would have loved that. My father, too. Leeson clearly did: "Discovering a new trout stream is a wonderful thing, and even if its whereabouts are common knowledge, to come upon the place yourself for the first time is nonetheless true discovery." You go, Ted!

Day before yesterday I started on the Big Green River (a misnomer as it's not big at all). According to Wisconsin's DNR, it's a Class One trout stream with a self-sustaining population of brown trout. In size, depth, and clarity, it reminds me of that delectable little spring-fed gem, Sand Creek, in eastern Wyoming.

I parked near the bridge at Collins Road, rigged up a 3-weight Orvis graphite rod and dove into my handy-dandy take-it-anywhere all-occasion nymph box for tandem selections: #16 Pheasant Tail, Gold-ribbed Hare's Ear, or La Fontaine Caddis Pupa on top, and smaller Zebra Midge, Brassie, or Crystal Serendipity as a tiny dropper, with one or two small pieces of shot depending on water depth and current speed. No indicator today as an extra test of skill. Worked well enough on four or five trout as I walked downstream from the bridge. I had others on, but I wasn't quick enough on the strike set as my head was often miles away.

Beautiful stream winding through open pasture land and beneath wooded slopes where trees were putting on their annual green. Comforting to see life going on. The ineluctable urge and rush and push of the green fuse. Air temperature close to sixty-five degrees and sunny, with a light breeze. Perfect conditions to while away the afternoon lost in thought, or maybe fishing for thoughts. I never quite know which is which. *Cast, drift, lift, pause, change flies, cast again, drift off in thought.* Maybe that's the true democratic space, the place we inhabit freely without impediments in our minds and hearts, here and now streamside.

When I went back to the truck to eat a sandwich around 6 p.m., the caddis activity ramped up, with bugs flying around the truck and over the bridge. Somewhere a switch had been thrown, and right on cue a door in creation swung wide and caddis by the thousands answered the call. I tied on a single #16 tan X-Caddis, which worked well for the grannoms. Fished leisurely upstream from the bridge and took seven or eight browns and rainbows on top. Nothing over 10 inches but all handsomely decked out and trim-looking fish.

Yesterday I packed up, checked out of the motel in Fennimore, said good-bye to its garrulous and entertaining owner, who regaled me with local stories and urged me repeatedly to be sure to fish with a Green Weenie, which he swore was the local secret "killer pattern." I drove north up Route 61 to Town Hall Road, turned west and found a parking place right next to Crooked Creek, another wild-trout fishery winding narrow and deep through bucolic pasture land. Not another soul in sight. No nymphing today, so no Green Weenie action. Dries were the order of the day, especially the Parachute Adams in #18 and #20. Small, comely-proportioned browns and rainbows hell-bent on attacking my fly as often as they could.

So the fishing's been intriguing enough to keep leading me on, but these days have also been an occasion for reflection and dream weaving. Leeson's apt metaphor of "meandering" fits the bill physically and mentally. No straight lines anywhere in this picturesque landscape, but a series of fluvial wanderings, driftings, jogs, zigs, and zags. Nothing preordained, no evident, dedicated conclusions in this geography, only a continuous series of thoughts, proposals, considerations, ruminations, and questions, questions, questions, coming at me like drifting duns on a dreamy river: *What have you lost?* the water says, *Who are you?* it whispers, *Where are you going?* it sings. These creeks, each small enough to fit in God's back pocket and each with a song of its own, are perfect for recovering part of what's been lost or forgotten or gone missing. A small crooked spring creek carries memories of my father back to me and I'm thankful. Grief seems to be containable within its boundaries. It's that small-stream allure and magic again.

I praise all watercourses, big and little, but especially clear, cold, healthy rivers, streams, creeks, brooks, and tributaries no matter how small or unassuming. It's not the sublime I'm after here, the transcendent big bang that lights up the sky, but something closer to miniature, hand-sized, so to speak, not a bear hug. The dry fly rather than the tarpon fly. These creeks are large enough to harbor many fish, but small enough to wade comfortably and even step across; they're close enough to see into without courting danger by grasping after a fleeting self-image and drowning like Narcissus.

Hemingway comes to mind: Nick Adams in "Big Two-Hearted River" journeying into the northern Michigan countryside to hold at bay grief and traumatic memories, probably of war, though the war is never specifically mentioned in the story. Nick doesn't head out to fish a huge brawling river, representative of the scale of war, but aims for smaller, more secretive and intimate water. He's a minimalist in that regard, packing light for recovery's long haul. Ted Leeson too. The death of a brother is a latent subject throughout *Jerusalem Creek*, just there out of direct sight, like a creek glimpsed through trees or at dusk, indisputable but also evanescent. When the days seem lined up against us, it's important to gain some measure of privacy and even control, important to enter a landscape that doesn't dwarf us with impunity. Intimacy is key; scaled-down perspective is all. Even small packages have their own coherent splendor.

Isos and *Big Fish*

19 June 2007

The first Father's Day in my life when my own father isn't alive. So in the company of nagging mind burrs and continuing grief pricks, not just about Dad's passing but how to handle moving my ninety-year-old mother from Connecticut to Ohio, Kate and I hauled over from Athens yesterday to stay again in "Whispering Brook," the cabin in West Virginia near the Elk River that we've rented several times in the past eight months. Good call on Kate's part. Recent immersion this spring in watery byways over here in Almost-Heaven West Virginia, and in Connecticut on the Farmington and Housatonic, and on Wisconsin spring creeks, has brought some needed solace and comfort. But face it, there are times when no amount of fly fishing can ease personal pain entirely, so finding Kate again after we went our separate ways with other partners nearly twenty years ago has been life-altering and more redemptive than anything I could have imagined. Lucky for me, she's a widow who understands bereavement.

Yesterday Kate stayed at the cabin to finish a writing project while I ventured down the road to the upper end of the catch-and-release area. I had the river to myself, a rare enough treat here, as this Elk Springs area is becoming more and more of an extra-local angling destination. Rigged a

4-weight outfit and fished nonstop from 6 p.m. until almost 9 p.m. Turned out to be one of my best sessions on the Elk. Started slowly with a single rainbow trout on a #18 Parachute Adams that popped off at the last minute, damn the luck, followed by a stretch of absolutely no activity at all, not even a rising fish. *Zero. Nada.*

I almost quit in disgust, but a profusion of spent *Isonychia bicolor* nymphal shucks on the sides of rocks at river's edge opened a door. I wasn't in the mood to set up a nymph rig with indicator, split shot, tandem flies, and do the whole-hog complicated chuck-and-drift routine in a river whose limestone bottom is so jagged that it invites constant snagging. It might have been the kind of activity that yielded foul, unwanted results. Emotionally and psychically, I mean. The Nick Adams effect again: fishing in a difficult place complicates life and becomes in Hemingway's words "a tragic adventure."

Well, that's melodramatic. It's not like I've returned wounded from war and suffering with PTSD. But to keep complications to a manageable size, I did want to fish more cleanly and simply and directly with a single visible fly. And though I know Elk River trout don't routinely tumble for the dun of *Isonychia,* I tied on a #12 CDC Leadwing Coachman pattern, anyway, just for variety's sake and a stab at the unknown. Nothing ventured, nothing gained. Cast thy dry fly upon the waters, and all that.

Right away I felt a tiny lift of optimism. The fly looked damned good and perky on the water. It was reassuring somehow. Though I admit to being dismayed that "Leadwing Coachman" has become its predominant popular name, with its dour sounding heavy-handedness, rather than the more appealing "Mahogany Dun" or Art Flick's "Dun Variant" or better yet, Ted Fauceglia's "Slate Drake," so named in his *Mayflies,* or my personal favorite, the way more apt and delicious-sounding "Chocolate Drake," "quite as dark as rich chocolate," Thomas Ames says in *Hatch Guide for New England Streams,* my well-thumbed little bible and vest-pocket on-stream companion. The point being, the bug is good enough to eat.

In my favorite section, the Valley Fork run, I had a few hits by eager juvenile fish out to earn their bones, then in a corridor edge between fast and slow water a lovely fish, shadowy and indistinct as thought at first, rose slowly from the bottom to inspect the fly as though it had all the time in the world and, like a *flâneur,* was merely out for a Sunday stroll on a Parisian boulevard, looking into street-front shop windows as it went leisurely on its way. The fish was clearly out to test my mettle.

I waited several minutes before casting back, and a 20-inch rainbow sipped the offering. But then, I thought, why shouldn't it? The *Iso* dun is an imposing creature as far as such fragile-winged ephemera go and it is one of our region's most beautiful insects. The dry that imitates it is a juicy-looking meal for a trout, though the shame is that, because the bug hatches above the waterline and often flies off into the trees to molt unimpeded, the adults don't present the same bobbing, floating midstream offerings for trout that other insects do, notably the sulphurs this time of year. But every so often the exception disproves the rule.

I was deliberately ignoring the few remaining sulphurs and sticking perversely with *Isos*. And even though I only saw a couple of *Iso* duns on the wing, not unusual for this peripatetic insect, they were still the menu order of the evening at the Elk River Diner. A parachute pattern fished in the film with a little twitch took a number of nicely colored browns. As evening came on, who knows why but the anticipated *Iso* spinner fall never materialized, but that did not deter a couple of truly special fish from falling prey to spinner memory and coming to net on a #12 mahogany-colored spinner—a chunky rainbow that shot up and down the run like a fire-breathing maniac and put every other feeder down for a few minutes with his wild antics, and a bully, head-tossing 17-inch brown, one of the most beautiful I have gotten on the Elk in the seven years I've been coming over here and proof that reports of goodly fish in this river are not exaggerated.

Thoughts of my father were with me the whole time, but concentrating on fishing properly, and paying attention to the goings-on in front of me, pushed them to the background where they registered like a dull ache and a kind of abiding absence, a phantom pain, rather than a debilitating wound. It helps for mourning's sake, I think, to go whole hog into an alternative universe. Fishing and writing do that for me. So does cooking. When I got back to the cabin, Kate had a bottle of Côtes du Rhône opened, and I dove into our groceries and made a simple dinner of angel-hair pasta with smoked salmon and capers sprinkled with fresh parsley and dusted with aged Parmigiana Reggiano that fed our stomachs and our souls. It was so satisfying that I felt guilty for feeling so good. The old Catholic in me, I guess. I like to think my father would have agreed. He adored his pasta.

Kate and I sat for a while on the back porch and listened to the night sounds, at their height this time of year. On a nearby hillside a pair of screech owls, whether red or gray phase I could not tell, serenaded us in stereo with their haunting, trilling duet that went on after we retired. Cathartic birds they are, doing their maniacal hooting for us. This morning, on the alpine bench behind the cabin, trillium were flowering in profusion, and greeted us as we drank coffee and whiled away the morning reading and writing and swapping stories. I picked a couple of flowers—one for Kate and one to paste into a blank page of this journal.

Last night I dreamed of my father again as I have done often in the past six months. He was a young man, with a full head of black hair, and we were walking, my hand in his, as fathers often do with their children, picking a path through the field toward our neighbor's iced-over pond near our home in Connecticut, where he laced up my Christmas skates and waltzed me out on the ice to give my first skating lesson. I was three or four years old and too cold to be suitably patient or receptive. "Get up on the horse again," he kept saying every time I fell to the ice, "or the horse will get on you." He wasn't being harsh or threatening, but matter-of-fact. After the fourth or fifth fall I woke up and the dream dissolved and I started to return to myself with an eerie sense of both sadness and relief.

Last year, a year of bodily diminishment before Dad's death, those memories, experiences, stories, yarns, and tales were sustaining to both of us, as was my mother's devoted, selfless care toward him. I took a leave of absence from Ohio University and spent a goodly part of six months living with my parents during those trying times so I could assist in every aspect of a day-to-day life that had taken on a cast far darker than either of my parents ever imagined. When Dad's time came this past January, after nearly a year of off-and-on illness, medical pokings and proddings, injections, therapies, and operations, during which he was always a model patient, I like to believe he was ready for the end, having grown increasingly philosophical and even resigned, though who can say this isn't a delusional rationalization on my part? I take as truth, though, that when "a man's stories are remembered, then he is immortal," as Daniel Wallace says in his novel *Big Fish,* and in that way he lives on, even if it is only in the secreted space of this homely journal or in the confines of his family's individual hearts and minds.

I was extremely lucky, though, to have been able to tell him, nearly daily, that I loved him, and to kiss his cheek in that old respectful Italian way that was our habit. I wish more men were able to do that with their fathers. When a window opened and I could slip away without feeling guilty, I sought refuge in my old standbys: the Norwalk, Saugatuck, and Housatonic Rivers. I discovered the Farmington, which I came to love, not only for its prolific hatches and its stunning trout, but also for my one and only (small) Atlantic salmon. Now and then, I wandered a bit farther away and I hit the legendary Esopus in the Catskills. Fishing was so-so, my mind was elsewhere, my heart was in flight from itself, but there were always stories to tell that Dad enjoyed hearing when I returned, especially my tale of five purloined trout.

In writing of my father, ever so briefly here, even now a chasm opens inside me that seems bottomless, and I know I will never not miss him. Grief is a hole in the heart that no number of brown trout can fill. Which says a great deal about true priorities. How the dead get inside us, I well know: I live off the interest from Dad's gifts and stories even now, and in some areas I have become more like him than I ever imagined possible forty years ago. He's with me every time I work in my garden, step into a trout stream, or dine with loved ones. "To find the father is to find oneself," that marvelous centenarian poet Stanley Kunitz once said. I am happy to aspire to that.

Kate and I spent the day reading and writing, and she listened to me air some thoughts about Dad, which flood in so fast I can hardly manage them. Then we fished a bit, picnicked in the woods, then lazed around again, and so in that way nearly the whole day went by in a flash. Around 5 p.m. we drove back over to the Elk Springs area for a serious go at fishing—we felt we had earned it—and walked down below the fly shop and the main Mill Pool past a couple of other anglers and worked our way back up the stream. Last month we spent the entire day on the Slaty Fork of the Elk River, where we hit upon a simple, workable partnering solution: sharing a single fly rod. Letting Kate carry the rod most of the time kept me focused on the teaching task and made me less inclined to go off fishing on my own and neglect her.

Same thing today: I gave her my tip-flex Orvis Trident 4-weight, 8-foot-4-inch rod for keeps—it's the right length and weight for her—and we swapped it back and forth as we worked upstream with a single fly, though truth is Kate did most of the fishing and I did most of the coaching, standing by her side in the cold, rushing water for safety's sake in case she slipped, and trying not to make her nervous by repeating too many instructions, injunctions, and caveats. Men too often confuse bullying with instructing, and we have a nasty habit of wanting to interrupt, so I have to keep a watch out for crossing the line into injudicious, blabbery behavior. Thank God, she won't stand for it. Now and then I stand behind her, put my hand on hers and we go through the casting motion together so she gets a direct feel for its speed and timing, but most of the time she insists on space of her own where mistakes and slipups and errors can be processed and assessed if not actually tolerated.

A #18 Parachute Adams brought Kate a number of hits, but she was unable to connect, so I switched to the #12 *Isonychia* pattern, my Parachute Chocolate Drake, that worked so well yesterday, and on that easier-to-see

floating contraption she caught her first trout on a fly—a 9-inch rainbow. The smile on her face was worth everything. We remembered Elizabeth Bishop's poem, "The Fish" and its climax: "everything/was rainbow, rainbow, rainbow!/And I let the fish go." Whoops, hollers, high fives, fist bumps, hugs, and a flashy photo op turned heads of those anglers up river from us who must have been wondering what all the commotion was. *She got one*, I wanted to shout, *the woman I love got one.*

Now, hours later, what's better, I wonder. Our shared moment on stream when everything came together, or its immediate aftermath, reflected

Kate Fox with Elk River rainbow trout.
Credit: Robert DeMott

upon and written about in this late-night journal entry after a lovely sexual encounter? Why quibble, why split hairs? Either way, the place of equilibrium, the dry-fly take, is at hand. It's a way of being *right here, right now,* at an intersection where all relevant needful forces come into play and corrosive elements are held at bay for the time being anyway. Fishing is *always* a hopeful act, no matter how dire the context. If that puts me in the minority or brands me as romantic, so be it. I know my father would have understood.

The Big Wet

20 August 2008

On the 12th, my fishing on the Madison ended in a heartbeat when I took a plunge and lost rod, reel, hat, fish, and dignity. I made a cryptic entry in my daily calendar that night: "lost rod 3.00 bridge—TU Sage rod—lost when I fell trying to net brown trout." But that snippet hardly told the story. My world turned upside down and I have been trying to make sense of what happened ever since. Falling in is one of fishing's ugly little secrets, a failure that can hardly stand public scrutiny. There is much more to be said on that score, but this private account will have to stand for now.

I was wading thirty or so feet out from the west bank of a section of the upper Madison River above $3 Bridge (that I had almost entirely to myself), and I was bringing up some nice trout on *Epeorus* patterns. It was one of those moments that happen too rarely: just the right conjunction of time, season, weather, water clarity and temperature, hatch action, and feeding fish. All the celestial bodies aligned, and vanity of vanities, I began thinking rather highly of my angling skills. Which, of course, is always a mistake.

A curve cast put the fly on a left-hand seam of water and a bully brown trout about 19 inches grabbed it. I got tight to the fish right away as it ran upstream to my left, looped around and charged back down on my right-hand side where it dropped into a deep, fast trough. At the edge of the drop-off, gaining line, rod pulsing in hand, I leaned over to net the fish, a handsome butter-colored male with a small kype, the fly inserted perfectly in the corner of his jaw. I noticed all this in one of those uncanny moments of clarity as I hoisted his head up and slid him to the edge of my net.

I can't remember stumbling or tripping, much less fainting or blacking out, but in the next instant I was in the Big Wet, facedown, running like a maniac under a long chute of fast water so my feet could catch up with the rest of my body and I could gain my balance and stand upright again. It never occurred to me that I might drown or that this was a near-death experience, but the emptiness in the pit of my stomach felt endless, as though I was free-falling into an abyss.

In fifty years of fishing I've fallen in plenty of times but always managed to pop right up like a cork and hang on to my rod without even getting overly soaked. This time, when I regained my feet, the rod, a brand new 5-weight Sage ZXL with a Lamson Konic reel, an incentive gift from Trout Unlimited for having become a life member last month, was gone, still attached to the rampaging trout, which immediately began putting on pounds and inches, at least in my imagination. My gut response was not just anger and cursing, but a kind of undirected fury that I'd been tricked by a nameless, malicious, cozening god, a master angler of deception and deceit. Okay. If that's the metaphysical gambit, then the instrument of my undoing had better be nothing less than the Boss Fish of the Madison, Moby Brown himself. Better to be undone by a colossal adversary rather than a dink. *I deserve at least that much*, I told my battered, blue-streak-cursing self. By the time I got out of the drink the trout was already a two-footer going on three.

A few minutes later, a bit steadier on my feet, and having gagged up enough river water to float a fish, I hobbled down the bank as fast as I could looking for my runaway outfit, then waded across and came back up the other side. I was hoping to see the rod tip sticking out of the water, or my eye-catching yellow fly line snagged around a tree branch or some other obstruction, but there's not a sign of errant graphite or demonic fish, both of which had no doubt plowed well downstream.

At dusk, hatless and rodless, and starting to chill in the cool evening air, I skulked like a beaten dog back to the truck, took off the soaked vest, waders, and clothes, put on a dry shirt, and began to sort out waterlogged aluminum fly boxes, a couple of which had been dented by my fall, though I have no recollection of having fallen that hard. The ring Kate gave me last year to mark our commitment is gone, though I haven't a clue why or how.

No broken bones, no lacerations. My left wrist was bunged up, and I felt shooting pain into my shoulder, but I was thankful that it wasn't my casting arm that'd been winged. My injuries could have been much worse. Having that stretch of river to myself suddenly looked like a mixed blessing: no one else around to share the fishing also meant no one else around to help in direst straits. But even at that sobering thought, the voice of my most frivolous, superficial devil advised me to look on the bright side—never mind that I wasn't badly injured, more importantly, there were no witnesses to compound the shame, so the blow to my ego was mine and mine alone. For better or worse, I'd live to fish another day.

The cause of falling in—still undetermined and by now, even a week later, probably forever unrecoverable—was such an anomaly that I have no neat compartment in which to place it. Even now I find myself stymied not so much by the fact that I dumped, but by my embarrassment at my anger and my inability to resolve the nagging allied questions raised by screwing up. Am I getting too old, or worse yet, too unlucky to be on the river alone? It seems like a classic paradox: the closer I get to solving these implications, the farther they recede from my grasp. Though my mishap paranoia grows each day, I am unwilling to concede that, at sixty-five, I might be getting too old to keep fishing, but a fisherman—self-delusion or not—I still claim to be.

By which I mean, no longer flashy, extreme, or jaunty, but more measured, balletic, and almost comfortable with the steady, incremental dance and march of days. Like that aged, white-haired gent I encountered one evening a few years ago on Pennsylvania's Yellow Breeches. He appeared to be well in his eighties (maybe older). Not at all athletic, he was trundling on anyway, "making haste slowly," to use Eugene Connett's memorable phrase about fishing deliberately. I watched him work up the river toward me, moving so methodically and painstakingly as he laid out each cast that he might have been a heron in another life. When he reached me, he laid his cane rod on the berm, then got down on his hands and knees at stream's edge and crawled up the bank to the Allenberry Inn's lawn. Then, straightened up to the best of his ability, he ambled off toward the parking lot and was gone. I did not speak to him and don't know if he caught any fish, though his deliberate method had much to recommend it. *Good for him,* I thought. *That's looking the Death Trout square in the eye; that's a way I'd like to be if I don't croak first.* With more years behind me than ahead of me—the past is most of what I have—so the best I can do right now is follow a fantasy route and wish for a couple things.

First, I'd wish that I had a photo of the moment of going ass over tea kettle into the drink, a glossy snapshot that caught the utter surprise and incomprehension on my face. That would be a photo I'd most want to have, a trophy of the moment when the world turned upside down and I'm on the wrong side looking out. That photo would stand as a reality check, the thing about our human foibles, angling mishaps, and tenuous felt-soled hold on existence we should never forget and can neglect only at our own risk. But as falling in is one of angling's most frequently suppressed secrets, that taboo photo would never appear in any glossy, well-scrubbed fly-fishing magazine, so I'd paste it in the pages of this fishing journal and let it go at that.

Second, I'd wish like hell that some fortunate soul found that runaway fly rod and reel before it got trashed by the elements. I hoped it would be a young person, new to our sport, who could benefit from an instant upgrade in equipment. When he or she picked it up, I'd give anything to know if a lively brown trout was still tethered to the rig, still hauling the freight to Ennis. Surprise of surprises, that would be the best story of all to hear, a story something like redemption, something like a second life rising from a river of doubt, though of course it would be too early to tell whether that story was my own.

Co-Ed Angling

6–8 June 2009

What I love most about driving over to the Elk just about every other weekend this spring, is that it's like going back in time, so Kate and I get to experience two flowerings instead of one, two blossomings of redbuds, forsythia, rhododendron, mountain laurel, multiflora rose, lilacs, Siberian irises, peonies, woodland phlox, instead of a paltry single emergence. Drive the four-plus hours from lowland Athens to elevated Monterville and it's like turning back the clock. Just when I'm starting to feel cheated by the too-rapid passing of spring at home, there's more of it yet to come on the Elk. It's had the effect of slowing life down in an agreeable way, giving us a magical second shot at existence, like a parade passing us twice. That can't be said about too many things. Lilacs past their peak in our yard show up in full abundance in the hinterland where so many dooryards feature a well-heeled lilac colony, some house-tall, with luscious clusters of deep lavender flowers, and here and there, the occasional white-headed stepchild. Every flowering on the Elk coincides with a different hatch, so there is that added benefit of witnessing the natural progression. And there's the indescribable pleasure of sharing this all with Kate, the truest life partner I will ever have.

The best part of the trip is the last stretch from Elkins south to Monterville. There anticipation runs highest. Below Huttonsville, skinny Route 219/55 twists like coiled fly line as it follows the Tygart Valley River south to unincorporated Valley Head where we peel off on Route 15 toward the upper Elk. The country is deep there and has breadth and vista, and when it's bathed in moonlight like it was a couple of nights ago, the foothills of Cheat Mountain to the east look blue and icily remote in the moon's silver wash. By this point in our trip I've pretty well shucked the work-a-day professorial mind-set. The Doors or Jimi Hendrix or Tom Petty blasting from the speakers helps. As we get closer to Elk Springs I devolve. The cell phone no longer has a signal, air temperature is always at least ten degrees cooler than at home, foliage is less advanced, and I know I've arrived at an earlier moment of my own existence.

Kate and I stay at various inns, cabins, lodges in the area. This time we rented a small cabin at Elk Springs Resort near the river. Rainy and misty when we arrived. Elk is high and roily. Kate stayed in to read and write, but I walked to the Mill Pool to throw streamers, a useful tactic here under the constant drizzle and coffee-water conditions. Got one trout, lost one.

Next day, we share one rod so I can keep focused on her improvement. River a bit high but it's come down and is now of good color. Below the Valley Fork confluence I help Kate ease out to mid-river and direct her cast to the far bank, then follow her drifting fly. She hooks a nice rainbow when I say "Strike!" and fights it briefly but can't coordinate feeding line when it runs so it breaks off. I put on a Fran Betters–inspired Sulphur Usual and she casts over some eager fish, one of which came up for the fly three times in a row before chowing down. It's nice brown trout, hooked with only a little technical coaching from me, but with lots of enthusiastic vocal encouragement. She lands two more browns, then hands the rod to me and I do the same. We are in trout heaven and in no hurry and don't want to rush the experience so we relax streamside, break out our sandwiches, eat a late lunch, drink some water, and rehash the day so far. There is much to be savored.

When we start again, it's her turn and on a single Parachute Sulfur she has several hits and catches two nice browns, one of them a thick bodied, butter-colored brown of about 14 inches. It fills her whole hand when we take its picture. It's the best trout she's ever caught and we whoop it up in celebration. Best of all she did it herself. Not one iota of instruction from me. She casts, mends, tracks fly, strikes perfectly when the trout comes up. We had seen it rising a few times earlier and she patiently cast and cast again for the right float and angle of approach. A few minutes later she lands another brown, this one 12 inches, and I know it will be a long time before I get so much exquisite joy from fishing. In all the fly-fishing literature I've read in recent years I can't think of many writers who treat co-ed fishing in a positive way. Not misogynist Maclean, who believed women and trout should never mix. John Atheron praised his wife Maxine in *The Fly and the Fish*. Another I can think of is the elder statesman Theodore Gordon, who called the mystery woman with whom he fished the Neversink River in the early 1900s, the "best chum" he ever had in fishing. I know how he felt.

As evening came on Kate handed me the rod and turned back to the cabin. I was missing her already as I re-rigged with a Coffin Fly on top, followed by a Rusty Spinner as a trailer. The latter is paler and more muted than the ones I normally use. When I examined some captured spinners the other night they were a few shades lighter than rusty red. Trout were up in droves all over the run, some rising within a few feet of my waders, and I realized I'm witnessing a much-hyped "snout soup," a rather colorful way the local fly-shop mavens have of describing the frenzied feeding activity that occurs in the last thirty minutes of daylight. A boiling cauldron of hungry, chomping trout. I hooked three in quick succession, including one chunky brown near dark that was especially gratifying.

I watched spent sulphur spinners wash downstream without cessation. It's almost incomprehensible the number of tiny creatures that have to be born to keep the genetic thread alive. Nature's appalling fecundity and its harsh directives give me pause on this quick-footed river in Appalachia, where I have had no choice before *now* becomes *then* but to get with the speeding express, to put up or shut up, in this land of root-and-bud essentials that some nervy contemporary theoreticians say don't exist. I've heard about the "red fog" sulphur spinner fall here for a number of years but never saw it in its full blizzardy majesty. Words don't do it justice. I wished some of those misguided postmodern scholars, who claim nature is not real, were standing there with me. They might mend their ways.

Mayflies have been hatching all week in obscene numbers: true ephemerals, candles in the wind, lit and snuffed in mere hours, born without mouths and unable to taste, born only to fuck then die. *Here today, gone tonight.* Whitman had it right: "Urge and urge and urge,/Always the procreant urge of the world." I closed my eyes and tried to think of nothing beyond nothing.

It was enough to stand where trout rose freely to sex-crazed sulphurs and green drakes, where Virginia bluebells tipped their hats in profusion, where the woman I love more than anyone else told me again a little while earlier she loved me that way too, and where all around me in the fading light, an audience of thousands watched the watcher.

Front-Door Trout

15 August 2010

According to Montana's Fish, Wildlife, and Parks Department, the Madison River is one of the three most popular trout streams in the state. Thousands of hours logged here by anglers from the four corners of the globe in pursuit of this river's fabled wild trout. Finding an untouched honey hole in Disneyland is nearly impossible. Every so often, though, a stretch of river in this public-friendly area from Cameron downstream to Ennis presents itself that isn't pounded to death by Tom, Dick, and Mary.

Walked out the front door of our rental cabin and walked to the river. Fished the easterly bank of the Madison, the one nearest us, for two hours. No delicate match-the-hatch stuff on a 3-weight rod today. I'm all in for a brute. After yesterday's spring creek debacle I'm hot for a shooting-star connection. Rigged my Orvis 6-weight with a Chaos Hopper and a black Crowe Beetle as a dropper. Excellent conditions. Wind at my back made casting upstream a breeze, plus with the sun on the western horizon over my right shoulder, there was no glare in my eyes, and I had a clear panoptic view of the river and my scrumptious-looking lures.

A couple times each summer when I feel a homeboy urge to stick close, and don't feel like driving to the Gallatin, West Fork of the Madison, Grayling Creek, or Duck Creek, say, I take this handy front-door fishing route and work up the cabin side of the river moving like a heron step-by-step, as slowly as if I'm watching paint dry. Stalking I guess it could be called.

Moving deliberately lets me think about a hundred other things, but not so abstractly that I miss what's in front of me. I love fishing the edges next to the bank. I stand three or four feet out from the bank, throw upstream fifteen or twenty feet, and with a snap of the wrist try to curve my cast tight left to the willow bank and beneath delectable-looking porch overhangs and deck abutments. Trout hide in those protected pockets next to the bank waiting for lunch to come their way in the faster outside currents.

Nothing new or revolutionary in that, but what makes this gig special is that I have never seen anyone else fishing here. As far as I can tell, this section never gets touched by drifting anglers because fishing from a boat isn't allowed in the Madison above Lyons Bridge. I've seen guides cruise down the opposite side, anchor their boat, and encourage clients to wade around the small island off the west bank, but no one I've ever seen comes this way toward our shore. I'm not boasting superior knowledge, only a luck-of-the-draw, plug-lucky turn of events. This sheltered section is close to private summer residences and is not easy to negotiate on foot, which may help explain why it harbors some secret trout.

This is the third year in a row I've waited to see someone else fish here and for the third year in a row, not wanting the resident trout to get lonely, I've decided it might as well be me. Today was no different. It took me about two hours to stalk up the bank about 100 yards, but it was worth the effort, as I caught two plump browns, each about 16 inches and each in such perfect condition that I'll bet neither one had ever been hooked before or harried by the resident ospreys. Not the bruisers I know live here that I've tangled with before on spruce moths and nocturnal stonefly patterns, but lovely gifts nonetheless. The first, a yellowish-colored male with a slight hooked lower jaw, exploded on the hopper so violently that it startled me. The second was a less dramatic-looking creature that took the black beetle but it too hooked itself by main force. I had forgotten my net, so I had a lively time keeping both fish close to the bank and away from heavy current, which required easing into softer water under the willows and getting poked in the back by sharp limbs as I went about my unhooking business. Small inconvenience, though, considering the reward.

As I write this, I'm sitting at our picnic table looking out toward the stretch of river I just fished. In the slanting sunlight it looks like a swath of molten silver, too brilliant and mirror-reflective to gaze at for long without sunglasses. Our bird dog Meadow is sleeping at my feet after her stint walking along the river while I fished. Kate's gone to shop in Ennis and I look forward to her return so I can tell my story. I'm pleased with my outing, but don't want to read too much into it, don't want to get smug about success, no matter how modest. How twisted is that? No matter how content I am, I'm never not bedeviled by the maddening riddle of fly fishing. It's a refrain in my journals, like a nagging cough or a bad debt. Down one day, up the next; up one day, down the next.

Remember January? On two consecutive trips on Biscayne Bay, I got my first bonefish, an ecstatic moment, and followed that with a day in which neither my guide nor I spotted a single bone or permit. Tough to swallow at $600 a day. Yesterday I had a complete bust on DePuy's Spring Creek—lost every one of the few exasperating fish I hooked—yet today it went swimmingly, as though some superior intelligence had planned it down to the last detail. Over a long life of fishing perhaps those peaks and valleys even out in the end, reaching some kind of equipoise through the inscrutable law of averages. Or maybe that's the wrong way to consider progress. In *Going Fishing*, a book I've been reading lately that deserves to be better known, the world-wandering journalist Negly Farson says, "What you get out of fishing is infinitely more than fish," and that "neither size nor numbers should matter much," because "fishing should be the exercise of your skill—and its reward the spots it brings you to. If these are not your main objectives, then you don't know fishing." I get that. To truly "know" fishing means, among other things, not berating myself over issues I can't control, and no matter what the outcome, keeping this narrative moving toward the elusive horizon.

Slaty Fork Takes
Before It Gives

26 September 2011

Back from Montana on September 4 after six weeks away and nearly thirty straight days of fishing. But by September 7, neck deep in household chores, bill paying, catching up on mail, I was already itching to fish again. Endured several more weeks of homebody stuff and necessary further editorial work on *Astream,* a collection of fly-fishing essays (starting to round into shape thanks to excellent work by contributors), then, conscience cleared and all squared with the world at large, took off to West Virginia for three days with Kent Clements, my angling-obsessed friend and ex-student. We rented the tucked-away cabin at Hidden River Farm in Monterville that is perched above the "Dries" section of the Elk River connector a few miles upstream from the huge springs that create the catch-and-release section of the Elk where Cowger's Mill used to stand.

It's the parched, yellow, egg-yolky time of year, the cusp of summer/ fall when green-going-gold is everywhere: black-eyed susans, goldenrod, heliopsis, and tick seed in profusion. The turning leaves of maples, syca- mores, and river birches flicker in the dark alleys of hardwood stands. This late in the carryover season the connector is often completely dry, as it is now, so there is no sound of burbling water to provide a backdrop to our moment-to-moment life in this squirreled-away little cabin. Set in an over- arching grove of trees, it has an appealing bower-like quality, fit for contem- plation, reflection, relaxation, and daydreaming.

We fished the main Elk River catch-and-release section Saturday afternoon, the 24th, for three hours with no firm luck, no in-the-hand action. One or two halfhearted hits on dries by silly baby fish and that was all. Otherwise nothing. But then we weren't on top of our game. We packed it in and drove over to tiny Slatyfork for dinner at the Elk River Inn, a superb restaurant, the best in any direction for a hundred miles. The spicy Thai spring noodles and craft beer did not disappoint.

Sunday was better. It was raining when we got up so we prolonged breakfast, drank a few extra cups of coffee, and plotted strategies for the day. I dipped into a couple of angling memoirs—George Marzluff's *Fly Fishing Forever* and Glenn Busch's *Journey to the Final Cast*—and then scribbled some reading notes in the margins of Datus Proper's *What the Trout Said*. Bless her heart, Datus's widow, Anna Collins-Proper, recently gave me permission to use in *Astream* a long unpublished essay by her husband from his archive in the Special Collections library at Montana State University, so I have been reading everything else by him I can get my hands on in order to build an informed editorial background for myself. No question that Datus is among the great ones of the last three decades. I don't think anyone strikes a balance between empirical observation and philosophical musing quite like him. And I love the fact that he was a foreign-service diplomat not a professional scientist. His work gives amateurism a respected name. *What the Trout Said,* his great book on fly design, is full of intriguing insights and gists: "Innocence is a wild trout. But we humans, being complicated, have to pursue innocence in complex ways." But what choice do we have, I wonder? It's reassuring to know that Proper was out ahead of us on these issues. Either way, in arrogance or ignorance, we forge ahead, for better or worse. Look at Saturday's debacle.

We stopped at Elk Springs Fly Shop, poked around among the tantalizing goodies and hobnobbed with local angling legend and guide Dave Breitmeier. His well-earned nickname is "Elkfisher" because he plies the river 200 days a year and is on a first-name basis with most of its trout. From the fly shop we drove down to the Engine Hole. From there we hopscotched upriver, by foot and by auto, all the way to Sulphur Run, the Angle Hole, and then finally to the Valley Fork confluence. This took nearly all day and into the evening, and except for waiting out a rainstorm around 3 p.m. in my truck while we wolfed down some sandwiches, we fished hard the whole time with respectable results, including a fat 17-inch brown on a #20 Brassie and a similar-sized rainbow on a Zug Bug worked swimmingly back toward shore. That one made me feel especially skilled and savvy. And lucky.

The hits kept on coming, including some misguided pecks at my float-ing strike indicator by more of those silly baby fish. Kent was a happy camp-er, too, with several decent fish on dries. It was not the same river we fished yesterday, sure proof of Heraclitus's famous dictum, though I doubt he had fly-fishing results in mind 2,500 years ago. On second thought, Heraclitus *must* have been a fisherman of some kind, and a trout fisher at that, to have understood the fickle and changeable nature of the aqueous medium. Maybe what's needed is to invent a fly—a streamer, let's say—called the Heraclitean Special, which changes shape and color every time you cast it to keep pace with changing currents in our rivers and more importantly in ourselves.

Hindsight is always 20/20: today—Monday—we probably should have gone back to the Elk Springs section. But one of the attractions of the Hidden River Farm cabin is that you can walk out the back door to the abandoned rail bed behind it and in twenty-five minutes or so of hoofing, reach the lower end of the Slaty Fork section of the Elk. That gives access to four-plus miles of river beyond where it disappears in the mysterious "Blue Hole" and runs underground (beneath the Dries section) through Randolph and Poca-hontas County limestone karst another four-plus miles where it gushes up again at Elk Springs, right above the fly shop and cabins. The whole place is a geographical-mystery theme park.

The Slaty Fork of the Elk is one of the most maddening, challenging rivers I know, right up there with the legendary Railroad Ranch section of the Henry's Fork in Idaho, Benhart Spring Creek on the Milesnick Ranch in Montana, and the LeTort Spring Run in Pennsylvania. Because the river is sequestered, there is no getting accurate information about its current, real-time conditions. It exists in a fog of vagaries, a loose wash of innuendoes. Which means you have to invent the wheel every time you fish there.

It's a river that separates ambition from skill, a river that gets inside your head. Although only about one percent of all the hundreds of miles of viable trout water in West Virginia is under special regulations/catch-and-release rules, thankfully, this is one of them. The trout in Slaty are all stream-bred, as the West Virginia DNR stopped stocking it with fingerlings in 2004. Now, the railroad bed, once necessary for logging and mining operations, is degraded and washed out in many places. There is no car-worthy access road paralleling the Slaty Fork, the railroad tracks are no longer passable by mechanized means, so the only way to reach the river is on foot. Walking (and wading) requires patience, attention, and endurance. Hiking in requires some energetic bushwhacking to navigate around rotten cross timbers and fallen trees, all the while keeping a wary eye out for aggressive copperheads, several of which I have met over the years sunning themselves in the warm cinder openings between crossties. *Beware vipers in the midst of paradise,* I imagine warning people who express interest in fishing there.

Given all those obstructions and hazards, one of Slaty Fork's consummate attractions is its relative solitude. You run into people here at either access end during the most vaunted hatches—especially sulphur madness of May—but at best you are utterly, sublimely alone or at worst have decent stretches of river to yourself. In his lyric chapter on the Elk River system in *Journey to the Final Cast*, Glenn Busch claims the Slaty Fork "represents fishing as it used to be—before pollution and environmental degradation reduced mountain trout streams from their original pristine state." True, as far as it goes, but the entire Snowshoe Mountain region to which this river belongs is under threat of extinction if a proposed pro-industry, anti-environmental plan for a raw sewage treatment plant near Big Spring Fork, one of Slaty's two headwater sources, is allowed to go through.

But I see what Busch is getting at: get down far enough in the Slaty valley, so that the whirring machines and buzzing saws of the Beckwith Lumber Company can't be heard, and you have the illusion that you are in a reclusive place. Depending on the season, your eye is entertained by long copses of blooming rhododendron and mountain laurel on the ridge and cliff sides, and lower down the slopes, my favorite—the gorgeously bright, down-hanging Canada lilies that look like brilliant church bells swaying from their tall stalks, some of them the color of a rainbow trout's crimson stripe. Also delicious ramps in profusion to be dug, cleaned, and cooked. Then, of course, there is the occasional ruffed grouse brood whose whirring flushes still startle, and now and then, if you are stealthy enough, you see mink doing the same thing you are doing—slinking around hunting for trout—and comical beaver to watch as they do their daily ablutions and now and then let loose a resounding tail slap. The Monongahela National Forest, big and deep, is wild enough for black bear, and though I have only seen one cub in there, I have more than once had some hunter's radio-collared bear hound come down to drink in the river and share half of my sandwich before trotting out to the county road, miles away.

In this present dry spell, water levels are way down (it's an annual oc-currence here in late summer/early fall) and fish sulk in the deepest holes and runs, trying to avoid not just the occasional angler but herons, ospreys, mink, and those most maniacal predators, the greedy otters, which lately have been gaining an increasing foothold here to the dismay of nearly eve-ryone concerned with the wild trout population. Well, if it ain't one threat-ening thing, it's another. Elkfisher confessed yesterday that he won't guide clients on Slaty during such extreme late summer conditions, even though there are *very* big browns to be had.

Fatalists that we are, Kent and I were not deterred. This falls in the realm of idiocy or blind faith. My attraction to rock-ribbed Slaty during the past decade is so visceral and irrational that I can't adequately explain it. Nearest I can come is to liken it to the unrequited love we've all had at some point in our lives—that primal, gut-twisting obsession for the raving beauty who doesn't know you are alive and wouldn't give you the time of day even if she did. It's her insouciance, her studied indifference, her untouchableness, that fuels your ardor, your fantasy of *What If?* It's a sign of your bullheaded-ness that you keep hoping for a different outcome, some sign from her of recognition or acknowledgment. Which of course will never come.

Desperate cause or not, Slaty pulls at me like that. I dream about it at night; I fish it over and over in my head when I should be doing more pro-ductive things with my time. The fishing is tough, the trout are wild and wary, the walking and wading is physically demanding and even dangerous, and the rewards are for the most part limited. Complaints about the river's difficulties are legion on the WVAngler.com chat board. "It just won't coop-erate," one says; "there's no fish left in there," another says. I couldn't count the number of respondents who, having been humiliated once or twice, refuse to go back.

I've been among that group of frustrated anglers; my indignant shouts have gone up in concert with theirs. After a spell of private ranting and rav-ing, though, I figured out that Slaty Fork, like many other wild streams, requires you to put your time in. Maybe it's a game of averages. Or maybe it's that the river will give you only what it is ready to give you. There is no easy solution, which of course is a disturbing realization when masochism is part of the picture. But perhaps time spent equals points laid up in angling heaven. Who knows? You might fish it six times in a row with zero-to-modest success at best, even in the midst of one of its abundant hatches, but then, say, on the seventh or eighth time the place will hand you a gift and it will be exceptional enough to keep you going through another half-dozen anemic trips.

Like the time several years ago when Dennis Hess and I walked its entire end-to-end, 4.6-mile stretch in a light spring rain and encountered a blessed rarity: trout after trout taking a Parachute March Brown until, tired of the sheer stupid numbers, we lost count. And earlier this year on May 21, the day before the world was supposed to end according to Harold Camping, octogenarian owner of Family Radio, I was on Slaty's upper reaches when I took a 22-inch brown on a Grey Fox Comparadun. It was my only fish of the day but on a 7-foot bamboo rod and light tippet it was my own version of the rapture, with a small *r*. *Thank you, Jesus!* I saw the light and was saved.

Slaty Fork takes before Slaty Fork gives. So when is an 8-inch trout a completely satisfying catch for the day? When it is a wild stream-bred rainbow, a zesty little jewel as brightly colored as a hand-painted Oriental plate, which today jumped on a black-winged ant pattern in the limestone-ribbed lower reaches of this glorious, maddening stream. It was the sole fish Kent and I caught today, but it was just enough to make our trudge back to the Hidden River cabin less mournful and dolorous than it might otherwise have been.

Cruel Sport of the
Angling Gods

15 August 2012

Today was more proof, if in fact I really needed to be reminded, that a large percentage—perhaps the bulk—of fishing adventures end badly or close to that. Daily temperatures for the past week have been unusually high, and this part of Montana, between Ennis and West Yellowstone, is baking yet again under oven-like conditions, aided and abetted by the umbrella effects of numerous regional forest fires. The ill effects of the Hebgen Dam bust-out are in full swing. Water in the Madison River has heated (and dropped at least eight inches in the past few days down to around 750 cfs), hatches have been hindered, fish have been sluggish and closemouthed. The sun, an angry red ball behind the smoke curtain, goes on beating down hour after hour. Evening fishing, usually the go-to solution for what ails us, has taken a dive lately. Yesterday, an afternoon of floating the Madison below Lyons Bridge in my drift boat with Dennis Hess, was a complete bust. "Shit-Point-Shit," as an old boss of mine used to say. Sometimes fishing can be more work than fun, and drinking cold beer and grilling bison burgers becomes the day's high point. We scavenge what we can, hone in on the morsels of good.

But last night the wind shifted and blew in a blessed front from the north. This afternoon, we hit the inexhaustible Madison again where we were greeted by a sight not seen much lately: the shift in weather pattern and barometric pressure had trout rising liberally all over the river with that kind of gusto that makes knees go weak and hearts sing. I rigged a two-fly juggernaut: a 12-foot 5X leader with a #17 tan Iris Caddis, then off its bend, twenty inches of 6X tippet with a #14 Pink Albert emerger. There are rare times when you have such supreme confidence in the patterns you are throwing that you know it will only be a matter of time before a fish takes. Not *if*, but *when*. This was one of those times when confidence and anticipation were running sky high. *Let me at 'em*, a voice inside your skull screams.

In a few minutes I had on the biggest brown I have ever had on in the Madison. I mean *ever*, as in twenty-three years of fishing this river. I saw it rising in one of the slack-water pockets near the bank. I knew it was a hefty, broad-beamed fish, but could not tell right off how hefty. I did not obsess about its size: I didn't want to get too jittery, didn't want to jinx the moment by throwing in pounds and ounces. But it was a pig, a toad, a beast, and so on through all the gradations of behemoth. It surprised me to see a brown that big working the surface for small stuff, but then I remembered that Bob Jacklin caught that infamous ten-pound brown several years ago between Hegben Lake and Quake Lake on a #14 caddis nymph. I stepped into the river, kept low and stalked as close as I dared—within fifteen feet. My first casts were too far right, but the third one, with a little left-hand curve induced by a turn of my wrist, landed above the feeding fish.

I saw the take in a highlight-reel moment. It was surprising how quickly the gulp happened and how simple and direct it was. The fish didn't balk, shy away, come short, or refuse. It only needed a leisurely arching roll to take the caddis. Its take looked like the most natural thing in the world, a perfect example of nature naturing itself without saying, *Look at me! Ain't I great?* No grandstanding, no showboating with this fish, just the supremely confident head-to-tail arc one expects from an accomplished riverine predator.

I held my breath and kept time in my head so I wouldn't strike too soon and pull the fly out of its mouth. "Just a shot away," the Rolling Stones sing, and on its downward path the fish took the fly and pretty much set itself with only some light pressure from me. Okay. So far so good. I saw it twice more when it jumped. At first the fish lolled in the calm water as it moved upstream against the bank, and I thought for sure I'd get it if it stayed in the less-turbulent water, even though I thought it unusual that it didn't make a beeline immediately for deeper flows and faster currents midstream, which, in my experience, is generally what the big Madison browns will do when stuck.

Just at the moment there was a glimmer of hope, the fish did its predictable thing, its default move, turned left and headed to deeper water. In a nanosecond, curse the blasted fucking luck, it wrapped itself around some underwater obstruction, some boulder, and the small hook pulled out of its mouth. Then he jumped again, for the third time, as if to rub it in, as if to remind me that the best laid plans of fishing men are destined to go awry.

I saw the fish clearly each time it leaped and hung in the air in all its glorious brown-ness, and I'd guess it was at least 25 inches long and weighed six pounds, maybe more. A truly respectable trout on my Loomis Stream Dance GLX 4-weight rod and a trophy in many places. Gone. Gone like a paycheck in a booze hall on Saturday night. And in its place shrapnel in my heart and a wooziness in my knees. I felt a kind of abject emptiness I had not felt since, as a teenager, I hooked a tuna off Cape Cod on a charter trip. I fought that fish on a stout rod, put my back into it, lived and died with its electric runs, then lost it when the abraded line parted. I never even saw the tuna but felt its size and power.

In his savvy *Rod and Line*, Arthur Ransome says perhaps "it would be better to say nothing about lost fish," even though you feel as bad as "Lucifer dumped into Hell," but he admits, "it is almost impossible to keep quiet about it." Yes, I know that now. Losing any fine fish creates a cry from the heart that must be vented. If I had any sense I would have called it quits then, gratified but not consoled that I had tangled with a bruiser, did my part as well as I could, and exited the field honorably, then gone home to contemplate the awe-ful Chaldee of the brown trout's fleeing visage over a couple of beers at the Grizzly Bar & Grill. But no, those cruel Fates, the angling gods, hungry for more sport of their own, were not done with me yet. Losing Moby Brown was just the beginning. Unlucky man, I didn't think things could get worse, but they did.

Back in the game, I was casting from the bank so that a modest elevation gave me better vision, aided, too, by the afternoon sun that was behind me and angled over my shoulder—it lit up the river and made it possible to see each rising fish and every surface take with remarkable clarity. In a couple of casts I was fast to a lovely rainbow. What followed was routine and by the book: I stepped down into the river—an easy drop of fifteen inches or so from the bank—and netted the fish. The whole action was flawless, clean as a whistle. The way fishing is supposed to happen. I even captured the moment in a photo before the release. I congratulated myself, sent a long-distance high-five to Dennis who was upstream into his own fish.

A few more casts from the bank and I was into a bully, strapping rainbow about 20 inches long. As I worked it toward me I stepped off the bank and into the water—same drill as previous fish a few minutes earlier—but this time, for reasons I cannot fathom, I slipped, dropped my beloved GLX rod in the water and landed full force on it with my right knee. I heard and felt it crack in half, with a sickening noise that caught in my bones, so I reached down to pick up the intact upper sections and continued to play the fish but couldn't get enough leverage with the slenderest tip-top part of the rod.

Then I did the stupidest damn thing imaginable: even as I grabbed the leader outside the top guide and started to haul the fish in hand-over-hand, I knew it was a bonehead move, bound to fail. And it did. The thrashing trout, by now supported in its wild-bucking flurries by the angling gods' perversities, pulled loose immediately and was gone. The strained spider-thin tippet left a red furrow on my hand, the little emerger, its hook nearly straightened, hung like regret in the air.

My response to the day's setbacks was vehement cursing and a desire to whip the river, like ancient King Xerxes of Persia, who ordered the Hellespont to be given a hundred lashes for stopping his army's advance. "You salt and bitter stream, your master lays this punishment upon you for injuring him, who never injured you." I read Herodotus's words when I was a college freshman and never forgot them, thinking even then they might come in handy at some appropriate future moment. And here the moment was. They could do no good in bringing back a lost trout and a busted rod, but just saying them felt delicious.

O'Dell Creek *Redux*

22 August 2012

Kate acted as photographer today while Rodger Gaulding and I fished with Patrick Daigle, O'Dell Creek specialist from Blue Ribbon Flies. We met Patrick at the Longhorn Ranch entrance, south of Ennis, transferred our gear to his pickup, and rode overland into the creek, which runs south-north for many miles through the heart of the Madison Valley. If you didn't know the creek was there, smack-dab in that wide, treeless savannah-like valley, you could hardly guess at its existence. People by the thousands zip up and down adjacent Route 287 at seventy-five miles an hour and never dream such a remarkable, brilliant place exists. Today was sunny and clear, except for more of that noxious smoke and drifting haze from regional forest fires. The O'Dell water stood at a chilly and fish-friendly fifty-five degrees when we started at 9 a.m., though it rose to about sixty by late this afternoon, still within a trout's comfort zone.

I've been here before, written about the place in my introduction to *Astream*, and yet it is one of those places that seems eternally new to me and sets in motion a complex of emotions and reactions each time I visit. I admit to being enamored of geographic places upon which books and paintings are based, and I've made a quirky hobby of gauging representational relationships—usually complex and fraught—between physical venues and their textual counterparts. I've pursued this oddball fascination from coast to coast for decades, whether snooping around the environs of Concord and Walden

Pond in Massachusetts with a copy of *Walden* in hand, to wading a section of the Niobrara River in Northwest Nebraska where parts of Harrison's *Dalva* are set, to strolling the ranch outside of Salinas, California, where Steinbeck set his coming-of-age novella, *The Red Pony*.

I've made a hundred such stops across the United States, jotting impressions in my notebooks, and snapping countless photos that I later showed my American literature students to assist them in putting a real place to a literary name or title. I guess it's the village explainer in me, who believes in the artistic importance of geographical loci. I have never been disappointed with my findings, never become tired of viewing what author X or artist Y saw at a given place that started their juices flowing. Mine, too, because as I prefer fishing spring creeks to any other kind of trout water, the pastoralist in me was already salivating. What is water—flowing, still, or tidal—but a blank sheet on which to inscribe our aspirations? "A field of water," Thoreau says, "betrays the spirit that is in the air."

I return to Longhorn Ranch water because Nick Lyons set his masterful memoir, *Spring Creek,* and part of the shorter, equally lyrical *Sphinx Mountain and Brown Trout* here after several extended stays. Books lead us on. I don't think it is possible to read *Spring Creek* or Kevin Begos's beautifully crafted limited-edition *Sphinx Mountain* book and not want to explore the Madison Valley waters where they originated. Both works are illustrated by wife Mari Lyons in her superb impressionistic style, thereby adding yet another layer of readerly and visual enjoyment. She, too, took her cues from the O'Dell landscape. For my part, in the grip of eternal curiosity, a couple of visits have hardly been enough to fill my pilgrim yearnings.

Some areas of the creek have silted in and shallowed, but efforts in judicious restoration have begun on a couple of thousand feet of its upper stretch to remove sediment, narrow runs, and deepen holes. Today the biggest trout, including Rodger's pair of glorious 20-inch browns, came from that area, so the reclamation work thus far looks extremely promising and ties in well with a highly successful, widely publicized, and much heralded wetlands restoration project on Jeff Laszlo's Granger Ranch upstream to the south.

Finicky and shy, tucked beneath treeless meadow cutbanks to escape summer's sun, which drifted like a giant yellow indicator in the August sky, the gorgeously marked and colored-up wild browns came intermittently to our hands on various small dries, mostly terrestrial patterns (the major summer hatches were over) tied on 6X and 7X tippet. Each fish, especially

Rodger's beautiful browns, I liked to think, might have been a descendant of those alligators Nick and ranch owner Herb Wellington (dedicatee of *Spring Creek*) and his other guests (A. J. McClane, Craig Mathews, Datus Proper, to name a few of the angling legends) caught and released more than two decades ago.

On the way out of the valley, we stopped at Le Fevre Point and looked back and down to survey the creek's interior distances and vistas. *Oohs* and *aahs* abounded. Sometimes all we need for pleasure and satisfaction is laid amply at our feet. Our wish is that we do our part well enough not to screw up the outcome. It's difficult not to wax lyrical about such rare, fleeting moments: I was on a pilgrimage and in the right frame of angling mind, and, speaking for my fishing partners as well, it would have been impossible to be disappointed in that little simulacrum of paradise no matter what the catch rate happened to be. Nick said it best: "Fly-fishing thrums with harmonies."

More and more, I realize the truth of Thoreau's proclamation that we fish all our lives without knowing that it isn't fish we are really after. It's something deeper, larger, and more lasting. Something like a genuine way of being in the world, something like becoming part of a web of circumstance that humbles us at the very moment it ennobles us. Stand anywhere in that dazzling, interlaced riverine cornucopia where fish, birds, mammals, and insects down to the smallest midges thrive, and it is possible to see that there are rare days when even the tiniest things seem connected to everything else, and the smallest gesture, the thinnest filament, is not an inconsequential integer but is linked to the whole fabric of earth, sky, and water, where it is possible to find yourself becoming part of what Datus Proper once called a "four-dimensional world of sense and spirit." It's what we passionate fly fishers live for, what we will go far to protect, what we will spill gallons of ink in praising, what we care to share with like-minded friends and lovers. The world comes back at us in all its stark reality soon enough, but when is that brief moment of splendor, before loss sets in, not worth the price of admission?

Honey Ants on the
Railroad Ranch

15 August 2013

Back again to the fabled and excruciatingly difficult, hand-wringing, teeth-gnashing, hair-pulling Railroad Ranch section of Idaho's Henry's Fork of the Snake River. On its hyper-demanding water, with its super-fussy fish, everything I thought I knew about fishing was put to the severest test; every skill I thought I possessed was inadequate; every cherished image of myself as an angler proved false. My Waterloo, my Armageddon. Dry fly water that attracts anglers from all around the world to test their hand, only to be what—vanquished? Humiliated? Humbled? Tom McGuane's statement in *The Longest Silence* that "the Henry's Fork has brought so many to tears," hits the nail on the head in a single stroke. It helps to be a masochist with a taste for humble pie.

A year ago today Bob Hendrix, Dennis Hess, and I played hooky from the Madison and fished the Fork on our own. Babes in the woods, so to speak, with commensurate modest results, a sprinkling of small catches by Bob and Dennis and nothing for me over a long, long day of casting, changing up, and not just hoping for better results, but under my breath muttering entreaties to God for deliverance. By the time I was done, I had bargained away most of my future. Last year's trip was the first time I'd been back to the Railroad Ranch in many years. Today, twelve months later, there is a twist on the old story of empty handedness, but it requires a backstory.

I have history with the Henry's Fork. One day, curious about the hype I'd heard touting the Harriman State Park section as exceptional dry fly water, I drove south from my rental cabin at Staley Springs to Island Park, and laid eyes on it for the first time. That was more than two decades ago, on 14 August 1991, according to my angling journal.

During the next several years I fished its eight-mile-long section just enough to become enamored of its water (the biggest, baddest spring creek in existence), but not skilled enough to become adept at catching its great fish. Things came to a head for me one still, hot August day when I was sneaking along the bank between Osborne Rapids and Osborne Bridge looking for "heads"—the large surface-feeding rainbows for which the river is famous. I found a 20-inch-plus bruiser on a rhythmic rise, and threw a downstream cast with a foam beetle. The fabulous creature came up and took the beetle, but in my impatience and inexperience I struck too soon and pulled the fly, with its small gap, out of the trout's mouth, and that was that. No one else saw the deed, however, and I was saved the extra embarrassment of being a public dunce.

That is, except in my own heart and the telltale pit I felt in my gut, which on some days even now I can still feel. It's unnerving how certain fish take such ferocious hold in memory. That trout must have slept with God at some time in its life. And though it was not much consolation, I learned later that being humiliated on that part of the Henry's Fork is pretty much the standard. It seemed to be such an impossible place to fish that I wanted to complain to someone—anyone—that I deserved better treatment. To me, the Harriman Ranch water always lends new meaning to the word *heartbreaking*.

So, except for occasional trips to the Fork's rough-and-tumble Box Canyon, below Island Park Reservoir, where in its fast currents the fish were decidedly more opportunistic and cooperative, and to the easy-to-fish Henry's Lake outlet stream on the Nature Conservancy tract at Flat Ranch (which held some delightful surprises in trout numbers and size and its portion of solitude), I stayed away from the Harriman Ranch water altogether for a long time. I admit, it was a cowardly thing to do, especially because it was a period when the river was experiencing hard times caused by severely restricted winter flows, anchor ice, trumpeter swan infestation, siltation, and who knows what else? All those trials and tribulations reduced trout populations severely. The river Ernest Schwiebert once called the best dry fly stream in the West looked like a dubious destination to the uninitiated by the early to mid-2000s.

I did my meager part (easing my guilty conscience along the way) by joining the Henry's Fork Foundation and even lending a volunteer hand on a few cleanup tasks. I kept holding my breath, though: maybe someday conditions would improve and I'd go back as an angler, ready and eager. In fact, I often mused that, if I could fish only one place for the rest of my life, it would be the Ranch section of the Henry's Fork. Although the learning process would be so slow as to seem glacial, I reasoned that if I could fish that river often in all its various guises, temperaments, moods, and conditions, I could probably confidently fish almost any other trout stream on Earth. Given the Railroad Ranch's astonishing insect populations, its stunning geographical setting, and its drop-dead gorgeous rainbow trout, I kept telling myself that the humiliation of a steep learning curve ought to be worth every minute of effort. Who knows? I might even come out of the process a better person.

Meanwhile, the Madison, my grand home-away-from-home river, was filling my needs and then some.

A couple of months after Hendrix, Hess, and I washed out on the Fork last year, I bought a copy of John McDaniel's 2012 book, *Fly Fishing the Harriman Ranch of the Henry's Fork of the Snake River: Lessons Learned and Friends Made Sight Fishing to Selective Trout* and read it over last winter and spring and early summer with a close eye and a ready pen, circling, underlining, making marginal notes as I went, if only to talk back to its author, who I thought at first must be exaggerating his success.

When I came to study McDaniel's intriguing book, with its mouthful of a title, I was delighted to find that he's a retired anthropology professor, an academic like myself, who had done exactly what I fantasized I might have done had my life entered a different register. Only instead of wimping out and whining and gnashing his teeth, McDaniel, who started fishing the Harriman section in 1983 and then guiding summers on it in 1998, stuck with the place through thick and thin. The book is a love song to a unique public river. It records his journey from attraction (which I get) to mastery (which I will never get) on trout "as difficult to hook as any in the world of fly fishing." Given my dismal history with the Harriman Ranch section, I hoped Professor McDaniel's book at least would change my belief in its impossibility.

The only thing better than reading *Fly Fishing the Harriman Ranch* is fishing with the author himself, which brings me to today because Bob Hendrix and I reserved a trip with McDaniel. Masochist that I am, having been too long without a proper ass whipping, and feeling a bit more able than I once was as a result of reading his tome, I screwed up my courage and returned to face the dreaded Ranch again.

Today was a long day on the water. Sunny and warm but the water was cool enough to keep us body-temperate. In the afternoon a wind came up that made casting our cane rods a bit more demanding than usual. My 7 1/2-foot, 5-weight Orvis Battenkill wasn't always the best choice, but I played the hand I had dealt myself, even though I might have fared better with a longer graphite rod. Not making excuses, but just sayin'. . . .

The river is shallow enough in most places to wade across almost anywhere you choose, and standing in it, looking at its broad, flat surface unbroken in most places by boulders, log jams, or obstructions, is like looking at a silvered, dimpled mirror. Gaze at it long enough on a cloudless summer day, and you begin to understand how the Narcissus in all of us, angling for truth, beauty, love, and the catch of a lifetime, could lose balance, plunge in, and drown seeking his fleeting image in the alluring waters. Fish hard for nine hours straight on a brilliant summer day, and there comes a point when all of it—the whole collective of earth, sky, river, ospreys, sandhill cranes, cedar waxwings, muskrats, aquatic foliage, dragon flies, anglers, even a noisome aerial mapping drone—becomes surreal and hallucinatory, and you enter a dreamlike state where everything bleeds into everything else, boundaries blur, and you hold your breath waiting for the strike that does not come. Not for nothing the painter Galen Mercer labeled it "bewitchingly beautiful."

We did have strikes today—Bob and I had nine of them—so McDaniel's guiding is as good as his writing. We were supremely lucky to be present at a full-blown honey ant hatch, an event some anglers would give their eyeteeth to experience. I am not saying fishing today wasn't frustrating, but the adrenaline-rush action of hefty rainbows gluttonously rising for those oddball honey ants (are they aquatic wasps or land-born termites?) was fast, exciting, and truly memorable despite our losing *every* whopper we hooked, *every single one*, including the crowning glory of the day: Bob's 26-inch giant at Third Channel that popped the hook just inches from John's outstretched net. It was a larger trophy than any mentioned in McDaniel's book, a bigger monster than any he had seen in recent memory, a fish that qualified for legendary status, and while I might have been inclined to commit suicide or shoot the guide were it my lost fish, the equanimity that gentleman Bob Hendrix displayed underscored the true soulful meaning of the Railroad Ranch's culture: "lessons learned and friends made."

Come to think of it, not just the Harriman Ranch culture, but the true spirit of fly fishing everywhere. Even though all our fish got away, McDaniel himself, suitably apologetic for the lost bruiser, proclaimed the day a success, and if *success* can be equated with *memorable*, then who am I to disagree? Maybe McDaniel is correct—maybe the Ranch waters are not impossible, as I have long thought, but merely perplexing. Like The Dude, The Harriman Ranch water abides. I think I can live with that until the next humiliation.

Strange Courage

30 August 2013

The usual routine for wrapping up an annual fishing sojourn in Montana. I stowed my drift boat and trailer behind Jim Harrison's writing studio. With luck next spring some of the Hungarian partridge that frequent his place will nest again under the axle and he'll be able to send me humorous reports about the brood's progress. Meantime I kept a wary eye out for rattlers in that little hinterland behind the bungalow. Then to Chico Hot Springs where Kate and I took one of the small guest rooms on the third floor of the main lodge. Trudge up, trudge down. Not the most convenient accommodation, but frill-free and pet friendly for Meadow, our travel companion.

Kate stayed at Chico to take the thermal waters while I went to DePuy's Spring Creek to take the chilly waters. Only two other anglers signed up, so I had free passage all over the creek. I fished the bridge run above Dick's Pond where Walter Bennett and Paul Schullery and I have spent some pleasant hours in recent times. An easy place to navigate and wade, as long as you keep close to the bank. The currents are tricky and make for challenging presentations.

Moss and weeds in the water. *Cast, drift, clean flies, repeat process.* Ninety minutes of that without one iota of success. Then a small brown jumped the emerger, and gradually action picked up and fish slowly began working on pale morning duns as did a squadron of aerobatic cedar waxwings flitting around my head. I could watch their aerial acrobatics all day. A nice brown started working rhythmically at the far edge of the creek bank opposite me, and I kept my sights on it as I re-rigged with a PMD Sparkle Dun on 6X, trailed by a nondescript #20 olive emerger on 7X. First cast, the fish came up to look at the dun, decided it didn't like what it saw, then turned and slowly sucked in the emerger. I saw the take under the water and made a quick solid hook set. Steady side pressure kept the trout out of the weeds and into the net. An 18-inch brown, deep bodied and beautifully marked. A gem out of DePuy's bounteous, limpid waters. Most satisfying fish of the entire month, and one that coincided with a perfect storm of correspondences.

Almost without warning, a darkened sky snuck up behind me from a compass direction I had been ignoring. A downpour set in, so I trundled back to the truck to wait it out. I shed my gear, turned on the heater to dry off, opened a Pepsi from my cooler, ate a half bagel with cream cheese saved from breakfast at Chico, then remembered I had some oatmeal cookies in the backseat of my truck for dessert. Lunch at Babbo could not have tasted better. Smoked the rest of a Macanudo cigar while the rain and storm lashed on, the heavy drops *tat-a-tat-tating* on the roof, even as the clouds came down so close I could hardly make out the line of Absarokas to the east. Adult yellow warblers flitted in and out of the nearby streamside willows like quick bursts of sunlight, *here we are, there we go.* The air temperature chilled to sixty-two degrees, a far cry from the forecasted ninety. Something sublime and evanescent was in the air, like sweet music, Ralph Vaughan Williams's "The Lark Ascending" coming closest to the moment.

Scribbled in my vest-pocket notebook with sudden sad realization that nothing I wrote could adequately contain the ecstatic moment, which moved so fast through a series of changes of wind, light, temperature, and mood that I felt breathless and broke out in an involuntary laugh, though slap-my-knee humor was the last thing on my mind. But I felt light inside, buoyant and weightless. And through all the commotion, the creek flowed on unabated toward the great Yellowstone, carrying all I saw with it before I was able to get a handle on the previous minute, or the ones before that. Thoreau was onto something righteous when he said, "Time is but the stream I go afishing in."

I can't explain why, in the rush of activity, I was so content, but it was a deliriously happy moment, one of those rare times of giddy well-being when everything falls into place and things happen as you always wished they would. A month of slow fishing coalesces into a prime moment, an unexpected spot of time. A nice fish is feeding, you make a good cast, and one of the flies looks sexy enough for a bite, and even the gossamer-thin tippet holds without breaking, a rarity in itself. An earned moment, a boost in confidence, sure, but it is way more than that, way more than an uptick on the physical skills meter. It has to do with the felt but often unseen connections to the whole surround. For a brief instant, a veil lifts, and we are not just *in* nature, but *of* it, mystical and naïve as that sounds. I suppose, though, much as we wish for a continuous stream of numinous highs, a whole opera made up of arias, if such success happened more often than it actually does, we might become sated or, worse yet, jaded. I never thought I'd say this, but may the fish gods keep that from ever happening.

After lunch, the rain subsided. I changed into a dry shirt and went back to the same gliding run of DePuy's. As afternoon wore on, sulphurs started popping, the word went out in the fishy kingdom, and the trout multitudes began stirring in earnest. It was the most energetic top-water activity I had seen in any one place all month. I got two more browns and one cutthroat, each more lovely in their darkly burnished colors than the one before it, but they required changing flies often, as no single pattern worked consistently and I had numerous refusals as well. Five of my half-dozen fish today were on Xinked plain-Jane emergers tied on 7X tippet and fished in the film or just below it. Best of all, I did not lose a fish today. Just lucky, I guess. Around 5 p.m. I quit after a thirty-minute stretch during which I could not fool another trout and realized they had my number and were sticking it to me in their fishy way. Steinbeck on fishing: "It has always been my private conviction that any man who puts his intelligence up against a fish and loses had it coming." Enough abuse: I took my rod and got out of there.

I stopped at the Harrisons' house on the way back to Chico. I had missed Jim when I dropped off my boat. Earlier today he had left a message on my cell phone, his nasally smoker's voice sounding like it has been filtered through sandpaper. "Come for a beverage when you're done, Bobby. Okay. Bye-bye." So I stopped.

I had not seen him since our two so-so afternoons of fishing on the Yellowstone River in late July when we floated from Carbola to Point of Rocks, then Carter's Bridge to Mayor's Landing. SLOW action on a few suicidal fish, the way it's been during these recent dog-day summers the last several years. The heat enervates Jim so our floats were short. The after-effects of his brutal shingles affliction and a radical back operation last year makes it difficult to predict how he will feel day to day, so he has to take each day as it comes, though nothing keeps him from his appointed daily rounds at the writing desk. The monster browns the Yellowstone is famous for keep eluding us, though he always tells that story of pulling his fly away from what he thought was an otter and realizing too late that it was a giant brown trout.

Every year, Jim gives me a food gift for the trip back to Ohio. This time it's a fennel salami from Salumi, the Batali family salumeria in Seattle. Linda was at the house, presiding over dinner preparations in her expert way, and so was daughter Anna. We gathered around the worn wooden kitchen table as we always do, opened a bottle of Tempier Bandol, nibbled some exotic cheese and tart olives, and swapped stories. Jim hadn't fished much lately and he was aggrieved by that, though Peter Matthiessen, who Jim has known since their days at Stony Brook in the 1960s, had arrived for their annual Yellowstone fishing junket, for which he had high hopes, despite Peter's ailing health. But Jim always likes to hear my latest angling report, though the super-stealthy 7X stuff is no longer his game, if indeed it ever was. "I was a poor poet and they let me fish for free," he wheezed, after I told him DePuy's daily rod fee is now $100. I never tire of hearing his tales about the Paradise Valley spring creeks in the late 1960s when he and Brautigan, McGuane, and Chatham first discovered the area. I'm just a lowly footnote to their body of pioneering angling work.

More than that, though, today's entry would be grievously incomplete if I neglected what happened next. One of those arresting experiences occurred that, let's face it, rivals and perhaps even eclipses all the fishing memories I'll ever have. It wasn't part of my fishing life per se, and yet it was. Realism trumped romanticism; reality outmuscled myth.

Doug and Andrea Peacock arrived, and Doug immediately removed his shirt. He and Jim sat shirtless at the table because the lingering effects of their back and heart surgeries made them so super-sensitive to touch that even the minimal weight of a shirt on skin was unbearable. Then Peter Matthiessen, who had arrived earlier in the day, came down from napping in an upstairs bedroom and joined the kitchen group. In his mid-eighties, tall, long-limbed, still imperially handsome, he looked gaunt and frail from chemo treatments. It was a somber moment when no matter how socially well-schooled or civilly mannered you are, no matter how tough and seasoned you think you are, you still don't know what the hell to say, so better to say nothing and not risk betraying your inadequacy.

I excused myself, afraid that had I stayed longer I would have wept like a child to see three of my elder contemporaries, longtime literary heroes renowned for their physical endurance and vitality, beset with body betrayals. Three great lions, three of the greatest writers, novelists, poets of my time, all of whom were not just intrepid but were ageless forces of nature (in my mind, anyway), reduced to taking it gingerly, step by step. But the next day would be a fishing day, a tradition renewed among friends. More power to them. Poet and physician William Carlos Williams understood the "strange courage" such shining stars give us. Can we ever ask for more from the people we most admire?

Looking for Joe Brooks

1 September 2013

Moved slowly yesterday morning, the grizzled visages of Peacock, Harrison, and Matthiessen still with me when I woke. Into Livingston to hunt for books at Saxe and Fryer's and Elk River Books. This quest too is part of my angling routine. Fisherman's luck comes in all shapes and sizes: at Elk River I found a cloth-bound ex-library copy of Joe Brooks's encyclopedic *Complete Guide to Fishing Across North America* and snapped it up for $5. His book is as hefty as a trophy trout. Published in 1966, much of its information is dated, but his laudatory assessment of Montana as a fishing destination remains accurate and true.

Brooks's photograph of the Wall of Fame in Dan Bailey's Fly Shop, which features a host of wooden plaques with tracings of trout over four pounds, sent me again to the original site. I snooped around Bailey's bargain room but failed to find anything I couldn't live without, except a redolent memory of the first time I entered Bailey's decades ago and saw a gang of local women tying flies here. That whole situation gone now but not forgotten, because of Tom McGuane's movie, *Rancho Deluxe,* where a scene with those women is preserved like a time capsule. I read just about every one of the Wall of Fame plaques, too, not without a little envy for the anglers who scored such prodigious trout. McGuane is on the wall; so is Danny Lahren. Joe and Mary Brooks (she held her own as an angler) account for several four- and five-pounders, all from the Yellowstone River on big Muddler-type streamer flies.

Kate and I made it to Nelson's Spring Creek Ranch, south of Livingston, about 4 p.m. yesterday. It's our final stop before driving east. What's not to like about the place? Staying here is like visiting family, if your family happens to be fourth-generation owners of a working cattle ranch, a fish-propagating business, and a world-class trout stream. And it's pet friendly, so Meadow fits in and helps me fish by pointing out rising trout.

No fishing last evening. Instead talked again with Roger about Joe Brooks, who fished the creek starting in the early 1950s and gradually helped give it its reputation and put it on the map. It was Brooks who suggested to Ed Nelson, Roger's father, that the creek become a fee fishery around 1960 or so. That was several years after Joe and Mary began spending summers in one of the ranch's unused outbuildings. Before dark I wandered down to the creek and sat on the commemorative bench (courtesy of the Joe Brooks Chapter of Trout Unlimited) overlooking a key run, and jotted some journal entries as I watched trout rising eagerly up and down the line to spinners, a sight no doubt that stirred Joe and Mary Brooks and their hosts, Edwin and Helen Nelson, as it stirred me.

More than any other, Brooks's *Complete Book of Fly Fishing,* a patient, generous, inspiring, and above all, readable book, profoundly influenced me when I was just starting out in fly fishing in the mid-1950s. I checked it out repeatedly from the Norwalk Public Library. It was the right book to come into the hands of an utter neophyte. We never quite shake off our formative early influences. Thinking about Brooks, meditating on his reputation as a world-class angler and by all

Memorial bench at Nelson's Spring Creek.
Credit: Robert DeMott

accounts a fine gentleman, too, I am struck that one aspect of fly fishing I'm thoroughly enamored with is its individual histories, its maker's and shaker's stories, whose presences and accomplishments lend a human face to fly fishing. But there is the salvation angle as well that has hooked me. I'd heard that Brooks was a heavy boozer at one point in his life, but cleaned up after marrying Mary. Love and fly fishing brought him a new lease and he made the most of it, a development I can relate to personally in my redemptive life with Kate the past six years. I was not a problem drinker, but I had my share of waywardness to redeem.

In his eulogy for Brooks, A. J. McClane, another of the guiding angling lights of my youth, said: "Buried in Livingston, Montana, the country he loved, he is home again." That's the kind of information that can't be ignored. So this morning, I swallowed part of my daily rod fee and postponed fishing in order to seek out Brooks's gravesite. It felt necessary to pay homage to him before casting the first fly of the day on water he helped make renowned. I've been meaning to do this for a couple of years and at last the time was right. No more excuses.

Kate and I found his and Mary's plot south of Livingston in the unpretentious Park View Memorial Gardens off East River Road on a rise above the Yellowstone River. There was no headstone or raised marker, just a modest, unadorned inground marker that took us nearly an hour to locate.

> JOSEPH W. BROOKS JR
> MARYLAND
> BM2 US COAST GUARD RES
> WORLD WAR II
> SEPT 29 1901 SEPT 20 1972

Lefty Kreh, arguably Brooks's most accomplished disciple, once said that fly fishermen under the age of fifty have probably never heard of Brooks, but "owe him a huge debt of gratitude." So I was heartened last spring on a fishing jaunt through Brooks's native Maryland to discover that there is an imposing brick-and-stone memorial dedicated to him on the banks of Big Hunting Creek. But there is no extended biography of him, as there is for other angling eminences such as Lee Wulff, George Griffith, G. E. M. Skues, and Frederic Halford, say, though I've heard there is a documentary film on Brooks in production that I hope sees the light of day. I know there's plenty of film footage of Brooks from the 1960s when he appeared on the

ABC television series *The American Sportsman*. I have a hunch Brooks has
been eclipsed by the rising tide of narrow-gauge technical experts, but that's
a pity as he still has much to teach us both in skill and in attitude. My visit
to pay respects was forty years overdue, but better late than never. Before I
ever wet a line today, I had made the catch of the day. Everything else would
be gravy.

After the cemetery excursion, I watched the frenzied feeding activity in
Nelson's commercial fish sluices for a while. It is possible to see there the
commodity value of rainbow trout, the opposite side of viewing them as
wild, mystical, or holy creatures, though of course they are that too in
many peoples' eyes. Best not to forget that, where trout are concerned,
dollars-and-cents economy undergirds many of our exalted notions, a
point made brilliantly by Anders Halverson in *An Entirely Synthetic Fish:
How Rainbow Trout Beguiled America and Overran the World,* a book that
ought to be required reading for every angler with trout stars in his or
her eyes.

Reality check aside, I walked down to the creek proper, rigged up a
9-foot, 4-weight Winston, started fishing, and kept at it all day long. This
is my thirtieth day of fishing out of the last thirty-four days. We start for
home tomorrow, so this afternoon I've been trying to land a fish on ridiculously small-gauge tippet. Difficult conditions, too: sunny and bright,
which meant relying on 7X and 8X tippet at the end of long leaders, 12
feet long and more to get an edge, real or imagined, on Nelson's finicky
fish. I had eight fish on today and brought in five (on 7X) but the ones
that got away (on 8X) were the most memorable and took part of my heart
with them.

Stalked and hunted and waited all afternoon for the right setup to present itself with a regularly feeding fish; finally just below the corral section I
found a hefty rhythmic riser. Crouched down and stalked as close as I dared
on my hands and knees and cast over that rainbow repeatedly before it finally
took my tiny sulphur emerger, though I came back too fast and hard, and
the 8X tippet snapped. A bit later farther up the same run, I had on a nice
cutthroat about 18 inches on the 8X dropper, but that one threw the tiny
hook, so there went my last chance to get a fish on 8X, which was my insane

goal all afternoon. But I should have been forewarned. I once heard Mike Lawson confess, "I'm not an 8X kind of guy." That from the man who wrote the Bible, *Spring Creeks*. So while I ought to know better and am thoroughly forewarned, my Quixotic quest continues.

Some drop-dead gorgeous fish in Nelson's. I watched them cruising the larger pools and setting up in various runs. I saw and/or spooked a number of 20-inch to 22-inch trout, an impressive array of fish destined to make my knees weak and mouth salivate. Their size and amplitude reminded me of the accommodating bruisers Craig Nova, Rodger Gaulding, Dennis Hess, and I used to encounter on McCoy's Spring Creeks in Dillon back in the day. Mouthwatering, tackle-straining trout big enough to get an otherwise reasonable human being talking to himself.

Today's trout, however, made me wish longingly for a pellet or worm fly because hardly any fish were taking sulphur duns, though from 3:30 p.m. to about 6 p.m. there were plenty of bugs on the water. Tried longer dropper, shorter dropper, various dry and wet patterns and styles, but good fortune today was sporadic and inconsistent. Unlike McCoy's eager fish, or those enormous 2-foot-long-plus triploid rainbows Kate and I caught without much difficulty on the Soque River in North Georgia a few years ago, Nel-

son's fish are tough to fool—the toughest I've encountered in a while. It's the kind of fishing where the trout rub it in my face, refuse my offerings with impunity and malice of forethought. All the Paradise Valley spring creeks are demanding, but I think Nelson's is the most demanding. Still, it is pleasant to be rewarded now and then. Joe Brooks: "The satisfaction an angler derives from fooling a distrustful trout is one of the things that make fly fishing." By that measure I got my money's worth today. Viva Joe Brooks!

Meadow pointing trout on Nelson's Spring Creek. Credit: Kate Fox

Déjà Vu All Over Again

13 August 2014

Last evening Kate and I hosted our friends Bob and Mary Hendrix and Harold and Katie Perkins for dinner at our rental cabin. California meets Ohio. We ate and drank, we told stories, we laughed. Hopes for today's fishing were sky high, despite the fact that when Bob and I got back from another ass-whooping on the Henry's Fork yesterday (concluding with a forty-minute march from Bonefish Flats to the truck at day's end), the temperature of the Madison near the cabin stood at sixty-eight degrees, dangerously close to the cease-fishing range. But overnight a good rain and cooldown moved in and prospects turned cheery once again.

On the Madison today I saw two anglers taking turns nymphing the same run over and over. While one fished the other would recline on the bank, leisurely as you please, and soak it all in between puffs on a cigar; then, as if on cue, they would switch roles without ever moving from that spot. I watched them for about fifteen minutes on my way in, and then again another ten minutes or so on my way upriver. I was standing on the rise above and behind them so I could not tell what flies they were using under their outsized indicators (one used white, the other yellow), but they cast the exact same length of line each time and ran the flies through the exact same run over and over without ever taking more than a step or two up or down the bank. Fascinated by the laid-back French anglers on the Seine River in Paris, who rarely caught anything of note, Steinbeck said once in his humorous essay "On Fishing," that he considered himself the foremost observer of other people's fishing, success notwithstanding. I can see why. Voyeurism has its attraction. I never saw either man catch a fish, but it was mesmerizing to watch them. *No fish? So what!* They looked at ease with themselves and their method, which I guess is what matters most.

They reminded me of a stranger I saw once years ago on the Stanislaus River in northern California. He issued forth from a beat-up old VW microbus (its windows plastered with Grateful Dead stickers), set up his three-legged stool at the river's edge, put on his floppy oilskin hat (it was a bluebird day), and cast his fly, which looked to me like a long section of yellow yarn. His casting was beautiful and accurate and rhythmic, and pretty soon a couple of children who were camping nearby came over to stand by him and watch the goings-on. He apparently did not care whether he caught fish or not, and I guess he hoped that enticing one to strike would be reward enough. The assembled group of children soon got impatient with his fishless aestheticism and quit the field. But years before I ever heard about anglers on the West Branch of the Delaware River casting flies that were not just barbless, but hookless as well, Bartleby the Fisherman was plying his metaphysical game. He preferred not to, that lone angler way back then already bravely hinting at a vanguard method, as a practical way of bridging the gap between old-style acquisitiveness and new ecological sensibilities, like today's fascination with the Zen-like Japanese Tenkara fishing style. But then perhaps it's as simple as saying Mr. Bartleby had read Steinbeck's "On Fishing."

Bob, Katie, Harold, and I—we all got into some fish today, the best being Bob's 17-inch brown on a beetle pattern. Fishing was, once again, sporadic for us all morning. I worked a double nymph setup with my brand new 9-foot Loomis NRX Lite Presentation 5-weight rod and managed a couple of smallish rainbows. It cast like a dream, even with a 12-foot leader and tandem nymphs—a brown Serendipity on the upper tag and a red-collared "French" Pheasant Tail on the lower tag—under a small indicator and two small split shot pinched at the bottom of the leader, drop-shot style. Light in the hand, responsive, tracked well, nicely balanced, accurate in close and at a distance. I could feel the nymphs right down to my rod hand. All the hype about the rod was true. I could hardly ask for better.

How to say this? What karmic retribution has come my way? Had the fish gods, the regulators of angling justice, taken note of my indiscretions and stored them up for future use against me? Who knows? Fanciful guesses aside, the undisputed fact is that this is the fourth year in a row, on almost exactly the same day, in almost exactly the same spot, I've busted a fly rod. This has to be some sort of weird smash record. Mid-August, just down-stream from $3 Bridge on the Madison River, so it must be the time and the place to break another rod! Four for four, no less!

In 2011 (August 15) it was my 10-foot, 4-weight Helios; in 2012 (August 15) it was my 9-foot, 4-weight Loomis GLX Stream Dance; in 2013 (August 13) it was one of the two tips on my forty-year-old Orvis Battenkill bamboo (especially heartbreaking and ten full months coming back from Orvis's repair shop); today it was my brand new NRX, a rod I felt especially enamored of, not only because it had shown so well in one of the Yellowstone Angler's fly rod Shootouts, but because I bought it for a song, more or less, having sold a couple of older graphite rods before I laid money on the barrel-head for this one, thereby substantially easing my conscience and my wallet.

There was something different about today, though. I took full respon-sibility for breaking the other three rods by clumsy accident or errant back-casts, but today's break was in a category of its own, because a fish caused it. After I passed the cigar boys on my way back upriver, I drifted nymphs through a deep slot about twenty feet out from the bank. A solid fish took the Pheasant Tail, made a strong run into heavy current before I got it snug on the reel and worked it to within a foot of my outstretched net. Then *POW!* Like a gunshot or a firecracker going off, the top of the second section of the NRX exploded. "*Déjà vu* all over again" in Yogi Berra's immortal words. This time I had my wits about me and I used the broken upper sections of the rod to steer the fish, a hefty 18-inch brown, into my long-handled net.

Apparently the fourth time is a charm. I took a couple of photos, then, because I didn't feel like walking back to the truck and rigging up another rod, I quit and watched my friends fish instead, admiring their skill and all the while composing a letter in my head to send to the parent company Shi-mano explaining why I refused to pay the $100 fee for an expedited Loomis replacement rod. The fault this time was neither in the stars nor in myself, but in the rod, broken, for the first time in my life, by a fish. Surely the com-pany higher-ups will honor that.

The Fisher as He Fishes

1 September 2014

Forty-ninth day of fishing this year, which equals around 150 pages in my journal thus far. Montana sojourn drawing to an end. It started with a memorable late April week on the Ruby Habitat Foundation's Woodson Ranch in Sheridan fishing a *Baetis* hatch in a snowstorm and is closing out here once again on Nelson's Spring Creek fishing midge patterns the size of pinheads in pre-autumn weather. Between then and now, in my first year of full retirement, I've fished all over—Ohio, West Virginia, Michigan, Maryland, Pennsylvania, Maine, and Florida. I closed out my professorial life for good in 2013. Now instead of classes structuring my day, it's writing, gardening, cooking, fishing, and upland bird hunting. The pleasures of retirement for a dyed-in-the-wool outdoor geezer. I should feel guilty but I don't, as long as I keep learning new tricks to keep the game lively.

I have been trout-obsessed for too long, too trout-centric, and need to mend my ways. I realized that two years ago when on a single January day I made a modest big-fish slam on baby tarpon, redfish, and snook in Florida. They piqued my interest in other species. Now, for the first time ever, there were carp in my life. I've been hearing enticing accounts about carp fishing for years but never tried it until Jerry Dennis invited me up in late May to fish with him in Lake Michigan. We started in bone-chilling, waist-deep water, casting to fast-moving fish that scurried by us and were gone in a nanosecond. After an hour of fruitless casting even my brain was numb. Problem solved when we turned toward shore and waded in among more leisurely carp cruising and tailing in the warmer, shallower flats of Grand Traverse Bay. Shoals of carp, battalions of carp, armadas of kingly and queenly carp. Royal flotillas with fish as big as torpedoes doing their carpy business right under our noses.

We spooked a number of fish by errant casts and sloppy presentations. Under a bright sun, our fly lines' shadows would fire their jets. Carp are more challenging and wary than I would have thought. They have their own allure. They are not as dazzlingly colorful as trout, but are beautiful in their own stolid, resolute way. They reminded me of the fallfish I caught earlier this summer on the Androscoggin in Maine and for which I felt enormous affection and found in them a kind of beauty that belied their chub origins, especially a bruiser all of 2 inches in length, a fish so small that it looked as though the nymph had caught it rather than the other way around.

Anyway, seeing carp take the fly, whether it was stripped or stationary, has a jarring immediacy all of its own. Then hang on for dear life. Jerry and I started off with a double, then in the next hour or so landed three or four more each. They were big—several were around twenty pounds—and I was glad for an 8-weight rod, ample backing, and stout tippet. Carp don't sizzle the way bonefish do on their first run for the horizon, but they plow forward, more like a redfish, in a relentless, deliberate, bulldog kind of way on long runs. They're more like fullbacks than wide receivers. But keep steady pressure on and they eventually tire more quickly than I would have imagined. Grab a tired carp by its tail, steady it in the water, and pop the jig fly from its mouth. No mess or fuss and straight away everyone involved is back in business.

Lake fishing seems to invite participation and digressions. What comes, comes in due course; what happens, happens organically. In July my Ohio University colleague Pat Washburn and I fished Lake Snowden near home, in his 17-foot Lund walleye boat, a sleek, carpeted craft that puts my creaky old drift boat to shame. Lake fishermen have it easy, what with a big outboard and an electric trolling motor to get them around. We cruised around like royalty in and out of the scallop-edged shoreline working the foot pedal on the trolling motor and casting popping bugs and fluffy attractor dries under drooping tree branches and over inky drop-offs and through likely looking weed patches.

A relaxing way to spend a warm summer afternoon poking along in a leisurely manner, without one iota of angling pressure or anxiety, a deserved, luxurious respite from hatch matching, curve casts, and drag-free floats. And of course as we lazed along in our measured periplum, we were solving this and that local and global problem, as ex-professors are wont to do, all the while dealing with maniacal sunfish attacking our lures with abandon, and every once in a while a feisty largemouth, with an appetite bigger than its modest size, smashing a popping bug like a juggernaut. Snowden opened its coffers and placed its scaly gifts in our hands. It answered our prayers and gave us "our daily fish," in the great Pablo Neruda's words. Home-water fly fishing reduced to its least-complicated equations.

A few busy days to catch up with and I'll be current in this journal. On August 29, got my last fishes on the Madison for this year: an 18-inch rainbow and a 15-inch brown, both on a pink-post caddis pattern I got from Frontier Anglers' guide Mike Saputo a few weeks ago when he and I and Rodger Gaulding floated the Beaverhead. The brown, after leading me helter-skelter downstream on a merry chase, came to hand at dusk, emerging out of the darkening water like a dream suddenly given form, substance, and color. The whole mystery of the moment took my breath away, and once released, that surprising butter-belly was gone, dissolved back into its watery medium as if it had been a sleight-of-hand trick all along, a brief glimpse behind reality's veil. But its soul, as Ezra Pound once said, still "floats over the stream/Like a little wafer of light."

A bit mystical and starry-eyed perhaps, but a fitting exclamation point anyway on a fine sojourn out here this summer. The last two weeks on the Madison were spectacular, with dry-fly activity as strong as I've witnessed in a number of years. The cool weather front and afternoon rainstorms dropped the water from a dangerously unfishable sixty-nine to sixty-one degrees in a matter of a few days. Ideal temperate zone for jump-starting bug and fish activity. Nights have been in the forties and have kept a check on rising air and water temperatures. Nearly daily rain in the valley equaled snow above 8,000 feet on the peaks of the Madison Range, so even in the latter weeks of August, autumn extended its hand toward us.

This has been a drastic departure from conditions during the last several late summers when fish and fisherman and even the drowsing river itself seemed to have the doldrums. Since 2008, when Hebgen Dam foundered and repair work started, water flows out of the lake from the surface, not from thirty feet down, which has always been the case. The past several years the over-the-dam, extra-heated, upper-cline water has jacked up the river's temperature by ten degrees and made August fishing on the Madison hinky and problematical.

The recent fall-like weather and off-again, on-again stormy conditions squelched what little hopper activity had started on the Madison, but in a delightful compensatory move, Nature, bless her fickle heart, brought on the lovely luscious *Baetis* in good numbers. Low clouds up and down the Madison Valley sat like a lid on a pot, and socked-in conditions kept the fish comfortable and looking up.

Twice last week Rodger Gaulding and I spent afternoon and evening times on the Madison near the Squaw Creek confluence and enjoyed the best dry-fly days either of us had experienced there in years. It's an inviting, sexy piece of water, with wide sweeps, side channels, variations in depth and current speed, all of it made even more attractive—to me anyway—because John McDonald, the great Theodore Gordon scholar, fished this area in Cameron on occasion. He once summed up his angling on this stretch by saying the "fishing was beautiful." Simple, direct, and true.

We found beautiful browns and rainbows up in considerable numbers on a variety of top-water flies, including a couple of Blue Ribbon Flies concoctions: a Royal Coachman Cripple and Hare's Ear Cripple, both of which float like corks in that broad expanse of choppy water; and the stone-cold killers, a #20 BWO Cripple with a black post for daytime and a #20 Olive Spinner for evenings, both from Kelly Galloup's bins at The Slide Inn and both good imitations for *Baetis* and *Attenella margarita*. Even my kinky Purple Haze took fish as did a pink-hued *Glossosoma* Caddis Pupa dropper, and of course Craig Mathews's Zelon Midges, which have become the go-to pattern in recent years for evening fishing on the Madison, while other bulkier emergences have dwindled. I hated to leave such grand goings-on.

Then two days ago, Kate and I hauled our drift boat up to Livingston to store it behind Harrison's studio for the winter. The usual routine so I don't have to trail the boat two thousand miles back to Ohio. From Harrison's we drove to Nelson's Spring Creek Lodge. Yesterday I hit the creek at 9:30 a.m. and fished all day until dark, with intermittent stretches of writing in my vest-pocket notebook. Nymphing in the morning was especially fine on a #18 Zebra Midge. The fish were active below surface in the earlier hours of the day. That it was overcast and cloudy certainly helped. Started at the lower section of the creek just above the boundary with the Dana property and worked my way upstream. Then an exquisite, pinnacle experience: a decent brown trout moved out of the weeds into the mid-water column and hovered there, suspended the way trout often do, to set itself up for feeding, and I hooked it by watching the fish's gills work and its mouth open and close—shades of G. E. M. Skues on the River Itchen! I never felt more dialed in to an angling moment in my life.

I guard against giving myself airs, or jinxing myself, but I feel as though I'm finally getting a handle on this rarefied, fine and far-off process. At least I feel more competent than I have in the past. It's only taken forty years! I bought a copy of John Mingo's *Fly-Fishing the Montana Spring Creeks* and when I finally read it closely, I realized that I've discovered some of his se-crets on my own by common-sense trial-and-error process, the best kind of empirical education. Mingo elaborates his strategy and components down to the nth degree, as one would expect in a book intended to instruct, but my formula, such as it is, works for me most of the time: the double-taper fly line attached to 12-foot-long Maxima or Rio Powerflex 6X leader to the first fly; 2 feet of 6.5X or 7X TroutHunter fluorocarbon tippet for the dropper; tiny flies fronted by a miniscule #6 split shot placed 12

Journaling on Nelson's Spring Creek.
Credit: Kate Fox

to 14 inches above first fly, with second split added for deeper runs; smallest neon paste-on or roll-on indicator possible (or none at all when I'm feeling especially cocky as I was today); 3- or 4-weight, 9-foot rod with sensitive tip. Of my nine fish today I lost only two. That qualifies as a record for me on Nelson's tricky water.

In one of his essays, Aldo Leopold speaks of the kind of experiential knowledge that comes to the "digger as he digs," an archeological metaphor that I shamelessly amend for my own purposes to "the fisher as he fishes." It is the soul and essence of heurism. Which is to say, we need forebears, we need mentors and guides, we need book learning, history, and tradition, we need the expert John Mingos, but our truest education is a self-generated trial-and-error process of discovery. Even in the space of a single angling year, it's a winding route from down-and-dirty lakes to fragile spring creeks. Yet every stop on the way is part of an overarching scheme: at first nothing, then something, then everything. These spots of time, these supernal moments, have a way of hooking up with each other in a vast panoply of remembrances worth crowing about. I hereby grant myself permission to ride the good-fishing gravy train, temporarily anyway, because luck can change overnight and darken prospects.

Finale, for Now

27 October 2015

Fly fishers, attuned to natural cycles of dispersal and renewal, have an inside track on the recurrence of history. Wait long enough, be patient enough, and another circle closes, a loop repeats itself, time swallows its own tail, another hatch cycle plays its rounds. In July a group of us were on hand when Nick and Mari Lyons returned to O'Dell Spring Creek on the Wellington family's Longhorn Ranch for the first time since 1999. In August Jim Harrison and I floated the Yellowstone River again with Dan Lahren after missing last year. Later that month I managed a hefty cutthroat at Nelson's Spring Creek on 8X tippet. And after decades of striking out miserably, another private quest came to a happy end when I fooled a glorious Railroad Ranch rainbow on a callibaetis spinner. It was the fish of the year, given how long it was in coming. Having nothing left to prove, I've even entertained never having to go back to Harriman's again—*been there, done that*—but I'm not that smug, and know I won't be able to resist its siren call when the time comes.

Once, out of the blue, as a result of an offhand referral via three or four degrees of separation by someone at Bressler's Western Rivers guide school, a Montana lodge owner offered to hire me as a guide. He preferred having teachers on his seasonal staff. "You all know how to get along with the public," he brayed over the phone. Many of his clients were CEO types and corporate high rollers who usually got their way and demanded a clean ship: "No beards or long hair, no tattoos, no dope smoking, no talk about politics or religion" were his only other personnel requirements.

Until that moment, when I was being addressed as a mindless integer, servant to God-knows-what upper-crust, mega-buck strivings, I had no clue that I would turn down a summer guide job, a position I had once hoped would be an agreeable way to augment my academic life and salary. The speed with which I said "No" surprised me and turned my fixed idea on its ear. I thought of Oscar Wilde's quip that the only thing worse than not getting what you want is getting what you want. That's what gut instinct is for: it shouts *pull back* and *run for cover* before making the next move.

So despite completing guide school and casting certification, I never became a full-time fly-fishing guide, never worked for a Western fly shop nor outfitter nor lodge, never put out a shingle as a full-time casting instructor. And I know now that I never will. And I have no regrets, either. Full-on Western guide work is too strenuous, too physically taxing for a seventy-plus relic like me. Taking punishment day in and day out marks it as a younger person's game. Besides, what time would be left for other things that matter?

And then there's the boat business. Several years ago, when I was still hoping to establish my *bona fides* as a versatile, multi-threat guide, I shopped around for a reasonably priced drift boat and found one in Livingston. It was a 14-foot Lavro Lazy Drifter built in the 1970s and had more in common with Ahab's *Pequod* than with today's sleek top-end boats. Then I spent nearly as much money having it refurbished at Ro Boats in Bozeman, they of the greatest corporate catchphrase ever ("All who drift are not lost"). The total package still cost less than many used Clackas and Hydes, so I felt ahead of the game on that score.

It's an indestructible craft in a clunky, antediluvian, bathtub kind of way, but its high sides make it susceptible to winds, and as I row mostly on the Madison River—maybe the gustiest stretch of trout water on the continent—handling the boat adds an extra layer of complication to directing someone else's fishing fortunes. I've done it successfully, but never with the kind of full confidence and authority that I see evidenced by twenty- and thirty-something guides. At the very least, my adventures in drift boating reinforced how demanding Western river guiding is. I think of that cautionary day on the Big Hole three years ago when Graham Klipp and I came on a swamped boat with a guide and his two elderly clients hanging on for dear life. We spent several hours getting them across the river to safety. The guide was a veteran, too, so if an accident could happen to him, it could happen to anyone. My admiration and respect for the athletic men and women who guide anglers day in and day out with or without mishap is boundless. Those who ply that trade love the work, certainly, but earn by sweat and blood every penny of their meager fee. Proof plenty that people are attracted to guiding for reasons other than a paycheck.

I never retired from Ohio University as soon as I could have. One thing after another kept me on, which made cutting ties to the students and the intellectual life of the campus difficult. At some point while I was still officially employed, my bearings shifted from wanting to earn a supplementary income to augment my pension toward voluntarily giving back to the sport that had offered me so much for so long. Dennis Hess and I co-taught our Trout Unlimited chapter's eight-week fly-fishing class, where all the conjoined elements came into play—casting, knot tying, selecting flies, reading water, fishing, and of course telling yarns. Now and then I gave private casting lessons and for several years instructed at the annual West Virginia Trout Unlimited fly-fishing school, but my guiding became a strictly no-cash, ad hoc deal. In fact, I didn't consider it guiding, but rather hosting, accommodating, or accompanying; by whatever name, it's been limited to escorting and mentoring relatives, friends, friends of friends, and students on various waters in Montana, Pennsylvania, Ohio, and West Virginia. As with guides everywhere, however, I get as big a charge out of a companion landing a good fish as I do if I had caught it myself.

Muck around in fly fishing long enough and unexpected things happen. Recently an opportunity to guide walk-and-wade trips on West Virginia's Elk River fell in my lap. The timing was right, the conditions were perfect, the setting familiar, and this go-round I couldn't say no. The scale of the prospect fit my current ability; the nature of the employment fit my current wants. Not permanent, but flexible, part-time, occasional, now-and-then, as needed. Like a zillion other middle-class retirees on a fixed pension, some occasional extra moola is welcome, as is the call to return to a kind of teaching, which is, of all things, what I know and love best.

Years ago I imagined a fly-fishing niche of guiding senior citizens, and over the last couple of days, working out of Elk Springs Resort, I've done exactly that. It was a lucky draw: my clients, two dentists from Columbus, were fifty-nine and seventy-nine. The former was a beginner who required lots of coaching and casting instruction, but what he lacked in skill and knowledge he made up for in curiosity, enthusiasm, and quick learning. The latter was already a smooth, rhythmic caster and experienced steelheader, though limited in physical mobility, who benefitted from close and careful attention and a steady hand at his shoulder. Both men exhibited that compensatory goodwill and graciousness that sometimes comes to us elders if we are fortunate. Between their two poles of experience I found teachable common ground. It was sweet to see both men catch rainbows on tiny #20 and #22 Blue-winged Olive nymphs and emergers, neither ever having used flies that small before. Like the cricket on the wagon axle, I wanted to chirp, "See what a dust I have raised!"

Besides bringing some fish to hand, more importantly, no one impaled a hook in his eye, fell on the rocks, had a stroke, broke a fly rod, squeezed a trout to death, or went in over his waders. I enjoyed their company, their good cheer, their stories, and the way they took each day's fortunes in stride. I even received generous tips—more than generous tips—which if I had had my wits about me, I would have declined as being too lavish. But I was out of practice on that score, not having been offered a gratuity of any kind since I was a seventeen-year-old caddying for the winning golfer in the Connecticut Open. I was gratified, but embarrassed too by so much largesse. Is nothing unalloyed in this life?

"Just keep fishing," Jim Harrison says in his essay "Older Fishing," "and you'll have a nice life." Times like this, I know he's right. I think of my older friends who are still fishing in their mid-seventies and early eighties—DuBack, Kelly, Lyons, McGuane, Ornduff—and I give a *sotto voce* salute and huzzah to those troopers who keep on keeping on. I carry them all a long way in my heart. That's what the age thing is about: not letting go when all the signs in the universe tell you otherwise. By which I mean still being present as fully as possible even in twilight when the world recedes from us; still doing what lights us up despite the frailties of our bodies, the liabilities of our senses, the vagaries of our minds; still drifting on at our own pace, even if it's a single step at a time. Maybe it has taken these thousands and thousands of words to arrive at this place of momentary, therapeutic repose, to reach the sustaining thing itself that has been lurking urgently behind a life with fishing all this time, like a shadow under water. The permanent knot, the indispensable nexus, the constant lodestar always was and always will be about *more* than fishing, and it has many names—but *blessing* is the one I like best.

I think I'll leave this journal now, for the time being anyway.

PART III (2016–2018)

"There's something strange about . . . fishing, that *requires that it be written about* . . . It's the most *writerly* of sports."

—Gordon Wickstrom, *Late in an Angler's Life (2004)*

Slow-Handedness

18 March 2016

A quick run forty miles up the road to Clear Creek to try out my long awaited cane rod from Vandalia Rod Works. Philip Smith made the rod to order for me over the past sixteen months: an eight-foot, three-piece, two-tip, 5-weight built on Jim Payne model 201 formula. I drove over to Spencer, West Virginia a week ago to pick it up. Darkish caramel-colored cane with burgundy wraps tipped with gold. An indulgence for my three-piece rod fetish. A gorgeous bit of rod building I was almost hesitant to take on the water. But I am an angler not a collector, and a rod like this earns its chops by being put to use. So my reluctance lasted about two minutes. I was hoping for some holdover browns today, but no such luck. Zero fish in two full hours of trying. Windy and cold. Not prime conditions for split bamboo. Action-wise, it is more on the medium side than fast, and heavier in the butt than I like, but no complaints otherwise. The more I cast it the more it struck me as a niche rod: single dry fly in calm conditions at medium-to-close range, where I know it will prove its worth.

Where's the time go? No fishing at all since last October. Kick started this angling year a couple of weeks ago when Kate and I drove to Sullivan's Island in South Carolina to get out of Ohio's winter and get the lay-off cobwebs out of my head. Fished for redfish with Jeremy Mehlhaff of Charleston Shallows guide service on a cold and windy, windy day, my head wrapped in the thickest wool ski cap I own. But being in and among those miles of unspoiled and primal estuaries, smelling the salt air, riding his bucking boat from spot to spot, called up my youth fishing for all kinds of finny quarry––flounder, weakfish, snapper blues, baby stripers––on Long Island Sound. Completely enjoyable experience then and now, with a few nice reds thrown in this time for extra measure.

Today, other things on my mind. *Angling Days* is due out in a few months, and I would think I had had enough of writing after-fishing entries, yet I can't give up the diary habit. Obsession, internal compulsion, habitual tic––whatever it's called–– is a hard master to overthrow, not that I'd ever want to do so. Journaling is a life-long habit, on the order of an automatic reflex or an itch that can never be scratched or relieved. There is a progressive seriality to keeping a journal; it goes on as long as we are alive and kicking, one entry leading naturally and eventfully to the next, so it ends only when we do. The horizon stretches out ahead in varying degrees of length depending on age, health, and condition. The only conclusion is the final one, which in my case at seventy-three is nearer at hand than farther. "Ripeness is all," Shakespeare says in *King Lear.* But who knows if we are ever ready?

In that, I suppose, writing and fishing are alike. Writing sentences is like casting a fly line, in that both are repetitive, but more importantly both are rhythmic, hopeful, and of course necessary, as well as being partly intuitive and partly thoughtful. Words plug me into the larger panoptic and expansive purview of the whole shebang, beyond just the river and its fish. Pushing a pen and wielding a fly rod–– both gratifying physical and metaphysical acts––still strike me as being good for the soul and worth indulging.

Meantime, writing every day is one of the few acts I can personally control in an increasingly chaotic, polarized world. For me, writing makes a statement all of its own about continuance, about playing the past forward, about linking up with what sustains and nurtures, both physically and mentally. And there's this, too: journaling lends material aid to memory, which is notoriously shifting and unreliable, the older I get. In my most extreme moments I think words are the realest part of reality. Words are imperfect, sure, but they still keep me honest and on task, even in this digital age—*especially* in this image and quick-view–oriented age of social media. Why do it, then? If writing seems somehow retrograde in the reigning era of Face-book, Go-Pro, Instagram, Pinterest, Snapchat, Twitter, and YouTube––all of which seem to target the crotch-rocket moments and glorify the latest broad-grinned brand ambassador who represents this or that angling entity, company, or institution––I consider my slow-handed old-fashionedness to be subversive and rebellious. Going slow is a way to follow my own peculiar bent, the way casting a bamboo rod symbolizes an alternative to other forms of rod play. I say less technology, more poetry and philosophy, is what's needed in these uncertain times. Give me that old time religion any day! And at the very least, no redfish or trout are harmed in the production of a sentence. That can't be said about every endeavor.

In my geezer years I'm fishing less than I once did. This no longer strikes me as a sad fact, or a bitter disappointment. Other aspects of life––too numer-ous, varied, and ho-hum to list here, but the kinds of things oldsters are heir to, the kind of things I once either put on hold or thought I could willfully escape or ignore––seem to have redoubled in recent years. It's called aging. It leavens us all, requires an alternate mind set from the hurry- up-and-cast way of doing things I've been accustomed to since my teen years. Recently I've averaged about forty-five to fifty angling days a year. The truth is, after six decades of fly fishing, I don't need to fish as much now, so making the most of this new regimen seems paramount in my so-called golden years.

John Steinbeck once said that if he didn't bait his hook he wouldn't be bothered by a fish biting when he was thinking about other things. I see the wisdom in that now. At times I practice sit fishing: plant my ass down on a river bank or fallen log (the Madison has the greatest bank-side sitting logs in the universe), rod at the ready, and do nothing at all until I've watched the water a long time for some clue as how to proceed. It's a habit that's great for schooling patience and inviting reverie. More often than I care to admit I tie on a bushy dry fly or rubber-legged foam concoction no respectable trout would ever hit and cast it for the sheer bodily pleasure of the repetitive, maybe even mindless, motion, the unadulterated joy of immersing myself in a physical action. Muscle memory takes over, history and personality fall away, my mind is elsewhere, preoccupied with this or that issue, problem, person, and while my eye sees the fly my gaze is well beyond it, too. Reverie, rumination, grass-growing mood—all enhanced by a river's siren call. In the rare instance that some foolish baby fish swipes at the fly, I'm startled by its impertinence but appreciate its enthusiasm and zest. In such ways time and the river pass and I come away reanimated, having communed with the quiet in my head or the stillness in my heart, at least for a little while. I know sometimes that's all I can ask.

Everything but Our Stories

25 October 2016

Despite best intentions, I've been slow getting serious about fishing this year. This is the 111th page of 2016's journal, so it isn't like I haven't been plugging away. But I've lost the taste for fishing alone. I've done my share this year but solo angling doesn't seem to compare to getting on the river with a friend or two. Lose one friend and they *all* seem more precious than ever, proving I guess that we anglers are all joined at the hip. Jerry Dennis says it best in *The River Home:* "Good fishing friends are hard to come by, but they tend to last." Their presences, woven into so many earlier journal entries this year, embellished my days, added a dose of blessedness and camaraderie to my angling adventures. And if not in the flesh, then in spirit.

Those are all on the plus side of the ledger; on the negative side Jim Harrison died last March. His death darkened a large portion of my year. We fished together for twelve years, so his passing leaves another hole in my heart that will likely never be filled. A loss not just to me personally but to a world-wide audience of followers, the "Tribe of Jim," Doug Peacock aptly calls it. Jim's passing dropped a shroud over my year, I see that now, and the unaccounted part of my past seven months, the part I haven't always been able to name or to forget, has been a gnawing grief over his death. He was one of a kind.

I went out to Livingston a few days ago to be part of a celebration of his and his wife Linda's passing, she last October 2nd, and he this past March

26th. He died a writer's death in the middle of writing a poem at his desk in his winter *casita* in Patagonia, Arizona. His seventy-eight-year-old heart stopped and he keeled over. That's the stuff of legend, like painter John Atherton dying in a river while he was fighting a salmon. I guess some people go the way they are meant to, as though they scripted their own demise.

Anyway, a crowd of around seventy-five family members, colleagues, compatriots, and friends—many famous, many just every-day folk were invited from across the United States, to convene at the Murray Hotel and the adjacent Second Street Bistro to partake of the spectacular multi-course dinner organized by daughters Jamie and Anna, and orchestrated by Chef Brian Menges. The evening was a procession of brilliant offerings that stretched for hours all the way to a dozen different desserts and a Calvados brandy finish. The independently wealthy and the self-employed, the celebrities and the work-a-day stiffs all carried on like there was no tomorrow. Jim brought us all together: eat, drink, and talk, eat and drink some more—what could honor his voracious appetite for life more fittingly than that?

And there was occasion for private recollections and somber memories. On our last float on the Yellowstone River in late August, 2015, with Danny Lahren and his constant companion, wonder dog Jacques, Jim looked about as stricken and physically challenged as I have ever seen him. He could not share rowing duties with Danny, a switch-up I had gotten used to over our years of fishing together. He could not have been comfortable with his physical ailments and body betrayals, but he never complained though the ninety degree heat and wildfire smoke was outrageous—weather conditions he hated the most— and the fishing sporadic at best. I think he didn't want to disappoint me by staying home, bless his heart. And if going sapped his energy he did not let on. He was that kind of constant friend. "These fish have lock jaw," he lamented over and over. "Bobby, what can we do to shake these little dears from their torpor"? The lap of the oars, the wind in the cottonwoods, were our only answers.

Jim was expansive when we sat down later in his writing bungalow and started on the first leg of an interview on fishing: "You get hooked on the mystery rather early, or you don't," he wheezed, trying to explain the allure of a sport that had caught him since childhood, seventy years earlier on Michigan's Pine River when he caught his first brown trout on worms and a Colorado spinner. From there we covered the waterfront: brook trout in the UP on home-tied "bumble bee bi-visibles," tarpon and his first big permit in the Florida Keys, striped marlin in Ecuador, rooster fish in Baja ("If roosters lived in rivers no one would ever care to fish for trout again"). And his excitement fishing for October's hyperphagic, pre-spawning browns in the Yellowstone. "Obsession, that's what it is."

We completed about fifty minutes of audio taping, Jim reeling off in several directions at once, his good eye tearing up now and then in the wreath of smoke that circled his head, his breathing becoming more and more labored, the silences between speaking becoming more marked except for deep, alarming bouts of coughing, when Linda and Kate called us in to the main house for dinner. Afterwards, we talked another hour or so at the picnic table in the front yard, Jim bundled in his usual puff jacket against the cooling Montana evening, the last of the wine drained from our glasses, the next American Spirit cigarette at the ready for lighting, my own cigar just about ready to give up the ghost. His voice kept trailing off and his coughing ramped up. He looked rumpled, disheveled with his wild, ungroomed hair and nearly toothless grin, his pants slipped down his butt. It is an utterly indelible view of him, like his startling late-life black-and-white photos by Andy Anderson, that I will take to my grave. Realism out-muscles romanticism every time. After so many years of unstinting hospitality and largesse experienced in his and Linda's company, who would have thought it would be the last meal we ever shared? "Death steals everything but our stories," he said in *In Search of Small Gods*, a truism I have come back to a thousand times in the last seven months. Jim's one of the most quotable writers I've ever encountered and one of the toughest to replace.

The other night at the Murray we ate, drank, smoked (all civic bans against lighting up having been suspended), told stories, recounted the ins and outs of how Jim and Linda had touched our lives, made them demonstrably better and richer. But one thing remained: some of us needed to fish in order to complete the circle. Yesterday, with Danny Lahren, I signed us up for a day on Nelson's Spring Creek. It didn't seem right to fish it alone. After clearing our heads of the previous night's excesses at least to function reasonably, we had enough *oomph* left to mount a pretty good time on the creek. We had that blessed place all to ourselves, praise the Lord. It was a cool, overcast day and one of those times when the muted light added an extra level of depth and gravity to the entire scene. Everything seemed portentous, bound together by intense anticipation or maybe it was grief. It's hard to tell sometimes, even in glorious Montana, even in October.

Perfect conditions for a *Baetis* hatch, too, but in fact hard as we wished otherwise few risers appeared. Subsurface, where the meanings are, things were different, and small nymphs including a slim-profile #20 blonde Sawyer Pheasant Tail, a #22 beadhead Zebra Midge, and an anonymous #20 olive emerger (Jacquie Nelson's recommendation when we stopped at her fly shop) took their share of fish. We ended up having a banner day, every trout caught and released, every splash of brilliant aqueous color and muscular motion a tribute to Nelson's spectacular fishes. The cutthroats in particular looked like they had been burnished by an artist's hand. Their palette of colors, the music of their bodies, was astonishing, breath taking, arresting. Each one improved the autumn landscape. I'd never seen anything like it. The whole day was a testament to Jim's abiding spirit, his need for angling, and his love of "the improbable mystery of moving water." He was with us all day and we did not pretend otherwise.

Back home, I'm still full of the past week, trying to get it down before it fades to a long-gone blur. It's high autumn in the East. Throughout the Appalachians, rivers, not yet freighted with snow, take on their special fall clarity, littered here and there with dinner plate-sized-sycamore leaves. Brown trout are redding up and beginning to spawn. Male brookies are donning their harlequin mating colors. Teal have already flown the coop. Woodcock have had enough of the Northland and are traveling their flight lanes south, happy news to my setters, who, like me, become more restless for upland coverts every day. The quality and character of light has changed. As leaves drop and trees turn naked, the sky above them seems deeper and more intense, and those of us living under its dome seem more mortal and fragile somehow.

The mind's eye registers all and I don't even have to be on the water to see what passes forth. Hatches have dwindled, and the glories of spring mayfly time seem a distant memory. No matter, all will return in their own way in their own time. I counsel myself to be patient and remember my friend.

Shadow of the Death Trout

23 August 2017

A day in our lives as of yesterday: Bob Hendrix, Rodger Gaulding, and I stood on a bank of the Ruby River at the Woodson Ranch, site of the Ruby Habitat Foundation, in Sheridan, Montana, on one bright, clear third-week-of-August morning. We were all from somewhere else––California, Texas, Ohio––and had driven ninety minutes to get there, arriving early enough from our cabins over the mountains in Cameron to witness masses of *Tricorythodes* spinners drifting over the water like patches of iridescent gray smoke. We watched as the little buggers rose and fell in that tantalizing up-and-down, back-and-forth rhythmic dance so characteristic of spinners on the make. Cedar waxwings started their aerial show and we three Trout-men of the Apocalypse licked our lips in anticipation of epic morning action on feeding trout. While we waited we talked, we bantered, we joked, we laughed in a giddy sort of way about how great the morning sport was going to be.

Then nothing. *Nada. Zero. Zilch.* We kept waiting. Then, dumbstruck and disbelieving, we waited some more. All up and down the river, not a rising fish could be seen. Eventually, rafts of black-and-whites washed downstream, as though on a conveyor belt, untouched by a single trout. We held our breaths, poised without mirth or levity, until the very last second when some obliging fish might show itself so we could go to work harvesting our brief portion of joy. It was past noon when the door slammed shut. Utterly and profoundly fishless, we were faced with decisions about our next moves. What to do when fishing sucks? One of us suggested lunch, which suddenly seemed like a truly inspired idea: nourishment and reflection in equal portions, so we dove into our coolers and spread the bounty around.

Otherwise, prospects were bleak: the Great *Trico* Washout had set the tone for the remainder of our day and was fast becoming a symbol of this late summer's entire fishing fortunes. A few fish eventually came to hand from the Ruby and from adjacent Cattail Creek, but they were hard earned, and few and far between. We weren't skunked, having managed to salvage a tiny morsel of collective pride, but nonetheless our ride home was unusually somber. A way stop at The Gravel Bar in Ennis, a watering hole that never disappoints, highlighted our return trip. When in doubt, eat and drink. Later, the women in our lives wanted full particulars of the day, and of course we did our level best to a avoid telling the dismal truth.

In these disbelieving angling moments, when nothing occurs the way we think or hope it should, thoughts turn dark and despairing, and perhaps it is inevitable to want to blame something or someone. I'm not immune to casting blame. This August in Southwestern Montana, has been one of those times of despair, and qualifies as my worst stretch in twenty-eight straight years of fishing the country in and around the Madison River Valley. And I'm guessing that it was not just my bleakest moment, but that of others as well: forest fire smoke everywhere; long stretches of hot, dry weather, often near or in the nineties with little or no cooling rains and storms to temper what had become in recent years the hottest summers on record; dangerously warming rivers, and then this basic fact—trout were off their feed. It has been too damn hot for fish to eat.

The Madison below Hebgen Dam has run in the high sixties day after day while other rivers in this region are closed or under hoot owl restrictions. Normally reliable mayfly and caddis hatches stalled, dwindled, or disappeared, and even the once vaunted late summer hopper bite has gone into hiding, compensated only occasionally, thank God, by flying ant emergences. And everywhere there is ample evidence of increased angling pressure on Blue Ribbon streams, the Madison in particular, for which I too have been culpable and blame worthy. How much pressure is too much? It's an eternal question, especially relevant now when recent Montana Fish, Wildlife, and Parks surveys show the Madison gets an astounding 175,000-plus angler days a year in the last couple of years, up considerably from even a half decade ago.

Such pressure *seems* to have an effect, but in fact that is nearly impossible to gauge empirically. My own journals and photographs since the late 1980s indicate that the average size of trout in the Madison has definitely fallen. Remember when a *good* fish was fourteen, fifteen, sixteen inches? A *really good* fish was seventeen, eighteen, nineteen inches? A *bruiser* was twenty inches-plus? Now a good fish is eleven, twelve, thirteen inches, a very good fish is fifteen or sixteen, an excellent one is seventeen or eighteen. I'm happy to get them, but the memory of those larger fish—finny ghosts of the past—exert their nostalgic pull. It's one of those indescribable, anecdotal things you feel deep in your bones and guts. *Don't dare tell me I'm wrong!*

So maybe it's time for the state to regulate the boat traffic for a couple of seasons and see if the results look up. At the very least, ban boats from the Slide Inn to Lyons Bridge section. That stretch is supposed to be wade fishing only, but more and more anglers are float fishing it with impunity. I've had run-ins recently with several groups who think it is perfectly OK to fish right down my lane. A couple of times I've had to bolt out of the water to avoid being run over by this or that asshole in a raft or hard boat. Anyway, some kind of reduction or accounting would be an experiment worth trying, like what's been done on the Beaverhead and the Big Hole.

Anyway, while the deleterious effects of climate change seem obvious enough to me (and to many qualified scientists at the Northern Rocky Mountain Science Center, who have been ringing the alarm bell for years)—I mean obvious like a trout in a glass of milk—some otherwise reasonable and sober-minded anglers—perhaps having taken leave of their senses—have been blaming the total eclipse of the sun two days ago on the twenty-first as the real reason for the precipitous decline of angling fortunes. "The universe is out of whack," some old timers at the Grizzly Bar claimed, "what the hell are we to do?" I feel their pain, weird as their reasoning is.

Whether or not it's true that the trout gods have withdrawn their favors, current attitudes indicate a widely spread, cosmic sense of gloom and doom: the sun disappeared, the sky was falling, the heavens deserted us. In short, conditions are so hinky and intolerable that several fly shop owners, whose opinions and experience I have come to respect over the last three decades, admit that their clientele, including many regulars, had cancelled guide trips. Everything's going to hell in a wicker creel. News of fishing's crash in this part of Montana has spread like, well, wild fire. Some pundits, allegedly more prescient than most of us, have even taking to calling these conditions the "new normal," and urging that we get with our coping and adapting methods ASAP. I hate to admit that but I fear they might be correct.

As usual out here, I've fished every day (going on twenty-one days as of this entry), bearing down harder and harder as the burgeoning drought rolls on. Fly fishing is often a test of character and endurance rather than common sense, skill, or timing, but this prolonged vacuum is an especially grievous insult. I've had a few memorable days when I lucked into moments that were lovely and fulsome––dry fly hatch activity on the ever-chilly and under-hyped West Fork of the Madison––but overall this fishless fishing is playing havoc with whatever is left of my confidence and enthusiasm. Frustration loops like a bad piece of music in my head.

Fishing has become more like drudgery than pleasure, my sense of humor has taken a hike, and I know that the grim conditions have gotten into my skull in an ugly way. The Death Trout, with its sunken, sullen eyes, follows me everywhere; friends and family shun me. Maybe it was reading Marcelo Gleiser's *The Simple Beauty of the Unexpected: A Natural Philosopher's Quest for Trout and the Meaning of Everything* that put me over the edge––the author ends up walking away from fishing––but when I confided aloud to my dog that, after sixty years, I, too, am seriously considering giving up fishing altogether, I realize I've hit a wall and need a new approach, and pronto.

"The past is never dead," William Faulkner said. "It's not even past." So I dove into some earlier years of my angling journals looking for solace, searching for some thread of meaning, some shard of understanding, some clue buried in personal history that disaster has not always been the main narrative. I found in those pages something different than I expected. It had nothing to do with refining a repressed technique, rediscovering a forgotten honey hole, or resuscitating a killer fly pattern that had once worked wonders. What I found in a couple of older journals has nothing to do with physical skill, material success, or the numbers game, but everything to do with the essence of this maddening sport. Which is to say, angling in its entirety, even when fraught with discontents and failures, nudges us toward understanding and perspective. That's a good end, no matter how I cut it.

One entry in particular, written two Julys ago, hit the mark dead center because it chronicled a day of complete satisfaction and fellow-feeling. A mixed group of us on a Montana spring creek finding surpassing pleasure, tallied not in fish count, but in sharing a day of angling together. It was one of those moments when we fly fishers, attuned to natural cycles of dispersal and renewal, seem to have an inside track on the window of history. Wait long enough, be patient enough, and another circle closes, a loop repeats itself, time swallows its own tail, another hatch cycle plays its rounds, and so on. To fish storied trout water, to count as friends talented, proficient anglers, and to be in the midst of such natural plenty, is a reminder that the way we enter history is through a web of related factors that coalesce, rather than through one single defining event that outstrips all others. Myriad elements cannot be separated or dissected, but must remain intact to work in concert. Shitty fishing, even if it is preponderant, has to be seen in balance with good fishing. That's my version of the unified field approach to angling. Every skein, every thread, every filament whether good, bad, or indifferent—they all matter, they all link up somewhere, though the where is not always immediately apparent. Which is to say, the best fishing begins and ends with ideas.

The summer of 2017 rolls on in its implacable way. Remainder-of-August fishing these coming ten days or so will probably stay tough and inconsistent, and I should prepare myself for that. But after my journal dive I feel calmer, less cranky and desperate, more inclined to go with the riverine flow, whatever that proves to be. At the very least, I feel a return to normalcy, a restoration of equilibrium. In this late summer of disappointing conditions and encroaching self doubt, revisiting earlier journals page by lingering page—in effect rereading myself—brought back the good, honorable, small moments that provide a measure of reassurance, even redemption and transport. And a resolve: I've decided, after all, not to give up fishing. At least for now.

The Mirror of Fly Fishing

31 May 2018

Dodge a health bullet like I did in February and everything afterwards seems like gravy. Recovery took a while but at least it progressed as it should have, or so I was told by the gifted team of doctors at Riverside Hospital. There were times in intensive care when my body felt like it had turned to smoke, so insubstantial and free floating had it become, and I wasn't sure I'd ever see my routine life again. Or any life, for that matter. In helplessness we are blessed by others who aid our survival. I would not be writing this if it weren't for Kate and my daughter Liz, bless their loving hearts. They were by my side during the entire ordeal. These unwanted, unexpected setbacks in our lives remind us not just how fast cataclysmic change happens, but if we live through them and come out the other side they highlight what is truly valuable in our existence. Mortality, life span, our days on earth—it's all just smoke up the chimney or water under the bridge if we aren't careful or fortunate. Mindfulness helps. So does gratitude.

In those winter nights when the void was closer than I realized, my thoughts dwelled naturally enough on family, friends, and loved ones. Then I replayed as many of my most grievous and shameful indiscretions and malfeasances as I could bear—promising myself never to repeat such idiocies again—before turning to the far more pleasing memories of rivers, streams, and creeks I've known. To while away the interminable hours between medical checks, I fished as many waters as possible in my head. In the nether gaps between needles, tubes, and pills, the alluring, reflective slate of moving water came back to me again and again with increased longing and clarity.

One visitation was haunting and I mind-fished for one trout on one stream in particular over and over: a glorious, dream-worthy brown trout close to two feet long I met up with on the middle section of Nelson's Spring Creek last August. It rose regularly for ninety minutes, scarfing down sulphur emergers and now and then a dun, too, with a kind of deliberate insouciance that said everything about its alpha status. No other fish in the pod challenged its position in the water column. It had one lane all to itself and made the most of its dalliance. I fished patiently, humbly, then beseechingly and imploringly over that trout: I changed patterns half a dozen times or more, lengthening my leader with 7x and then 8x tippet to fourteen feet. On one occasion Mr. Brown moved slightly toward my newest offering, then backed off at the last second. My heart was in my mouth. *This is it,* I thought. *He's going to eat.* But his perfunctory nod was just enough to let me know he was on to me. He had my number and was intent on teaching me humility, I guess, in the face of failure. *Not this time, buster.* And so it is we beat on, fly fishers against the current, resilient enough and able enough and hopeful enough if we are fortunate to turn every angling episode into an object lesson. *Maybe next year,* I thought.

Sometimes, all the rivers, creeks, and streams—those special places we have fished and come to love and revere—hook up in one grand torrent and run together through us, through our memories and dreams, through the landscape and geography of our desire. It isn't a stretch to say our choice of waters defines us, gives us a grammar for the art of fly fishing, and a lexicon for understanding the sport and its relatedness to our lives. Whatever their size, rivers mirror our own individual character and return to each of us only what we are capable of giving ourselves, even if (and when) we are flat on our backs.

When conditions improved and I was cleared for activity by my doctors and by Kate and Liz, I was crazy to make up for lost time. I've gone on a fishing tear to Tennessee (Watauga and South Holston) and now West Virginia (Elk and Tygart Valley). I'm part way through my planned road trip and have visits this coming week to Pennsylvania (Yellow Breeches and LeTort), New York (Mongaup), and Connecticut (Housatonic). I've not fished the latter, one of my former home rivers, in a decade. I never cracked its code and don't expect great results, but my hospital dreams told me I should return before it's too late. Anyway, luck could change. So I think of my Eastern periplum as exacting revenge on the void, testing my physical endurance, and adding some store of pleasure to my recovery.

Like here, yesterday and today. There are few places I'd rather be in late May than on the upper catch-and-release section of the Elk River. Summer heat not yet ramped up and the very best of burgeoning spring all around. Everywhere I look there is greenness in profusion and circuses of full-blown flowering plants. Water from the main springs is at optimal temperature for prolific sulfur and green drake hatches and for active trout. It's cooler after rain and the river is a bit discolored but with decent visibility nonetheless and a flow that's manageable for wading. Surprising for this hatch-active time of year, there was no one else up or down the Valley Fork run, my favorite stretch on the whole river. It's a hallowed place, and looks like one of the troutiest stretches of water on the planet. Runs, riffles, undercut banks, long glides, deep, shaded pools: a model of an Appalachian limestone stream, just perfectly delicious in every regard and now, lest I forget, under threat of extinction by the obscene Atlantic Coast Pipeline project that will cut not just fairly close, but way too close for comfort.

I remember nearly every trout I've caught here in the last couple of decades, as well as the ones Kate caught when she first took up fly fishing and we plied this section together. It's a storied place, too—many of those moments made it into my angling journals and became part of this cumulative narrative, my evolving history of the place. That's the way fishing is: experiences, memories, words rise out of the geography of a particular place. Not to put too mystical a turn on this, such places become part and parcel of a rarefied, seemingly sanctified landscape: Thoreau at Walden Pond, Voelker at Frenchman's Pond, Lyons at O'Dell Creek. Impossible to plan such fortuitous revelations ahead of time. You have to be present in the midst, and attentive, too, when the boat arrives from wherever it launched.

Toward evening, fog and mist moved in, like a rolling swath of smoke, and suddenly sharp outlines blurred. The scene turned surreal and insubstantial and eerie, too, and I felt as though I was an actor inside someone else's dream. I had just caught a handsome brown trout on a #18 Copper and Bunny sulphur emerger, one of Dave Breitmeier's great patterns, fished a few inches below the surface. I waded back to the bank, pleased with the first fish of the night. I plunked down to watch the water and wait for the next tell-tale rise. Along the opposite bank another trout started feeding and I kept my seat until it got into a regular groove that seemed to keep time with a distant whippoorwill's rapid-fire call.

Just then, down stream, a woman angler appeared out of the bordering woods, entered the river, and started wading toward the rising fish, though I don't think she saw it. I almost said she materialized out of the murkiness, but that's mythologizing the moment more than it can bear. In the gathering mist she didn't see me either, and not wanting to startle her, I said quietly that she was about to spook a feeding fish if she kept wading. She turned and saw me hunkered down in the thick of streamside foliage, apologized, and started to back away.

The mind moves faster than flowing water at times like those. I could have taken umbrage at her intrusion, gotten huffy and self righteous— typically dumb masculine responses when acquisitiveness is on the line—but what's the point? The ethics, the spirit, the meaning of fly fishing teaches us otherwise. She hadn't set out to trespass or encroach and she was probably as surprised to find me there swathed in fog and mist as I was to see her. I thought of many acts of generosity and kindness I had witnessed in sixty years of fly fishing. I remembered the number of people who had given me great angling traps—rods, reels, flies, books—and the far more precious gift of themselves by sharing their angling knowledge, their honey holes, and their ways of being. Incident after incident of no-strings-attached generosity came to mind, all in a flash. I had returned the favors myself many times, too, and once again, here it was my turn to give back. I love the random-ness, the unpredictability of such a summons. You never know when the call will come. Refuse the summons and a whole lifetime of endeavor might be diminished.

Besides, no one has exclusive rights to trout in a public river (it's the genius of our democratic sporting tradition), so I asked her to try for the ris-ing fish. She was an accomplished caster, already had a sulphur pattern tied on her leader, and so it wasn't long before she hooked and landed that trout. It was a very fine, deft bit of angling and I felt honored to have had a ring-side seat for the action and was able to cheer her on. I even managed some photos but who knows if they will turn out in such low light?

We didn't speak much, both of us content with the silence, except for the on-again, off-again chant of that hidden whippoorwill, the perfect sound track to spring evening fishing. We shared the water and moved a number of fine trout. When it was too dark to see our flies any longer, we walked out to our vehicles, and started the ritual end-of-day stowing down and packing up. We bantered a bit, swapped information, and traded good wishes. Her name was Rosie and she hailed from Virginia, Roanoke, I think she said. She was in West Virginia with a group of women fly fishers on their annual outing, but had struck out on her own for the evening. She'd been fly fishing a long time and had the kind of finesse and skill all the best anglers possess. I wished her continuing success and many future converts and disciples among her peers and students. I don't know that I'll ever see her again.

On a wooded ridge behind me that lone whippoorwill kept up its dusky tremolo, only louder and more persistent now that I had come closer to its lair. They have declined throughout their range, so it's a rarity to hear one now, which only makes it more special, I suppose, like a gift out of the darkness. It was reassuring to know it was up there just out of reach, its song part of the air I was breathing, and would probably keep up its commotion until dawn, long after I left. Brown trout, pale evening duns, trillium and blue bells, whippoorwill, an unexpected angling partner—all part of the linked fabric of a thankful spring evening. They gave me their onliness and I gave them my lastness.

About the Author

Robert DeMott is Edwin and Ruth Kennedy Distinguished Professor of English Emeritus at Ohio University, where he received six major teaching awards and published numerous books during a career that spanned from 1969 to 2013. *Steinbeck's Typewriter* won the Ohio College English Association's 1996 Nancy Dasher Book Award, and *The Weather in Athens: Poems* won the Ohioana Library's Poetry Award in 2002. In 2006 he was given the National Steinbeck Center's Trustees Award for his sustained scholarly contributions to Steinbeck Studies. He is the chief editor of the Library of American's four-volume anthology of Nobel Prize-winner John Steinbeck's major writings (1994-2007) and is a member of the editorial board of the *Steinbeck Review* and of the Board of Directors of *Quarter After Eight*, a literary journal. A life-long fly fisherman, he is a Fly Fishers International Certified Casting Instructor and a life member of both Trout Unlimited through its Blennerhassett (WV) chapter, and of Northern Kentucky Fly Fishers. His recent books include *Afield: American Writers on Bird Dogs* (2010) and *Astream: American Writers on Fly Fishing* (2012), both published by Skyhorse, and *Conversations with Jim Harrison, Revised and Updated* (2019). A native of Connecticut, he lives in Athens, Ohio, with life partner Kate Fox, a poet, freelance writer, and editor.

About the Author